HOMETOWN
COOKING IN
NEW ENGLAND

The Very Best Recipes from
Community Cookbooks

Compiled and edited by Sandra J. Taylor

Down East Books / Camden, Maine

Book Producer: Sandra J. Taylor
Book Designer: Eugenie S. Delaney
Cover Designer: Faith Hague
Cover Photographer: Angelo Caggiano
Illustrator: Paul Hoffman
Food Stylists: Mariann Sauvion, William Smith

Printed and bound at BookCrafters, Inc.

6   8   9   7   5

Down East Books
P.O. Box 679, Camden, Maine 04843
Book Orders: 1-800-766-1670

Contents

${\mathcal{A}}$CKNOWLEDGMENTS

*T*RUE TO THE SPIRIT OF COMMUNITY COOKBOOKS, this one relied on a network of individuals for help—outside New England as well as within. Consequently, I am extremely grateful to a vast number of people. To begin with, my thanks go to the staff at Yankee Books and Rodale Press, who helped guide me on this book: Bill Gottlieb, Ed Claflin, Jean Rogers, Jane Knutila, Faith Hague, JoAnn Brader, Sarah Dunn, Laura Herzog, Linda Johns and Lisa Andruscavage. Thanks also to Eugenie Delaney for her excellent design, to Paul Hoffman for his outstanding illustrations, to Barbara Jatkola for her skillful copyediting, to Faith Hanson for her careful proofreading, to Jacinta Monniere and Linda Ottavi for their accurate and speedy keyboarding and to Nanette Bendyna for her expert indexing.

In addition, I'd like to thank Sue Hanna, whose personal collection of community cookbooks gave a tremendous boost not only to this project but also to my spirits. Thanks also to her husband, Archie, who provided assistance as well. For passing along leads, loaning me copies of their own cookbooks and testing and evaluating recipes, my sincere thanks go to Dolly and Benny Pearson, Sheryl and Candice Burton, Kenneth and Mia Burton, J. P. and Dorothy Taylor, Preston and Diane Taylor, Richard Pisciotta, Petr Hochmann, Ann Demeranville, Joan Dunning, Janet Rood, Martha Wilder, Laurette and David Carroll, Eugenie Delaney, Rux Martin, Celia Tuttle, Carla Richardson, Kathie Raleigh, Marjorie Romanoff, Carrie Strong, Susan McClellan, Sara Oot, Deb Wright, Cindy Cadot, Camille Gibson, Leonard Bolonsky, Rose Roman, Kathy Oliver, Edith Foulds, Pat Higgins, Millie Stewart, Susan Thompson, Sheila Kirkpatrick, Bob Ottavi, Rosemary Duggan, Carol Rosswaag, Ruth Batterman, Nancy Morris, Cathy Behrens, Mary Schacht, Linda Bensinger, Melissa Lawless, Jean Bacon, Helen van Ham, Ernestine Phipps, Cyndi Richards, Bea Achorn, Sue Carita, Patti Powers, Ann Harkleroad, Rich Roth, Nancy Adams, Anne Skotty, Rashell Ambrosini, Shelton Davison, Pamela Harwell, Joanna Bower, Maudie Willbern, Donna Mays, Charles and Susan Elder, Cathy Horecka, Mary Kay Jax, Monica Dunton, Pam Barrington and Susan Tait, as well as the many town clerks, librarians and bookstore owners and managers I contacted throughout New England.

INTRODUCTION

*W*HAT A PLUM ASSIGNMENT!" said my friend and former coworker Rux Martin, responding to a letter I'd sent about the cookbook I was compiling and my need to obtain more than 100 community cookbooks throughout New England. Given the popularity of these books, you'd think they would be simple to track down, but they aren't. Many are produced by church groups, hospital auxiliaries and small-town committees and are seldom found outside their own backyards, so to speak. So what was I to do?

First, I mailed a sort of chain letter, sending it to just about everyone I could think of in the region, describing the book project, requesting any leads they might have and asking that they please pass the letter along to someone else who might have such information. Unlike a traditional chain letter, however, this one promised nothing and made no threats—it simply asked for help. As the responses trickled in, I realized that I needed to take a more aggressive, grassroots approach, so I picked up the telephone and started calling complete strangers at bookstores, libraries and town offices, explaining who I was, what I was looking for and why.

When Rux telephoned, I had just hung up from my umpteenth call and was beginning to feel somewhat overwhelmed by the task before me. But she got me into gear again by giving me the names of half a dozen cookbooks and organizations and suggesting that I contact Edith Foulds in Burlington, Vermont, who might have further leads. I immediately called Edith, who told me about the *College Street Congregational Church 125th Anniversary Cookbook,* which had been published some years before and sounded as if it had the kinds of recipes I was looking for (see Vermont Spring Chicken on page 196 and Maple Baked Beans on page 279). It had gone out of print, so there were no new copies available, but she offered to loan me her own book. I happily accepted. Then she told me to call Janet Rood, who had worked on a couple of other church cookbooks.

When I reached Janet, she had a houseful of guests visiting from Texas, but this didn't stop her from listening to my predicament. I told her how difficult it had been trying to find a wide variety of community cookbooks, since I wanted to include small-town endeavors as well as big-time fundraisers. She said she'd send me a copy of *Out of Vermont Kitchens*, which has been reprinted repeatedly since 1939 (with a couple of revised editions), and a copy of *Vermont Kitchens Revisited*, a newer book (first published in 1990) that was still selling well. "You need to talk with Sue Hanna in Branford, Connecticut," she said. "Sue has been collecting community cookbooks for more than fifteen years, so she'll surely be able to help you."

I wasted no time in contacting Sue Hanna and learned that she had amassed a collection of more than 800 volumes from all over the United States plus several foreign countries. When I told Sue what I was trying to do, she not only offered to loan me some of her books but also invited me to come to her house and select the ones that seemed most suitable. A few days later, I made the 3-hour drive to Branford and had the privilege of seeing what an extensive yet well-organized collection of community cookbooks she has—due in part to her husband's influence. A professional book collector and bibliographer, Archie Hanna is the former William R. Coe Curator of the renowned Western Americana Collection at Yale University. When Sue decided to start collecting cookbooks, it was Archie who suggested that she specialize, so Sue chose charity cookbooks.

After a delicious lunch (including Spinach & Sprouts Salad, see page 106) and an enjoyable visit with Sue and Archie, I looked through the books that Sue had pulled from her shelves, based on my criteria that they be fairly recent editions (since 1980) and only from New England. By the time I left that afternoon, I had a boxful of cookbooks to bring home with me and the good feeling that my search, finally, was well under way.

Community cookbooks reflect the personality of a neighborhood, the generosity of a nonprofit organization or the character of a community. It is no wonder they are so beloved. Most often used as fund-raising tools, they generally are compiled by small, local groups. Proceeds from the sale of a cookbook may go toward supporting a town's fire department, renovating a church steeple or preserving a grange hall, country inn or other building of architectural significance. In the same spirit with which community cookbooks are compiled and produced, people all over the region—and beyond—continued to give me their assistance. Everyone pitched in—from church ministers and secretaries, garden club presidents, quilter's guild members and hospital volunteers to bookstore owners and employees, librarians and town clerks, as well as my own family, family of friends and hometown neighbors.

Hancock, New Hampshire, resident Pat Higgins, for instance, not only provided me with a copy of *A Hancock Community Collection* but also patiently checked the shelves at the Hancock Market to confirm the sizes of cans and bottles for various ingredients. Martha Wilder, another Hancock resident, loaned me 11 of her own community cookbooks; Laurette Carroll of Warner, New Hampshire, sent me 6; Rose Roman of Woonsocket, Rhode Island, sent me the 2 copies she had—well loved and well used.

And then there was the minister I telephoned one morning. His wife said that he had just been called away to attend to something and that she'd have him return my call when he got back later that day. He did call back, apologized for taking so long and listened to my request for a copy of his church's cookbook, which he said he'd put in the mail right away. Then he told me what had happened earlier that morning—a tragedy that had claimed the lives of two of his fellow townspeople. A few days later, his cookbook arrived, exactly as he had promised.

After receiving a broad and varied collection of more than 100 cookbooks, I began to page through each one, selecting recipes that not only sounded delicious but also fit into particular categories—breakfast and brunch; breads, rolls and muffins; main dishes; desserts and so forth. The next step was testing the recipes, and that was done by a host of women and men who prepared the recipes according to the ingredients and directions given in the cookbooks and then evaluated the results. The testing ran smoothly until the Christmas holidays approached. As more and more testers turned their time and attention to other, more pressing matters, fewer and fewer recipes were being tested, and the program almost came to a screeching halt.

Once again I got on the telephone, seeking help wherever I could find it. My first call, of course, was to my mother in Colorado. In spite of the fact that she and my stepfather were expecting two rounds of guests, one immediately following the other, she said that she'd love to help out and to send as many recipes as I wanted. Although she had already cooked up a storm for her company, she began it all over again—this time with recipes she'd never seen before. Fortunately, they all turned out and were well received by her guests. In fact, she's made them a number of times since then. (The Zucchini Chocolate Chip Cake on page 313 is a particular favorite.)

Then I called my friend Joan Dunning in Northern California. I discovered that she was in the middle of writing and illustrating a book that was on deadline, but she took the time to contact friends and called me back later that day with the names and telephone numbers of four people who were willing to get involved. My next call was to my father and stepmother in Texas, who also elicited help from friends and relatives. When my sister returned home on Christmas Day after visiting our mother and stepfather, she began a marathon of recipe testing. So did her son, who had just arrived for the holidays from Cornell. They tested the most recipes in the shortest period of time—and were delighted with the results, adding several to their own repertoires (see Curried Apple-Zucchini Soup on page 134, Chatham Stuffed Leg of Lamb on page 184 and Gingered Pear Pie on page 289).

Once all the test reports were in, I began selecting the recipes that received the best evaluations. They range from old-time favorites to updated creations, from wholesome and hearty to light and nutritious. In all, more than 400 recipes fill the pages of this heart–of–New England cookbook. Each recipe is accompanied by the name of the cookbook it was taken from, plus the name and location of the organization that sponsored it. (The Directory starting on page 354 gives details about ordering these books.)

With 300 to 400 different individuals' recipes represented, I had just as many recipe-writing styles that I wanted to make consistent so they would be easy to follow. At times when the directions were brief, I filled in between the lines. Whether cooking is a necessary chore or a delightful pastime for you, I guarantee that you'll be able to prepare any of the dishes offered here.

I've also tested some of the recipes with ingredients that are lower in fat and sodium. Provided they're just as good as the heartier (but less healthy) originals, I occasionally suggest alternative ingredients or cooking methods. For example, when appropriate, I may suggest plain yogurt as an alternative to sour cream or sautéing in a small amount of oil rather than deep-fat frying.

A couple of times, I have included more than one recipe for the same dish. Take clam chowder, for instance. Rather than offer only one way to prepare this New England classic, knowing full well that there are about as many variations as there are people in the region, I included three slightly different versions. To some, a thick, creamy chowder is the only way to go. To others, the addition of flour and water is unheard of. To still others, it's the salt pork that makes the dish "culinarily" correct.

Another example is cranberry relish. Why limit the choices to only one when three variations on the same theme are all equally good? The differences may seem insignificant, but the end results are distinctive and well worth having available to you.

Whatever your needs—early-morning eye-openers, late-night snacks, holiday specialties or simple yet savory suppers—*Hometown Cooking in New England* provides you with heart-of-the-home cooking at its best. I hope you enjoy not only this taste of New England but also the view of its communities as well.

Sandra J. Taylor

BREAKFAST
&
BRUNCH

$\mathcal{G}$RANNY'S GRANOLA

⁂

Cereals of this kind are fun to make because the ingredients and their amounts can be determined by what you have on hand and personal preference. Using this version as a rough guide, you could double the amount of oats, reduce the wheat germ to $1/2$ cup, use sunflower seeds instead of nuts, use brown sugar instead of honey or maple syrup and so forth. The combinations are endless. The main thing to watch, however, is the baking. Granola can overcook and burn during the last few minutes, so make sure to keep an eye on it and stir more frequently as you near the end of the baking time. Serve this with milk as cereal, use as a topping for ice cream or frozen yogurt or eat as is for a nutritious snack.

1 cup rolled oats	$1/2$ cup instant nonfat dry milk
1 cup wheat germ (optional)	1 cup honey or maple syrup
1 cup walnuts or pecans	$2/3$ cup water
1 cup unsweetened coconut	$1/2$ cup oil
1 cup dried fruit (raisins, prunes, apricots or dates, or a combination)	1 teaspoon vanilla
	$1/8$ teaspoon salt

Combine the oats, wheat germ (if using), walnuts or pecans, coconut, dried fruit, milk, honey or maple syrup, water, oil, vanilla and salt in a large, deep roasting pan and mix well. Bake at 350° for 30 minutes, stirring every 5 minutes, until lightly browned and fairly dry. Cool thoroughly and store in tightly covered containers in a cool place or in the refrigerator.

Makes about 8 cups.

Maine-ly Good Eatin'
American Cancer Society: Maine Division, Brunswick, Maine

$\mathcal{A}$PPLE PANCAKES

The taste and texture of the cornmeal combines beautifully
with the soft chunks of apple. The pancakes can break easily
when turned over, so handle them with care.

1¼ cups cornmeal	½ teaspoon salt
1¼ cups unbleached flour	2 eggs
¼ cup sugar	1¾ cups milk
1 tablespoon plus 2 teaspoons baking powder	¼ cup plus 2 tablespoons oil
½ teaspoon ground cinnamon	2 apples, peeled, cored and finely chopped

In a medium bowl, mix the cornmeal, flour, sugar, baking powder, cinnamon and salt. In a small bowl, beat the eggs, then add the milk, oil and apples. Add the egg mixture to the flour mixture, stirring only until the dry ingredients are moistened.

Cook on a greased griddle over low heat until the rim of each pancake is full of broken bubbles and the underside is golden brown. Flip and cook until done.

Serves 6 to 8.

Liberal Portions
Unitarian Universalist Church, Nashua, New Hampshire

$\mathcal{B}$LUEBERRY CORNMEAL PANCAKES

Here's an appetizing remedy for those
who've gotten up on the wrong side of the bed.

1 cup unbleached flour	1½ cups orange juice
1 cup cornmeal	3 tablespoons oil
2 tablespoons baking powder	1 egg, beaten
1 tablespoon sugar	1 cup fresh or thawed frozen blueberries
½ teaspoon salt	

In a medium bowl, mix together the flour, cornmeal, baking powder, sugar and salt. Add the juice, oil and egg and mix well. Gently fold in the blueberries.

Heat a lightly greased griddle to medium-high. Pour the batter onto the griddle, using approximately ¼ cup batter for each pancake. Cook until bubbles appear. Flip the pancakes and cook until done.

Serves 4 to 6.

Mystic Seaport's Moveable Feasts Cookbook
Mystic Seaport Museum Stores, Mystic, Connecticut

ORANGE BUCKWHEAT PANCAKES
✥

Garnish these with grated orange rind or orange slices and serve
with sour cream or plain yogurt and warm maple syrup.

2 **eggs**	2	**tablespoons sugar**
2 **cups buttermilk**	2	**teaspoons baking powder**
¼ **cup oil**	1	**teaspoon baking soda**
1 **cup unbleached flour**	1	**teaspoon grated orange rind**
1 **cup buckwheat flour**	½	**teaspoon salt**

In a large bowl, beat the eggs, buttermilk and oil. Add the unbleached flour, buckwheat flour, sugar, baking powder, baking soda, orange rind and salt and beat until smooth. Spoon the batter onto a lightly greased hot griddle, turn as soon as bubbles form and cook on the other side until golden brown.

Serves 4.

Marshfield's Overdue Cookbook
Cliff Rodgers Free Library, Marshfield Hills, Massachusetts

ROCK FARM PANCAKES

Don't let this recipe title mislead you.
There's nothing hard or heavy about these pancakes—even though
they contain wheat germ and whole-wheat pastry flour. The crêpelike
batter yields cakes that are light, tender, delicate and delicious.

1 **cup whole-wheat pastry flour**	2 **cups milk**
¾ **cup unbleached flour**	½ **cup plain yogurt**
¼ **cup wheat germ**	2 **tablespoons butter or**
1½ **teaspoons baking powder**	**margarine, melted**
1 **teaspoon baking soda**	2 **eggs, beaten**
¼ **teaspoon salt**	

In a large bowl, mix together the whole-wheat pastry flour, unbleached
flour, wheat germ, baking powder, baking soda and salt. In a small bowl,
blend the milk, yogurt, butter or margarine and eggs. Stir the liquid ingredients into the flour mixture until combined, then cook on a lightly greased
hot griddle, making the pancakes as large or as small as you prefer.

Serves 4 to 6.

Poker Hill Cookbook
Poker Hill School, Underhill, Vermont

$\mathcal{P}$OWERFUL PANCAKES

These pancakes are just as the name implies: hearty and healthful. Serve them with applesauce or maple syrup for breakfast or accompanied with a mild sausage for lunch or supper. Because the oats need time to soften, you might want to mix the batter the night before so you don't have to lose time waiting in the morning. The batter will keep in the refrigerator for days.

2½	cups milk	¼	teaspoon vanilla
1	egg	¾	cup raisins
¾	cup rolled oats	¼	cup sunflower seeds
2	tablespoons honey (optional)	¼	cup sesame seeds
1¼	cups whole-wheat pastry flour or whole-wheat flour	¼	cup wheat germ
2	tablespoons oil	¼	cup bran
1	tablespoon baking powder	1	apple, shredded

Beat the milk and egg together in a large bowl. Add the oats and honey (if using), stirring to blend. Set aside for 10 to 15 minutes.

Add the flour, oil, baking powder and vanilla and mix well. Stir in the raisins, sunflower seeds, sesame seeds, wheat germ, bran and apples. Cook on a well-greased medium-hot griddle.

Serves 6.

The Andover Cookbook II
Phillips Academy: The Ladies' Benevolent Society, Andover, Massachusetts

PUMPKIN-CHEESE PANCAKES

Be sure to use fresh pumpkin or another kind of
winter squash, not canned or cooked. These are savory instead of
sweet and can be served for lunch or supper as well as brunch,
accompanied with sour cream or applesauce.

2 tablespoons butter or margarine	**Ground nutmeg**
2 large scallions, sliced	**2 eggs**
2 cups grated peeled pumpkin or other winter squash	**¼ cup plus 2 tablespoons milk**
Salt	**¼ cup plus 2 tablespoons unbleached flour**
Ground black pepper	**¼ cup shredded Jarlsberg or Swiss cheese**

Melt the butter or margarine in a heavy skillet over medium-low heat.
Add the scallions and stir for 1 minute. Add the pumpkin, salt, pepper
and nutmeg. Cook, stirring frequently, until the pumpkin is tender, about
6 minutes. Cool the pumpkin mixture slightly.

Mix the eggs, milk, flour and cheese in a food processor. Add the
pumpkin mixture and blend, using on/off turns.

Heat a large, heavy skillet or griddle over medium-high heat. Grease well
with oil. Spoon in the batter, using 1 tablespoonful for each pancake. Cook
until the pancakes are browned and set, about 45 seconds on each side.

Serves 4.

Marblehead Cooks
Tower School, Marblehead, Massachusetts

OVEN PANCAKE WITH CIDER SAUCE

This puffy pancake with its sweet-tart and spicy sauce
makes a fun family breakfast on the weekend.

PANCAKE

- ¾ **cup unbleached flour**
- 1½ **teaspoons sugar**
- 1¼ **cups milk**
- 2 **eggs**
- 1 **tablespoon butter or margarine**

SAUCE

- ½ **cup sugar**
- 1 **tablespoon cornstarch**
- ¼ **teaspoon pumpkin pie spice**
- 1 **cup apple cider**
- 1 **tablespoon lemon juice**
- 2 **tablespoons butter or margarine**

To make the pancake: In a medium bowl, combine the flour and sugar.
Stir in the milk, then add the eggs and beat until smooth. Put the butter or
margarine in a 10″ skillet and place in a preheated 425° oven until melted.
Tilt the skillet to cover the bottom with butter or margarine, then pour in
the batter and bake for 20 minutes, or until the pancake is golden brown
and puffy.

To make the sauce: Mix the sugar, cornstarch and pumpkin pie spice
in a saucepan. Stir in the cider and lemon juice. Cook until the mixture
thickens and boils. Boil, stirring, for 1 minute. Remove from the heat and
blend in the butter or margarine. Serve with the hot pancake.

Serves 6 to 8.

History in the Baking
Sunapee 2000 Beautification Committee, Sunapee, New Hampshire

GINGERBREAD WAFFLES

These are so good you'll want them morning, noon and night.
For breakfast or brunch, serve them with butter or margarine and maple
syrup; for dessert, top with whipped cream, frozen yogurt or ice cream.

2	cups sifted cake flour	½	teaspoon salt
½	cup sugar	¾	cup sour cream or plain yogurt
2	teaspoons baking powder		
¼	teaspoon baking soda	1	egg, beaten
2	teaspoons ground ginger	⅔	cup dark molasses
1	teaspoon ground cinnamon	¼	cup milk

In a large bowl, sift together the flour, sugar, baking powder, baking
soda, ginger, cinnamon and salt.

In a small bowl, combine the sour cream or yogurt, egg, molasses and
milk. Add to the flour mixture and beat until smooth. Cook in a hot waffle
iron according to the manufacturer's directions.

Serves 4 to 6.

Flavors of Cape Cod
Thornton W. Burgess Society, East Sandwich, Massachusetts

SUNDAY MORNING MAPLE WAFFLES

Tasty and good-looking, these waffles are packed with nutrition. Wheat
germ is somewhat high in fat, however, so you might consider using nonfat
plain yogurt and skim milk and reducing the oil to ¼ cup.

1	cup wheat germ	1	cup plain yogurt
¾	cup whole-wheat flour	1	cup milk
½	cup unbleached flour	⅓	cup oil
1	tablespoon baking powder	2	eggs
½	teaspoon salt	2–4	tablespoons maple syrup

In a medium bowl, combine the wheat germ, whole-wheat flour, unbleached flour, baking powder and salt. In a large bowl, beat the yogurt, milk, oil, eggs and maple syrup. Add the dry mixture to the wet and stir until smooth. Let sit for a minute, then pour out the proper amount for your waffle iron and cook according to the manufacturer's directions.

Serves 4.

The Mark Twain Library Cookbook, Vol. III
Mark Twain Library Association, Redding, Connecticut

MAPLE-BUTTER SPREAD

This is such a special treat that it makes a fine gift item, presented in small fancy jars or decorative tins. Serve with pancakes or waffles, or spread on warm, home-baked breads, rolls or muffins.

1 cup maple syrup   **¾ cup butter or margarine**

Cook the maple syrup in a heavy-bottomed saucepan over low heat until it reaches the soft-ball stage. Add the butter or margarine and stir until it melts. Pour the mixture into a deep bowl and beat with an electric mixer until thick and creamy.

Makes 1¾ cups.

Vermont II: Kitchen Memories
Montpelier, Vermont

ABBOT COFFEE CAKE

Just about everyone seems to have a favorite crumb cake recipe—
or at least a memory of one from childhood. This has the traditionally
crumbly brown sugar and cinnamon topping that complements the not-
too-sweet cake, which is finely textured and holds together well.

COFFEE CAKE
- **2 cups unbleached flour**
- **1½ teaspoons baking powder**
- **⅛ teaspoon salt**
- **3 tablespoons butter or margarine, softened**
- **½ cup plus 2 tablespoons granulated sugar**
- **2 eggs**
- **¼ cup plus 2 tablespoons milk**

TOPPING
- **⅓ cup unbleached flour**
- **¼ cup firmly packed brown sugar**
- **½ teaspoon ground cinnamon**
- **2 tablespoons butter or margarine, melted**
- **3 tablespoons ground nuts**

To make the coffee cake: Have all the ingredients at room temperature. In a
medium bowl, sift the flour, baking powder and salt twice. In a large bowl,
cream the butter or margarine until light, gradually add the sugar and
cream until well mixed. Beat the eggs and add to the sugar mixture,
blending thoroughly. Alternately add the flour mixture and milk to the
creamed mixture, then beat until smooth. Spread in a greased 8″ × 8″
baking pan.

To make the topping: Mix the flour, brown sugar and cinnamon in a small
bowl. Pour in the butter or margarine and mix by hand until crumbly.
Combine with the nuts and sprinkle over the cake batter just before putting
it into the oven. Bake in a preheated 350° oven for 40 to 45 minutes.

Serves 10.

The Andover Cookbook II
Phillips Academy: The Ladies' Benevolent Society, Andover, Massachusetts

SOUTH NEWBURY UNION CHURCH
COFFEE CAKE
❧

Frost this coffee cake with a confectioners' sugar icing and
decorate with ground nuts or cherries before the frosting dries.

¼ cup warm water	2 tablespoons shortening
1 package dry yeast	3½–4 cups sifted unbleached flour
¾ cup plain yogurt or sour cream	1 tablespoon butter or margarine, melted
¼ cup granulated sugar	½ cup firmly packed brown sugar
1 teaspoon salt	
1 egg, beaten	2 teaspoons ground cinnamon
2 tablespoons butter or margarine	¼ cup ground walnuts

In a large bowl, mix the water and yeast, stirring to dissolve. In a
saucepan, heat the yogurt or sour cream until warm (do not boil) and add
the granulated sugar, salt, egg, 2 tablespoons butter or margarine and shortening. Stir to dissolve the shortening and butter. When cooled, add to the
yeast. Add enough of the flour to make the dough easy to handle and turn
out onto a floured surface, kneading in the remaining flour. Let the dough
rise in a greased bowl until doubled in bulk. Punch down and let rest for
10 minutes.

On a floured surface, roll the dough into a 15″ × 9″ rectangle. Spread
with the melted butter or margarine and sprinkle with the brown sugar,
cinnamon and nuts.

Starting on the long side, roll the dough up tightly and seal well. Wet or
grease the two ends and pinch them together, forming a circle. With a
knife, make cuts ⅔ of the way through the ring at 1″ intervals, opening up
each cut.

Let the dough rise for about 20 minutes, then bake in a preheated 375°
oven for 25 to 30 minutes.

Serves 10 to 12.

South Newbury Union Church and Society Cookbook
South Newbury Union Church, South Newbury, New Hampshire

MAPLE JOHNNYCAKE

This maple syrup–sweetened corn bread, with a cakelike texture and butter-yellow interior, can accompany any meal and makes a satisfying snack as well. The batter can be baked in a muffin tin, if desired, but reduce the baking time to 12 to 15 minutes.

1⅓	cups unbleached flour	2	eggs
⅔	cup cornmeal (preferably stone-ground)	⅓	cup maple syrup
		⅔	cup milk
1	tablespoon baking powder	⅓	cup melted shortening or oil
½	teaspoon salt		

Combine the flour, cornmeal, baking powder and salt in a large bowl. In a small bowl, beat the eggs, maple syrup and milk. Add to the dry ingredients and blend. Stir in the shortening or oil. Pour the batter into a lightly greased 9" × 9" pan and bake in a preheated 400° oven for 20 minutes.

Makes 12.

Out of Vermont Kitchens
The Women of St. Paul's Cathedral, Burlington, Vermont

MOTHER SHAW'S BAKING POWDER BISCUITS

Serve these hot from the oven, accompanied with butter or margarine,
honey, maple syrup or preserves. If cut to a 3″ diameter,
the biscuits can be used for strawberry shortcake.

2	cups unbleached flour	¼	cup shortening
4	teaspoons baking powder	¾	cup milk
½	teaspoon salt		

Sift the flour, baking powder and salt into a medium bowl. Add the
shortening and rub it in with your fingertips or cut it in with a pastry
blender until crumbly. Add the milk slowly and mix to blend. Turn the
dough out onto a lightly floured surface and knead 4 or 5 times. Roll out to
a 1″ thickness and cut with a 2″ biscuit cutter. Bake in a preheated 450°
oven for 10 to 15 minutes.

Makes 12.

Cracker Barrel Cookbook
First Congregational Church: Newbury Women's Fellowship, Newbury, Vermont

BREAKFAST MUFFIN TREATS

This recipe gives you a great deal of leeway.
Instead of using nuts in the muffin batter, you could substitute
an equal amount of dried fruits—apricots, dates or raisins. The topping
is a nice embellishment, but if you're running short of time or have
just run out of brown sugar or walnuts, it can easily be omitted.

TOPPING (OPTIONAL)
- ⅓ **cup firmly packed brown sugar**
- ⅓ **cup chopped walnuts**
- ½ **teaspoon ground cinnamon**

MUFFINS
- ½ **cup butter or margarine, melted and cooled**
- 1 **cup applesauce**
- 1 **cup firmly packed dark brown sugar**

- 1 **cup unbleached flour**
- ½ **cup whole-wheat flour**
- ¼ **cup rolled oats**
- 2 **tablespoons wheat germ**
- ½ **cup chopped walnuts**
- ½ **teaspoon salt**
- 1 **teaspoon baking soda**
- ½ **teaspoon baking powder**
- 2 **teaspoons ground cinnamon**
- ½ **teaspoon ground cloves**

To make the topping (if using): Mix the brown sugar, walnuts and cinnamon in a small bowl and set aside.

To make the muffins: Mix the butter or margarine, applesauce and brown sugar in a small bowl. In a large bowl, combine the unbleached flour, whole-wheat flour, oats, wheat germ, walnuts, salt, baking soda, baking powder, cinnamon and cloves. Make a well in the center and lightly fold in the butter mixture. Spoon the batter into greased or paper-lined muffin cups, sprinkle with the topping (if using) and bake in a preheated 375° oven for 25 minutes, or until a toothpick inserted in the center comes out clean.

Makes 16.

Cox Community Cookbook
A.W. Cox PTO: Playground Committee, Guilford, Connecticut

MAPLE RAGAMUFFIN DESSERT

Although referred to as a dessert, this can be served with
the morning meal. The lightly browned biscuits are covered
with a thick sauce that has an intense maple flavor.

1½ **cups unbleached flour**
1 **tablespoon baking powder**
½ **teaspoon salt**
¼ **teaspoon cream of tartar**
¼ **cup shortening**

½ **cup (scant) milk**
2 **tablespoons butter or**
   margarine
1½ **cups maple syrup, heated**

In a medium bowl, mix the flour, baking powder, salt and cream of
tartar. Cut in the shortening until the mixture is crumbly. Blend in the milk.
On a floured surface, roll out the dough to about a ½" thickness and cut
out 12 small biscuits. Place the biscuits in a greased 12" × 8" baking dish
and dot with the butter or margarine. Pour the maple syrup over the top
and bake in a preheated 375° oven for 15 minutes.

Serves 12.

Sharing Recipes
Benson First Response Rescue Squad, Benson, Vermont

$\mathcal{A}$NNIE WINNIE'S PINEAPPLE SCONES
❧

These are a delightful addition to a breakfast menu.
The dough is quite sticky, so you may need to sprinkle it lightly
with additional flour as you pat it out into circles.

SCONES

- 2 cups sifted unbleached flour
- ¼ cup sugar
- 2 teaspoons baking powder
- ½ teaspoon salt
- ¼ cup shortening
- 1 egg
- 3 tablespoons unsweetened pineapple juice
- 1 cup drained crushed unsweetened pineapple

ICING

- ½ cup confectioners' sugar
- 1 tablespoon milk, heated
- ¼ teaspoon lemon extract

To make the scones: Sift the flour, sugar, baking powder and salt in a large bowl. Cut or rub in the shortening until the mixture is crumbly. Beat the egg and pineapple juice and stir into the flour mixture. Mix in the crushed pineapple only until the mixture is moistened.

Divide the dough in half and place it on a lightly floured surface. Pat each half into a circle about ½" thick. Cut each circle into 8 pie-shaped wedges. Bake on an ungreased baking sheet in a preheated 425° oven for 12 to 13 minutes.

To make the icing: Mix the confectioners' sugar, milk and lemon extract in a small bowl, stirring until smooth. Frost the scones while they are still warm and serve.

Makes 16.

The Vermont Symphony Cookbook
Vermont Symphony Orchestra, Burlington, Vermont

APPLE & WALNUT SCONES

Wonderful fresh from the oven as well as at room temperature,
scones also can be reheated. Wrap them in aluminum foil
and place them in a preheated 375° oven for 5 minutes, then
fold back the foil and heat for 3 to 4 minutes more.

2¼ cups unbleached flour
½ cup granulated sugar
2 teaspoons baking powder
½ teaspoon salt
½ cup butter or margarine
2 eggs, beaten
¼ cup milk

2 teaspoons vanilla
1 teaspoon grated lemon rind
1 cup chopped apples
½ cup chopped walnuts
¼ cup firmly packed brown sugar
1 teaspoon ground cinnamon

In a large bowl, combine the flour, granulated sugar, baking powder and salt, mixing well. Cut in the butter or margarine until crumbly.

In a small bowl, mix the eggs, milk, vanilla and lemon rind, then stir into the flour mixture (the dough will be sticky). Stir in the apples.

Grease an 11″-diameter circle on a baking sheet, place the dough on top and pat it into a 9″ circle. Mix the nuts, brown sugar and cinnamon and sprinkle over the top. Cut the dough into 8 wedges and bake in a preheated 375° oven for 30 to 35 minutes, or until lightly browned.

Serves 8.

Boston Cooks
Women's Educational & Industrial Union, Boston, Massachusetts

*F*RESH HERB SCONES

These scones have a pleasing light-brown color,
excellent texture and perfect balance of flavors,
with neither the cheese nor the herbs dominating.

2 cups unbleached flour	2 teaspoons lemon juice
1 tablespoon baking powder	2 tablespoons snipped fresh
¼ cup grated Parmesan cheese	chives or scallions
¼ teaspoon ground black pepper	1 tablespoon chopped fresh basil
½ cup buttermilk or plain yogurt	1 teaspoon coarsely chopped fresh thyme or oregano
¼ cup olive oil	½ teaspoon minced garlic
1 egg	

Combine the flour, baking powder, Parmesan cheese and pepper in a
large bowl, mixing well. In another bowl, whisk the buttermilk or yogurt,
oil, egg, lemon juice, chives or scallions, basil, thyme or oregano and garlic
until well blended. Stir the herb mixture into the flour mixture until a soft
dough forms.

Turn the dough out onto a floured surface and knead 10 to 15 times.
Gather into a ball and cut in half. Place both halves on a baking sheet and
pat each into an 8″ or 9″ round. Cut each round into 8 wedges and bake in
a preheated 375° oven for 15 to 20 minutes, or until lightly browned. Cool
on a wire rack for 5 minutes. Wrap loosely in a dish towel on the rack and
cool for at least 15 to 20 minutes more before serving.

Serves 8.

Liberal Portions
Unitarian Universalist Church, Nashua, New Hampshire

IRON-POT OVEN SCONES

If you do not have an iron pot, a ceramic one will do, as will any round
casserole with a cover. These scones are low in fat and cholesterol,
for they use no butter or margarine, but you'll never miss it.

2 cups unbleached flour	**½ teaspoon salt**
1 teaspoon baking soda	**1 cup buttermilk**
1 teaspoon cream of tartar	**1 cup golden or dark raisins**

Sift the flour, baking soda, cream of tartar and salt into a medium bowl
and stir to blend. Make a well in the center and add the buttermilk and
raisins. Mix the batter until it is soft and elastic. Turn it out onto a floured
surface and knead very lightly. Form into an 8″ round, place in an iron pot
and cover. Bake in a preheated 450° oven for about 30 to 35 minutes. Cut
into 6 to 8 wedges and serve. (Keep warm in a tea towel if not serving
immediately.)

Makes 6 to 8.

Derry Community Playground Cookbook
Derry Playground Committee, East Derry, New Hampshire

OAT SCONES

Quick and easy to prepare, these scones can be made at any time, but they really deserve to be enjoyed on a leisurely weekend. Savor them on Sunday morning with mugs of hot coffee or cocoa and homemade preserves, or while relaxing in the afternoon with a cup of freshly steeped tea.

1½ cups unbleached flour
1¼ cups rolled oats
¼ cup sugar
1 tablespoon baking powder
1 teaspoon cream of tartar
½ teaspoon salt

⅔ cup butter or margarine,
melted and cooled
⅓ cup milk
1 egg
½ cup raisins

In a large bowl, combine the flour, oats, sugar, baking powder, cream of tartar and salt. In a separate bowl, beat the butter or margarine, milk and egg. Add to the dry ingredients and mix until moistened. Stir in the raisins.

On a greased baking sheet, form the dough into an 8″ round. Cut it into 8 to 12 wedges and bake in a preheated 425° oven for 12 to 15 minutes.

Makes 8 to 12.

Marblehead Cooks
Tower School, Marblehead, Massachusetts

MAPLE-CINNAMON ROLLS

Large, lovely and luscious, these breakfast rolls have a delicate maple flavor and fine texture. They are not at all complicated to make and rise to any occasion: weekend brunch, holiday buffet or hostess gift.

1 **cup milk**	1/4 **cup warm water**
1/3 **cup plus 2 tablespoons butter or margarine, divided**	5 **cups sifted unbleached flour, divided**
1/2 **cup plus 2 tablespoons sugar, divided**	2 **eggs, beaten**
1/2 **teaspoon salt**	1 **teaspoon ground cinnamon**
2 **packages dry yeast**	1/3 **cup maple syrup**

In a saucepan, bring the milk just to a boil, add 1/3 cup of the butter or margarine, 1/2 cup of the sugar and the salt, stirring until the butter melts and the sugar and salt dissolve. Set aside to cool.

In a large bowl, sprinkle the yeast over the warm water and set aside for 5 minutes. Stir in the cooled milk and butter mixture, blending well. Add 2 1/2 cups of the flour and the eggs and beat. Mix in the remaining flour, turn out onto a floured surface and knead for 10 minutes. Place back in the bowl, cover and let rise for 2 hours.

Punch down, knead briefly on a floured surface and roll out into a rectangle about 1/2" thick. Spread the remaining 2 tablespoons butter over the surface of the dough and sprinkle with the cinnamon and the remaining 2 tablespoons sugar. Starting on the long side, roll up the dough and seal the seam. Slice into 12 pieces. Generously butter the bottom of a 13" × 9" baking dish and add the maple syrup, tilting the pan to coat the entire surface. Place the rolls on the syrup, cover and let rise until doubled in bulk. Bake in a preheated 375° oven for 15 to 20 minutes.

Makes 12.

A Collection of Maple Recipes
New Hampshire Maple Producers Association, Londonderry, New Hampshire

STICKY BUNS

Because this breakfast treat takes some time to make, you might
want to start preparations a day ahead. Chill the dough overnight
and keep it in the refrigerator until you are ready to prepare the pans.
Sticky buns are wonderful for holiday breakfasts, so double the
recipe at Thanksgiving and freeze half for Christmas.

1 cup hot sieved or mashed potatoes (save cooking water)	2 eggs
½ cup butter or margarine, softened	1½ cups warm potato water
	7 cups flour (approximately)
½ cup plus 2 tablespoons granulated sugar, divided	Brown sugar
	1 cup chopped walnuts
½ teaspoon salt	3 teaspoons ground cinnamon
1 package dry yeast	3 tablespoons butter or margarine, melted

In a large bowl, combine the potatoes, softened butter or margarine,
½ cup of the granulated sugar and salt. Cool to lukewarm and add the
yeast, eggs and potato water. Mix well. Stir in enough of the flour to make a
manageable dough.

Knead the dough on a floured surface until smooth. It should be moist
and somewhat sticky, so take care not to add too much flour. Place in a
greased bowl and let rise until doubled in bulk. Punch down and refrigerate until thoroughly chilled.

Use enough brown sugar to cover the bottoms of 3 greased 8" or 9"
round or square cake pans. Sprinkle on enough water to make the sugar
very wet, then sprinkle generously with the walnuts.

In a small bowl, combine the cinnamon and the remaining 2 tablespoons
granulated sugar. Remove the dough from the refrigerator and roll out on a
floured surface into a rectangle about ½" thick. Brush with the melted butter
or margarine and sprinkle with the cinnamon-sugar mixture. Starting on the
long side, roll up like a jelly roll and cut into ½"-thick slices. Place these side
by side in the prepared pans. Let rise until doubled in bulk.

Bake in a preheated 350° oven for 20 to 30 minutes. Immediately invert
onto a plate while hot, or the buns will stick to the pans. Serve hot or warm.

Makes 20 to 24.

Vermont Kitchens Revisited
The Women of the Cathedral Church of St. Paul, Burlington, Vermont

$\mathcal{B}$LUEBERRIES & DUMPLINGS

Fresh or frozen berries work equally well in this
delectable dish. It's terrific for breakfast or brunch and even
dessert, topped with vanilla ice cream or frozen yogurt.

1½ **cups fruit juice**	2 **teaspoons baking powder**
2 **tablespoons cornstarch**	½ **teaspoon salt**
1 **quart blueberries**	1 **egg**
1 **cup unbleached flour (or part**	**Milk**
whole-wheat flour)	

In a large saucepan, mix together the juice and cornstarch. Cook and stir
over medium heat until bubbly and clear. Add the blueberries and continue
to cook, stirring occasionally, until bubbly.

Meanwhile, mix the flour, baking powder and salt in a small bowl. Break
the egg into a measuring cup and add enough milk to make ½ cup. Beat
well, then stir into the dry ingredients. (The batter should be stiff.)

When the blueberries are bubbly, spoon the batter over the top, making
8 small dumplings. Cover, reduce the heat to a simmer and cook for about
10 minutes.

Serves 4.

The Community Cooks
Pine Hill Waldorf School, Wilton, New Hampshire

CHEESE-APPLE COBBLER

Appealing at any time of the day, this cobbler combines two
New England staples: apples and Cheddar cheese. A good baking apple like
a McIntosh or Granny Smith is recommended. Note that the cheese
topping is spooned over the apples and doesn't need to be spread on
evenly. If this is to be used as a dessert, you might want to increase the
sugar, although the sweetness of the apples should determine this.

6 cups peeled, cored and thinly sliced apples (about 2 pounds)	1½ teaspoons baking powder
	1½ cups shredded Cheddar cheese (6 ounces)
1¼ cups unbleached flour, divided	¼ cup butter or margarine, melted
½ cup sugar, divided	¼ cup milk
¼ teaspoon ground cinnamon	

Combine the apples, ¼ cup of the flour, ¼ cup of the sugar and the cinnamon in a large bowl. Toss together. Spread the mixture evenly in a lightly buttered 8" × 8" or 11" × 7" baking pan.

Combine the remaining 1 cup flour, remaining ¼ cup sugar, baking powder and cheese in a large bowl. Add the butter or margarine and milk, stirring until just combined. Spoon the cheese mixture over the apple mixture in the pan. Bake in a preheated 400° oven for 30 to 35 minutes, or until the topping is crisp and golden and the apples are tender. Serve warm.

Serves 8 to 10.

Anniversary Celebration Cookbook
Trinity Lutheran Church, Chelmsford, Massachusetts

ℬaked Eggs with Mashed Potatoes

An interesting and unusual breakfast preparation,
these also are great for lunch or supper. Depending on how you
like your eggs—soft or well-done—the baking time will vary.

2 cups mashed boiled potatoes **Salt and pepper** **¼–½ cup milk or cream, heated**	**3 tablespoons butter or** **margarine, divided** **4 eggs**

Beat the potatoes and salt and pepper to taste in a bowl. Add the milk or cream and 2 tablespoons of the butter or margarine and continue to beat until light and fluffy. Place in a buttered 9″ × 9″ baking dish and make 4 deep hollows in the potatoes. Carefully drop an uncooked egg in each hollow, dust with additional salt and pepper to taste and dot with the remaining 1 tablespoon butter cut into bits. Bake in a preheated 350° oven until the eggs are cooked, about 10 to 20 minutes. Serve at once.

Serves 2 to 4.

A Taste of Glocester
Glocester Heritage Society, Chepachet, Rhode Island

SCALLOP FRITTERS

Easy but elegant, these tender fritters are enveloped in a
crunchy crust. Serve them with lemon wedges.

½	pound scallops		Pinch of garlic powder
1	egg	1	teaspoon minced onions
½	cup dry bread crumbs	2	tablespoons butter or oil
½	teaspoon dried parsley		

Chop the scallops. In a medium bowl, beat the egg and stir in the bread
crumbs, parsley, garlic powder, onions and scallops.

Heat the butter or oil in a large skillet and drop the batter by heaping
tablespoonfuls, spreading each out into a circle. Fry gently, then turn over
and continue cooking until firm. Remove to a covered casserole until ready
to serve.

Serves 4.

A Collection of Favorite Italian Recipes
St. Anthony's Church: The Women's Guild, Woonsocket, Rhode Island

NEW MEADOWS RIVER FISH HASH

Leftover fish is ideal for this, for it will save
preparation time. And if a sauce was used, that's fine, too,
as it will add to the flavor of the hash.

2 medium potatoes, peeled and
quartered
1 medium onion, chopped
2 tablespoons oil, divided

1 small sole, haddock, cod or
hake fillet (about 1 pound)
Salt and white pepper

Place the potatoes in water to cover and boil until tender. While they are
cooking, sauté the onions in 1 tablespoon of the oil. Drain the potatoes,
mash and add to the onions. Remove from the heat and set aside.

Cook the fish in a small amount of salted water until it flakes easily with
a fork. Remove the fish from the water and break it up into small pieces.
Add it to the potatoes and onions, mixing well. Add salt and white pepper
to taste.

Heat the remaining 1 tablespoon oil in a skillet, add the fish and potato
mixture and cook until golden and crispy on both sides.

Serves 4.

The Maine Collection
Portland Museum of Art, Portland, Maine

$\mathcal{V}$ERMONT APPLE-RAISIN BREAD

Dark, moist and chunky with raisins and nuts, this bread
has just a hint of chocolate flavor, and the spices, surprisingly,
are equally subtle. Baked in a ring mold or Bundt pan, it looks and
tastes like dessert, although it also can be served with mid-morning
coffee or afternoon tea. Serve it plain or with cream cheese.

1½ cups unbleached flour	½ teaspoon ground allspice
1 cup sugar	1 cup applesauce
2 tablespoons unsweetened cocoa powder	½ cup buttermilk
	¼ cup butter or margarine, melted
1 teaspoon baking soda	
½ teaspoon salt	1 cup raisins
½ teaspoon ground cinnamon	½ cup chopped walnuts
½ teaspoon ground nutmeg	Confectioners' sugar

In a large bowl, combine the flour, sugar, cocoa, baking soda, salt, cinnamon, nutmeg and allspice. In another bowl, mix the applesauce, buttermilk and butter or margarine. Stir into the dry ingredients, mixing only
until moistened. Add the raisins and walnuts and blend lightly. Pour into a
well-greased and floured 6-cup ring mold or Bundt pan. Bake in a preheated 325° oven for 45 to 50 minutes, or until a toothpick inserted in the
center comes out clean. Cool in the pan for 10 minutes, then turn out onto
a wire rack. Sprinkle with confectioners' sugar.

Serves 18 to 20.

Vermont Kitchens Revisited
The Women of the Cathedral Church of St. Paul, Burlington, Vermont

APPLE-ANA BREAD

Diced apples and flecks of bananas provide visual appeal as well as their own sweet flavor to this quick bread, so the amount of sugar could be reduced. For a crunchy texture, add ½ cup chopped walnuts.

4	apples	1	teaspoon vanilla
1	teaspoon lemon juice	3	cups unbleached flour
3	large bananas	1½	teaspoons baking powder
½	cup shortening	1½	teaspoons baking soda
1	cup sugar	½	teaspoon salt
2	eggs		

Peel, core and dice the apples and put them in a small bowl. Sprinkle with the lemon juice to keep them from turning brown. Mash the bananas and add them to the apples.

In a large bowl, cream the shortening and sugar until light, then beat in the eggs and vanilla until creamy. Sift the flour, baking powder, baking soda and salt and add alternately with the apple-banana mixture to the creamed mixture. Divide the batter between 2 greased 8½" x 4½" loaf pans and bake in a preheated 325° oven for 55 to 60 minutes, or until a toothpick inserted in the center comes out clean.

Makes 2 loaves.

The Harvard Cookbook
Harvard Unitarian Church, Harvard, Massachusetts

CRANBERRY-ORANGE BREAD
❧

Keep extra bags of cranberries in the freezer so that you can
make this year-round, or bake large quantities of the bread at a time,
for it freezes very well. If you can resist the temptation to cut into a loaf
soon after it is baked, let it sit overnight before serving. Its flavor
will be even better the next day—and the day after that.

	Juice and grated rind of	**$^1/_2$**	**cup coarsely chopped**
	1 orange		**walnuts**
2	**tablespoons oil**	**2**	**cups unbleached flour**
	Boiling water	**$1^1/_2$**	**teaspoons baking powder**
1	**egg**	**$^1/_2$**	**teaspoon baking soda**
1	**cup sugar**	**$^1/_2$**	**teaspoon salt**
$1^1/_2$	**cups cranberries**		

Put the orange juice and rind in a measuring cup. Add the oil and
enough water to bring the level to $^3/_4$ cup.

Beat the egg and sugar in a large bowl. Pick over the cranberries and
rinse them thoroughly. Then add the cranberries, walnuts and orange mixture to the egg mixture, stirring to blend.

Sift the flour, baking powder, baking soda and salt into a small bowl.
Add to the cranberry mixture and stir well.

Pour the batter into a greased and floured 9" × 5" loaf pan and bake in a
preheated 325° oven for about 1 hour, or until a toothpick inserted in the
center comes out clean.

Makes 1 loaf.

Hospitality
Salem Hospital Aid Association, Salem, Massachusetts

GLAZED LEMON NUT BREAD

This is an old Nantucket recipe for a tea bread.
Let it cool completely before slicing and serving.

¼ cup butter or margarine, softened	2 cups unbleached flour
¾ cup plus 2 tablespoons sugar, divided	2½ teaspoons baking powder
2 eggs	½ teaspoon salt
2 teaspoons grated lemon rind	¾ cup milk
	½ cup chopped nuts
	2 teaspoons lemon juice

In a large bowl, cream the butter or margarine and ¾ cup of the sugar until light and fluffy. Add the eggs and lemon rind and beat well.

In another bowl, sift the flour, baking powder and salt and add alternately with the milk to the creamed mixture, beating until smooth after each addition. Stir in the nuts.

Pour the batter into a greased 8½" × 4½" loaf pan and bake in a preheated 350° oven for 50 to 55 minutes, or until a toothpick inserted in the center comes out clean. Let cool in the pan for 10 minutes.

Combine the lemon juice and remaining 2 tablespoons sugar and spoon the mixture over the top of the bread. Remove from the pan and cool thoroughly.

Serves 8 to 10.

From the Galleys of Nantucket
First Congregational Church: Ladies' Union Circle, Nantucket, Massachusetts

PEAR BREAD

This delicate bread freezes well, so you'll want to keep an
extra loaf or two on hand as a special treat for unexpected company.
Its fine texture and lovely appearance also make it suitable for
wrapping up and presenting as a hostess gift.

½ cup butter or margarine, softened	½ teaspoon salt
1 cup sugar	⅛ teaspoon ground nutmeg
2 eggs	¼ cup plain yogurt or buttermilk
2 cups unbleached flour	1 cup peeled, cored and coarsely chopped pears
1 teaspoon baking powder	1 teaspoon vanilla
½ teaspoon baking soda	

In a large bowl, cream the butter or margarine and gradually beat in the
sugar. Beat in the eggs, 1 at a time.

In a separate bowl, combine the flour, baking powder, baking soda, salt
and nutmeg. Add to the egg mixture alternately with the yogurt or buttermilk. Stir in the pears and vanilla and pour into a buttered 9″ × 5″ loaf pan.
Bake in a preheated 350° oven for 1 hour, or until a toothpick inserted in
the center comes out clean. Cool for about 15 minutes, then turn out onto
a wire rack.

Serves 8 to 10.

The Longyear Cookbook
Longyear Museum and Historical Society, Brookline, Massachusetts

HUBARB BREAD

Rhubarb rewards New Englanders in more ways than one.
Not only does it offer spectacular culinary possibilities for pastries
and other baked goods, but the sight of its green leaves pushing up
through the ground boosts our winter-weary spirits and proves
that spring has indeed returned to the region.

1¼ cups firmly packed brown
   sugar
1 egg
⅓ cup oil
1 teaspoon vanilla
½ teaspoon salt
1 teaspoon baking soda
1 cup sour milk (1 tablespoon
   lemon juice or vinegar plus
   enough milk to make 1 cup)

2½ cups unbleached flour
1½ cups diced fresh or frozen
   rhubarb
½ cup chopped nuts (optional)
½ cup granulated sugar
1 tablespoon butter or
   margarine

In a large bowl, beat the brown sugar, egg and oil. Stir in the vanilla and
salt. Mix the baking soda with the sour milk in a small bowl and add to the
egg mixture. Stir in the flour, rhubarb and nuts (if using). Pour the batter
into 3 greased 7¼" × 3½" loaf pans. Combine the granulated sugar and
butter or margarine and distribute over the top of the batter. Bake in a
preheated 325° oven for about 1 hour 20 minutes, or until a toothpick
inserted in the center comes out clean.

Makes 3 loaves.

Our Favorite Recipes
Holy Redeemer Parish, West Lebanon, New Hampshire

$\mathcal{S}$TRAWBERRY BREAD

This bread freezes well without the cream cheese topping, so make a double batch and put the extra loaf in the freezer until you need a taste of summer on one of those raw and blustery winter days.

1½ cups mashed strawberries	½ teaspoon ground cinnamon
1½ cups unbleached flour	½ cup oil
1 cup sugar	2 eggs, well beaten
½ teaspoon baking soda	1 package (3 ounces) cream
½ teaspoon salt	cheese, softened

Drain ¼ cup of juice from the strawberries and save for the topping.

Mix the flour, sugar, baking soda, salt and cinnamon in a large bowl. Make a well in the center and add the strawberries and remaining juice, oil and eggs. Mix gently until thoroughly combined. Pour into a greased 9" × 5" loaf pan and bake in a preheated 350° oven for 50 to 60 minutes, or until a toothpick inserted in the center comes out clean. Cool thoroughly.

Beat the cream cheese with the reserved strawberry juice until smooth. Drizzle over the top of the bread or serve separately as a spread.

Makes 1 loaf.

Just Desserts
Londonderry Women's Club, Londonderry, New Hampshire

CHEESE-APPLE-WALNUT BREAD

Almost a meal in itself, this stick-to-your-ribs bread is fabulous toasted for breakfast. It's also a hearty partner to soups and salads and rivals any breads served at New England's many fine inns and restaurants.

1/4 cup butter or margarine, softened
1/4 cup sugar
2 eggs
1 cup shredded tart apple
3/4 cup finely chopped walnuts, divided

1/2 cup shredded Cheddar cheese
1 cup whole-wheat flour
1 cup unbleached flour
2 teaspoons baking powder
1/4 teaspoon salt
1/4 cup skim milk

Cream the butter or margarine and sugar in a large bowl until light and fluffy, then beat in the eggs. Add the apples, 1/2 cup of the walnuts and the cheese and mix well.

In a separate bowl, combine the whole-wheat flour, unbleached flour, baking powder and salt. Add half the flour mixture to the apple mixture, stirring until moistened. Stir in the milk and the remaining flour mixture. Pour into a greased 9" × 5" loaf pan, sprinkle the remaining 1/4 cup walnuts on top and bake in a preheated 375° oven for 35 to 40 minutes, or until a toothpick inserted in the center comes out clean. Remove from the pans and cool on a wire rack.

Serves 12.

Boston Cooks
Women's Educational & Industrial Union, Boston, Massachusetts

WHOLE-WHEAT ZUCCHINI BREAD

Dark and dense, this bread slices nicely when it has thoroughly cooled. Serve it toasted for breakfast, with soup or salad at lunch, with just about any main dish or as a nutritious snack.

2 **eggs**	1 **teaspoon baking soda**
½ **cup firmly packed brown sugar**	¼ **teaspoon baking powder**
½ **cup molasses**	½ **teaspoon salt**
¼ **cup oil**	½ **teaspoon ground cinnamon**
1½ **teaspoons vanilla**	¼ **teaspoon ground nutmeg**
½ **cup whole-wheat flour**	1 **cup shredded zucchini**
¾ **cup unbleached flour**	¼ **cup raisins**
¼ **cup wheat germ**	¼ **cup chopped walnuts**
	Sesame seeds (optional)

In a large bowl, beat the eggs, brown sugar, molasses, oil and vanilla. In another bowl, combine the whole-wheat flour, unbleached flour, wheat germ, baking soda, baking powder, salt, cinnamon and nutmeg. Stir into the egg mixture. Add the zucchini, raisins and walnuts and mix to blend. Pour the batter into a greased 9" × 5" loaf pan and sprinkle with sesame seeds (if using). Bake in a preheated 350° oven for 50 to 60 minutes, or until a toothpick inserted in the center comes out clean.

Makes 1 loaf.

The Maine Ingredient
Planned Parenthood of Northern New England, Portland, Maine

BOSTON BROWN BREAD

Don't let the steaming discourage you from making this bread.
It's fun and a great change of pace. You can use a coffee can
(1-pound size) on a rack in a big kettle. If you have no rack,
use clothespins or an iron trivet to support the can.
Cover the can with foil, then cover the kettle. If you have a big enough
kettle, you can make 3 or 4 batches at a time. The new 13-ounce
coffee can may be too small, for the batter will rise as it cooks.

½ cup whole-wheat flour
½ cup cornmeal (preferably stone-ground)
⅓ cup instant nonfat dry milk (optional)
1½ teaspoons baking powder

¼ cup raisins or chopped dates (optional)
1 cup milk or plain yogurt
½ cup molasses
½ cup wheat germ

In a large bowl, combine the flour, cornmeal, dry milk (if using), baking powder, raisins or dates (if using), milk or yogurt, molasses and wheat germ. Pour the batter into a greased 1-pound coffee can or similar-size ovenproof dish and cover with foil. Set the container on a rack inside a deep kettle or pot. (If you use clothespins for a rack, set the container on them first, then add the boiling water.) Add enough boiling water so that it comes ½ to ⅔ the way up the sides of the container. Cover the kettle or pot and simmer for 2 hours. Take the container out of the water, pull off the foil and dry the top in the oven if necessary. Remove from the container and cool on a wire rack.

Serves 6.

Liberal Portions
Unitarian Universalist Church, Nashua, New Hampshire

STEAMED BROWN BREAD

This recipe has become a tradition in Milford, Maine,
where it's served at the annual town meeting dinner and
at baked bean suppers throughout the year.

1	cup unbleached flour	1	cup rolled oats
2½	teaspoons baking soda	2	cups water
½	teaspoon salt	⅔	cup molasses
1	cup whole-wheat flour		

In a large bowl, sift the unbleached flour, baking soda and salt and stir to combine. Add the whole-wheat flour and oats. Stir in the water and molasses and mix well, but do not beat. Fill a well-greased 1½-quart tube mold or two 1-pound coffee cans about ⅔ full. Cover with aluminum foil and tie tightly. Set in a steamer kettle or deep pot, add enough boiling water to come ½ to ⅔ the way up the sides of the mold or cans and steam for about 3 to 3½ hours for the mold, 2½ to 3 hours for the cans.

Serves 14 to 16.

Cooking with a Maine Accent
Gorham Woman's Club, Gorham, Maine

$\int$PIDER CORN BREAD

This bread gets its name from a cast-iron skillet that
was originally made with a long handle and short feet
so that it could be placed among coals on a hearth.

1⅓ **cups cornmeal**	1 **cup buttermilk**
⅓ **cup unbleached flour**	2 **eggs, well beaten**
¼ **cup sugar**	2 **cups milk, divided**
1 **teaspoon baking soda**	2 **tablespoons butter or**
½ **teaspoon salt**	**margarine**

Combine the cornmeal, flour, sugar, baking soda and salt in a large bowl.
Add the buttermilk, eggs and 1 cup of the milk. Beat with a spoon until
smooth.

Melt the butter or margarine in a 9″ heavy skillet. When the skillet is hot,
pour in the batter. Pour the remaining 1 cup milk over this. Bake in a preheated 350° oven for about 50 minutes, or until lightly browned. Cut into
wedges and serve.

Serves 8.

A Hancock Community Collection
First Congregational Church: The Guild, Hancock, New Hampshire

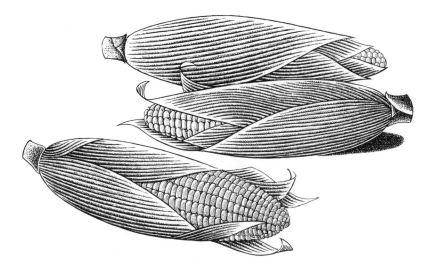

HERB CORN BREAD

If there's any bread left over after serving this,
store what remains in the same can it was baked in and
seal with the plastic lid to preserve its freshness.

1 **package dry yeast**	1 **can (13 ounces) evaporated**
½ **cup warm water**	**milk**
2 **teaspoons celery seeds**	2 **tablespoons oil**
(optional)	½ **teaspoon salt**
3 **tablespoons sugar, divided**	½ **cup cornmeal**
1½ **teaspoons dried sage**	3½–4 **cups unbleached flour,**
¼ **teaspoon ground ginger**	**divided**
¼ **teaspoon dried marjoram**	**Butter or margarine, melted**

In a large bowl, dissolve the yeast in the water. Blend in the celery seeds (if using), 1 tablespoon of the sugar and the sage, ginger and marjoram. Let stand in a warm place until bubbly, about 15 minutes.

Stir in the remaining 2 tablespoons sugar and the milk, oil and salt. Gradually beat in the cornmeal and enough of the flour, 1 cup at a time, to make the dough heavy and stiff, but not too sticky.

Divide the dough in half and spoon into 2 well-greased 1-pound coffee cans, or spoon all the dough into a well-greased 2-pound coffee can. Cover with greased plastic lids. (At this point, you may freeze the dough.)

Let the covered cans stand in a warm place until the dough rises and pops off the lids (45 to 55 minutes for 1-pound cans, 55 to 60 minutes for a 2-pound can). If the dough is frozen, let it stand in the covered cans at room temperature until the lids pop (4 to 5 hours for 1-pound cans, 6 to 8 hours for a 2-pound can).

Bake, uncovered, in a preheated 350° oven for about 45 minutes for the 1-pound cans, about 1 hour for the 2-pound can; the crust will be very brown. Brush the tops lightly with butter or margarine. Let cool in the cans on a wire rack for 10 minutes. With a thin knife, loosen the crust around the edges of the cans, slide the loaves out and continue to cool in an upright position on a wire rack. Once a baked loaf is sliced below the top of the can, it may be stored in the can with the lid on to keep it fresh.

Makes 1 large or 2 small loaves.

Patchwork Pantry
Monadnock Community Hospital, Peterborough, New Hampshire

QUICK WINTER HERB BREAD
❧

This bread has an unexpected but tasty combination of herbs,
nuts and raisins. It makes an excellent accompaniment
to homemade soup and even toasts well for breakfast.

1¼	cups unbleached flour	½	cup raisins
1½	teaspoons baking powder	½	cup chopped nuts
½	teaspoon baking soda	1	egg
½	teaspoon salt	2	tablespoons honey
½	teaspoon dried basil	¾	cup buttermilk
¼	teaspoon dried marjoram	¼	cup butter or margarine,
⅛	teaspoon dried oregano		melted and cooled
	Pinch of dried thyme		

In a large bowl, sift the flour, baking powder, baking soda and salt.
Sprinkle in the basil, marjoram, oregano and thyme and toss together until
evenly distributed. Mix in the raisins and nuts and toss again until evenly
distributed.

In another bowl, beat the egg until light and slightly thickened. Add the
honey and beat to blend. Beat in the buttermilk and butter or margarine.
Stir into the dry ingredients with just a few strokes. Turn the dough out
onto a well-floured surface and, using a pastry scraper, reach under the
dough and lift it up on top of itself. Do this several times, then pat the mixture together gently with floured hands. If it is very sticky, sprinkle on a bit
more flour, but be stingy.

When the dough just holds together but is still lumpy, put it into a buttered 9″ round cake pan. With lightly floured hands, pat lightly to fill the
pan.

Bake in a preheated 400° oven for about 20 minutes, or until lightly
browned and the middle feels springy when pressed. Do not overbake. Cut
into wedges and serve warm.

Serves 8 to 12.

Recipe Sampler
Shoreline Quilters' Guild, Branford, Connecticut

ℬOULDER FARM BREAD

"My great-grandmother made this bread every day in the summer
at her home in New Hampshire's White Mountains," wrote the
contributor of this recipe. "She would set the loaves to bake in the 'slow'
oven of her woodstove while everyone went off to do chores
around the farm. Bread and chores would be finished around the
same time, and all would gather for a lunch of piping-hot bread, slices
of mild cheese and a salad. Then off to the swimming hole!"

2½ **cups whole-wheat flour**
½ **cup bran**
½ **teaspoon baking powder**
1 **teaspoon baking soda**

2 **teaspoons hot water**
1 **cup buttermilk**
½ **cup molasses**

In a large bowl, combine the flour, bran and baking powder.
Dissolve the baking soda in the water and combine with the buttermilk.
Stir in the molasses. Add to the dry ingredients and stir to blend. Pour into
a greased 8½" × 4½" loaf pan. Bake in a preheated 300° oven for 40 to 50
minutes, or until a toothpick inserted in the center comes out clean.

Makes 1 loaf.

The Community Cooks
Pine Hill Waldorf School, Wilton, New Hampshire

HOBART'S IRISH SODA BREAD

This easy-to-make and attractive quick bread is irresistible fresh out of the pan and equally good toasted and served with jam for breakfast.

4 cups unbleached flour	**⅓ cup butter or margarine**
¼ cup sugar	**2 cups dark raisins**
1 tablespoon baking powder	**1 tablespoon caraway seeds**
1 teaspoon baking soda	**1 egg, beaten**
1 teaspoon salt	**1½–1¾ cups buttermilk**

In a large bowl, combine the flour, sugar, baking powder, baking soda and salt. Cut in the butter or margarine until the mixture has the consistency of coarse cornmeal. Stir in the raisins and caraway seeds. Gradually add the egg and 1½ cups of the buttermilk, stirring to blend. The batter should not be dry, so you may need to add about ¼ cup more buttermilk. Knead briefly and put into 2 greased 8″ round cake pans. Cut a bold cross on top of each and bake in a preheated 375° oven for 30 to 40 minutes, or until a toothpick inserted in the center comes out clean.

Serves 14 to 16.

Rumsey Rare Bites
Rumsey Circle: Rumsey Hall, Washington, Connecticut

COUNTRY CHEESE BREAD
❧

This bread gets even better with age. It's great used for a
ham sandwich or toasted and buttered and served with soup.

1½ **cups milk, scalded**	6–7 **cups unbleached flour,**
2 **tablespoons butter or**	**divided**
margarine, melted	7 **ounces sharp Cheddar**
2 **tablespoons sugar**	**cheese, shredded**
1 **teaspoon salt**	2 **packages dry yeast**
1 **teaspoon ground black**	1 **cup lukewarm water**
pepper	1 **egg yolk, lightly beaten with**
	1 tablespoon water

In a large bowl, combine the milk, butter or margarine, sugar, salt and
pepper. Set aside to cool. Blend in 2 cups of the flour and beat until
smooth. Add the cheese and stir to blend.

In another bowl, dissolve the yeast in the water, then add to the milk
and cheese mixture, blending in enough of the remaining flour to form a
soft dough that pulls away from the sides of the bowl as you stir. Turn the
dough out onto a lightly floured surface and knead for about 10 minutes,
or until the dough is smooth and elastic.

Place the dough in a buttered bowl, turning it so it is well greased on all
sides. Cover with a dish towel and let rise in a warm place for about 1 hour,
or until doubled in bulk. Punch down, turn out again onto a lightly floured
surface and knead lightly.

Divide the dough into 2 parts, shape into loaves and place in 2 greased
9" × 5" loaf pans. Cover with a dish towel and let rise for about 1 hour, or
until doubled in bulk. Brush the egg wash over the tops, then bake in a
preheated 400° oven for 30 to 40 minutes, or until golden brown. The
loaves should sound hollow when tapped. Remove from the pans and cool
on wire racks.

Makes 2 loaves.

The Andover Cookbook II
Phillips Academy: The Ladies' Benevolent Society, Andover, Massachusetts

DILLY BREAD

Some recipes for this bread use dill seeds instead of dill weed,
but this is simply a matter of preference.
Either way, the bread is aromatic and irresistible.

1 **package dry yeast**	4 **teaspoons dried dill**
¼ **cup warm water**	1 **teaspoon salt**
1 **cup creamed cottage cheese**	¼ **teaspoon baking soda**
2 **tablespoons sugar**	1 **egg, beaten**
2 **tablespoons minced onions**	2–3 **cups unbleached flour**
1 **tablespoon butter or margarine**	

In a small bowl, soften the yeast in the water. Combine the cottage
cheese, sugar, onions, butter or margarine, dill, salt, baking soda and egg in
a large bowl. Stir in the yeast and blend thoroughly. Gradually add enough
flour to form a stiff dough. Turn the dough out onto a floured surface and
knead for 8 to 10 minutes, adding more flour as needed. Place the dough in
an oiled bowl and rotate to coat the top.

Let the dough rise until doubled in bulk, about 1½ to 2 hours. Punch
down and shape into a loaf. Place in a greased 9" × 5" loaf pan and let rise
again until doubled in bulk, about 1 hour. Bake in a preheated 350° oven
for 35 to 45 minutes, or until the bread sounds hollow when tapped.

Makes 1 loaf.

Cohasset Entertains
The Community Garden Club, Cohasset, Massachusetts

HARPSWELL ANADAMA BREAD
✲

Wheat germ and rolled oats enhance this full-bodied,
full-flavored New England classic.

5 cups unbleached flour, divided	1 teaspoon salt
2 packages dry yeast	1 cup rolled oats
2 cups water	½ cup molasses
½ cup cornmeal	¼ cup butter or margarine
2 tablespoons wheat germ	2 eggs

In a large bowl, combine 2 cups of the flour and the yeast. In a
saucepan, bring the water to a boil, remove from the heat and stir in the
cornmeal, wheat germ and salt. Cook over low heat, stirring constantly, for
2 minutes. Add the oats, molasses and butter or margarine and cook for
3 minutes more. Remove from the heat and set aside to cool.

Add the eggs, 1 at a time, to the cooled cornmeal mixture, beating well
after each addition. Combine with the flour and yeast in the bowl and beat
for 2 minutes. Add enough of the remaining 3 cups flour to make a soft
dough that can be handled easily. Turn out onto a floured surface and
knead until smooth, about 5 minutes.

Place the dough in an oiled bowl, turning to coat, and cover with a dish
towel. Let rise in a warm place until doubled in bulk, about 1 hour. Punch
the dough down, cut in half, shape into 2 loaves and place in lightly oiled
9" × 5" loaf pans. Let rise again until doubled in bulk. Bake in a preheated
375° oven for about 40 minutes. Remove from the pans and cool on wire
racks.

Makes 2 loaves.

Merrymeeting Merry Eating
Mid Coast Hospital / Brunswick Auxiliary, Brunswick, Maine

FIVE-GRAIN BREAD

This slightly sweet multigrain bread also could be shaped
into free-form round loaves. For decoration,
sprinkle oats over the top after applying the egg wash.

1	cup rolled oats	¾	cup lukewarm water
¼	cup bulgur	2	packages dry yeast
¼	cup cornmeal	1	egg, beaten
¼	cup rye flour	½	cup molasses
½	teaspoon salt	1	cup whole-wheat flour
½	cup oil	6–8	cups unbleached flour
1½	cups boiling water	1	egg
1	tablespoon sugar		

In a large bowl, combine the oats, bulgur, cornmeal, rye flour and salt.
Add the oil and mix until well blended. Stir in the boiling water and let the
mixture stand until lukewarm.

Mix the sugar and lukewarm water. Add the yeast and let soften. Combine with the oats mixture. Add the beaten egg, molasses and whole-wheat
flour, then add enough of the unbleached flour to make a firm dough that
isn't sticky.

Put the dough in a lightly oiled bowl, cover with a dish towel and let rise
until doubled in bulk. Punch down and knead on a lightly floured surface
for about 10 minutes. Divide the dough in half, shape into loaves and put
into 2 greased 9″ × 5″ loaf pans. Beat the remaining egg and brush over the
tops. Bake in a preheated 350° oven for 50 to 60 minutes.

Makes 2 loaves.

The Community Kitchen Cookbook
The Community Kitchen, Keene, New Hampshire

PILGRIM'S BREAD

Great toasted for breakfast or for sandwiches, this bread combines the flavor of cornmeal with the whole-grain goodness of three flours.

1¼ cups cornmeal	2 packages dry yeast
⅓ cup firmly packed brown sugar	½ cup warm water
1 teaspoon salt	¾ cup whole-wheat flour
2 cups boiling water	½ cup rye flour
¼ cup oil	4–4½ cups unbleached flour, divided

In a large bowl, combine the cornmeal, brown sugar and salt. Gradually stir in the boiling water and then the oil. Cool to lukewarm.

Soften the yeast in the warm water and add to the cooled cornmeal mixture. Add the whole-wheat flour and rye flour and mix well. Add enough of the unbleached flour, 1 cup at a time, to make a stiff dough.

Turn out onto a floured surface and knead for 6 to 8 minutes. Let rise in a greased bowl for 1 hour. Divide the dough in half and shape into 2 loaves. Let rise in greased 9" × 5" loaf pans for 30 to 45 minutes. Bake in a preheated 375° oven for about 45 minutes.

Makes 2 loaves.

Seasoned with Love at St. James Lutheran Church
St. James Lutheran Church, Barrington, Rhode Island

MAINE POTATO BREAD

This is a good, basic white bread. Be sure to grease the waxed paper
that is placed over the dough while it rises; otherwise, the paper will
stick and mar the surface of the dough when it is removed.

1 **medium Maine potato, peeled**	⅓ **cup instant nonfat dry milk**
2½ **cups water**	¾ **cup warm water**
4 **tablespoons sugar, divided**	2 **teaspoons salt**
2 **packages dry yeast**	1 **egg, lightly beaten with**
9 **cups unbleached flour,**	**1 tablespoon water**
divided	**Sesame seeds or poppy seeds**
¼ **cup butter or shortening**	

Boil the potato in the 2½ cups water until soft. Let the potato and water
cool to lukewarm. Reserve 2 cups of the water, then pour it, 1 cup at a
time, into a blender or food processor and puree with the potato for 1 minute. Pour the pureed potato into a large bowl and add 2 tablespoons of the
sugar and the yeast. Stir and let stand for 5 minutes. Blend in 3 cups of the
flour, cover with a dish towel and let rise until doubled in bulk.

In a medium bowl, cut the butter or shortening into 3 cups of the flour,
then set aside. Mix the milk with the warm water. Stir down the risen batter
and add the milk mixture, remaining 2 tablespoons sugar and salt. Add the
flour-butter mixture and stir in 2 more cups flour. Turn the dough out onto
a floured surface and let rest for 5 minutes.

Using the remaining 1 cup flour, knead the dough until smooth and
elastic, about 10 minutes. Put in a greased bowl, turn to grease the top,
cover with a piece of greased waxed paper and a dish towel and let rise
until doubled in bulk.

Punch the dough down and shape into 3 loaves. Place in 3 greased
8" × 4" loaf pans and cover each with a piece of greased waxed paper and
a dish towel. Let rise until doubled in bulk.

Brush the egg wash on the tops of the loaves, then sprinkle on sesame
seeds or poppy seeds. Bake in a preheated 375° oven for 40 minutes, or until
the loaves sound hollow when tapped. Remove from the pans and cool on
wire racks.

Makes 3 loaves.

RSVP
Junior League of Portland, Maine

NEW ENGLAND OATMEAL BREAD

Although listed as optional ingredients, the wheat germ
and raisins contribute to both the flavor and the
texture of this bread, so you might not want to omit them.

1½ cups boiling water	¾ cup lukewarm water
1 tablespoon shortening	¼ cup molasses
½ teaspoon salt	¼ cup firmly packed brown
1 cup rolled oats	sugar
¼ cup wheat germ (optional)	5 cups unbleached flour,
1 cup raisins (optional)	divided
1 package dry yeast	

In a large bowl, combine the boiling water, shortening and salt. Stir in the
oats, wheat germ (if using) and raisins (if using) and let cool until lukewarm.

In a small bowl, dissolve the yeast in the lukewarm water. Add the
molasses, brown sugar and 1 cup of the flour and beat until smooth. Combine with the oats mixture and stir in the remaining flour, mixing well.

Turn the dough out onto a floured surface and knead until smooth,
about 10 minutes. Place in a large greased bowl, oil the top and let rise,
covered, until doubled in bulk.

Shape the dough into 2 loaves, place in greased 9" × 5" loaf pans and let
rise for about 1 hour, or until doubled in bulk. Bake in a preheated 400°
oven for 10 minutes. Reduce the heat to 350° and bake for 20 to 30 minutes more. The loaves are done when tapping them produces a hollow
sound. Remove from the pans immediately and cool on wire racks.

Makes 2 loaves.

Maine-ly Good Eatin'
American Cancer Society: Maine Division, Brunswick, Maine

POPPY SEED & MAPLE SYRUP BREAD

This bread rises high, has an extremely light texture and
is only slightly sweet. Those who prefer a stronger maple
flavor may want to increase the syrup to $\frac{1}{2}$ cup.

$\frac{1}{2}$	teaspoon sugar	1	tablespoon poppy seeds
2	cups lukewarm water, divided	1	teaspoon salt
		6–7	cups unbleached flour, divided
2	packages dry yeast		
$\frac{1}{3}$	cup maple syrup	1	egg, lightly beaten
$\frac{1}{4}$	cup oil		Poppy seeds for tops

In a small bowl, dissolve the sugar in $\frac{1}{2}$ cup of the water, add the yeast and proof until it is foamy.

In a large bowl, combine the remaining $1\frac{1}{2}$ cups water with the maple syrup, oil, poppy seeds and salt. Stir in the yeast mixture and 2 cups of the flour. Beat the mixture until it is smooth. Stir in 4 to $4\frac{1}{2}$ cups of the flour and knead the dough in the bowl for 2 to 3 minutes. Turn out onto a floured surface and knead for 5 minutes more, or until smooth and elastic, adding more flour if necessary.

Put the dough in a lightly oiled bowl, turn it to coat with the oil and let rise, covered, in a warm place until doubled in bulk, about 1 to 2 hours.

Punch down the dough, cut it in half and shape each half into a loaf. Put the loaves in lightly oiled and floured $8\frac{1}{2}'' \times 4\frac{1}{2}''$ loaf pans. Let rise, covered, in a warm place until the dough reaches the edge of the pans. Brush with the egg and sprinkle generously with poppy seeds.

Bake in a preheated 375° oven (on the middle rack) for about 30 minutes, or until the loaves are golden brown and sound hollow when tapped.

Makes 2 loaves.

1717 Meetinghouse Cookbook II
West Parish of Barnstable: Women's Guild, West Barnstable, Massachusetts

OLD-TIME RAISIN BREAD

This raisin bread makes delicious toast and sandwiches. Whole-wheat flour used in place of half the unbleached flour is a pleasing variation.

1 cup lukewarm water	1 teaspoon salt
1 cup milk, scalded and cooled	6 cups unbleached flour, divided
1 package dry yeast	
1 tablespoon plus ¾ cup sugar, divided	1 cup raisins
	Flour for mixing with raisins
¼ cup butter or margarine, softened	1 egg, lightly beaten with 1 tablespoon water

In a large bowl, mix the water, milk, yeast and 1 tablespoon of the sugar. In another bowl, cream the butter or margarine, remaining ¾ cup sugar and the salt. Add to the yeast mixture. Stir in 2 cups of the flour and beat until smooth. Cover with a dish towel and set aside to rise in a warm, draft-free place for about 1½ hours.

Meanwhile, soak the raisins in hot water for 15 minutes. Drain. Toss with some flour and stir into the risen batter. Add enough of the remaining flour to make a moderately soft dough. Knead until smooth and elastic, adding more flour if needed. Place the dough in a well-greased bowl, cover with a dish towel and let rise until doubled in bulk, about 1½ hours.

Divide the dough in half, shape into loaves and place in 2 well-greased 9" × 5" loaf pans. Cover with a dish towel and let rise for about 1 hour. Brush with the egg wash and bake in a preheated 350° oven for 45 minutes, or until the loaves sound hollow when tapped. Remove from the pans and cool on wire racks.

Makes 2 loaves.

Smith Neck Friends Meeting Cookbook
Smith Neck Friends Meeting of Dartmouth Monthly Meeting,
South Dartmouth, Massachusetts

$\mathcal{P}$ARMESAN BUBBLE LOAF

This bread makes a great deli-type sandwich. To make sure it
holds together well, don't coat the entire surface of the
dough balls with melted butter or margarine. Instead, just dip
them into the butter or margarine. For variety, roll the butter-dipped
balls in sesame seeds, then place them in the baking pans.

3	cups hot water	1/3	cup lukewarm water
1	cup grated Parmesan or Romano cheese	3	eggs
1/4	cup butter or margarine, softened	10	cups unbleached flour (approximately), divided
3	tablespoons sugar	1/2	cup instant nonfat dry milk
1 1/2	teaspoons salt	1/4	cup butter or margarine, melted
2	packages dry yeast	2	cloves garlic, minced

In a large bowl, combine the hot water, cheese, softened butter or margarine, sugar and salt. Stir until the butter or margarine melts, then set aside to cool.

Dissolve the yeast in the lukewarm water and stir into the cooled cheese mixture. Add the eggs and beat thoroughly. Sift 7 cups of the flour, blend with the milk and stir into the cheese mixture, mixing until fairly smooth. Add more flour to make a medium-stiff dough.

Turn the dough out onto a lightly floured surface and knead for 5 minutes. Place in a buttered bowl, cover with a dish towel and let rise until doubled in bulk, about 1 hour. Punch the dough down, turn out onto a lightly floured surface and divide into 3 equal portions. Divide each of these into 14 pieces, shape into balls and let rest for 10 minutes.

While the balls are resting, mix the melted butter and garlic in a bowl. Dip each ball into the garlic butter and place in 3 greased 8 1/2" × 4 1/2" loaf pans, making 2 layers in each pan and using 14 balls for each loaf. Press down lightly and set aside to rise until doubled in bulk, about 45 minutes. Bake in a preheated 400° oven for 30 to 35 minutes, or until browned and the bread sounds hollow when tapped.

Makes 3 loaves.

The Mark Twain Library Cookbook, Vol. III
Mark Twain Library Association, Redding, Connecticut

BRAIDED SESAME BREAD

Showcase your baking skills with this large, crusty braided bread.
It's fantastic served with spaghetti, lasagna or any Italian meal.

1½ **cups milk**
2 **tablespoons honey**
2 **tablespoons butter or**
  margarine
1 **teaspoon salt**
1 **package dry yeast**
¼ **cup warm water**

½ **cup wheat germ**
3½–4 **cups unbleached flour,**
  divided
1 **egg yolk, lightly beaten with**
  2 tablespoons water
  Sesame seeds

In a saucepan, scald the milk, then stir in the honey, butter or margarine and salt. Transfer to a large bowl and let cool.

In a small bowl, dissolve the yeast in the water. Add to the large bowl. Mix in the wheat germ and 2 cups of the flour. Beat for 5 minutes until the sponge is smooth.

Gradually add enough of the remaining flour to make a kneadable dough. Knead until the dough is smooth and elastic. Cover with a dish towel and let rise for about 1 hour, or until doubled in bulk.

Turn the dough out onto a floured surface and knead lightly. Divide into 3 equal pieces. On a floured surface, roll each into a sausage-type roll about 15" long. Braid the rolls loosely together, starting from the middle and working to the ends for an even look. Pinch the ends together and tuck them under the loaf. Place on an oiled baking sheet, cover with a dish towel and let rise for 20 minutes.

Brush the braid with the egg wash and sprinkle the top generously with sesame seeds. Bake in a preheated 375° oven for about 45 minutes. Tap the bottom of the loaf: if it sounds hollow, the bread is done; if not, return it to the oven for a few more minutes until thoroughly baked.

Makes 1 large braided loaf.

The Haystack Cookbook
Haystack Mountain School of Crafts, Deer Isle, Maine

THREE-FLOUR BRAIDED BREAD

The recipe tester for this bread wrote the following: "When my 85-year-old uncle picked up a third slice of this bread, he remarked, 'You know I don't eat a lot, but you are a witness to how much I like this bread!' "

4½ cups unbleached flour, divided
2 tablespoons sugar
1 teaspoon salt
2 packages dry yeast
¼ cup butter or margarine, softened
2¼ cups very warm water

4 tablespoons molasses, divided
1½ cups whole-wheat flour
1¼ cups rye flour
1 tablespoon unsweetened cocoa powder
1 tablespoon caraway seeds (optional)

Combine 2¼ cups of the unbleached flour with the sugar, salt and yeast in a large bowl. Add the butter or margarine and water and beat at medium speed for 2 minutes. Add another cup of the unbleached flour and beat at high speed for 2 minutes.

Divide the batter into 3 bowls. Into the first bowl of batter, beat 1¼ cups of the unbleached flour. Into the second bowl, beat 2 tablespoons of the molasses and the whole-wheat flour. Into the third bowl, beat the rye flour, cocoa, caraway seeds (if using) and remaining 2 tablespoons molasses.

Knead each dough separately until smooth and elastic, about 5 minutes. Cover with a dish towel and let rise in a warm place until doubled in bulk, about 1 hour. Punch each dough down, turn out onto a floured surface and divide in half. Roll each piece into a 15" rope. Braid together a white, a whole-wheat and a rye rope. Pinch the ends to seal. Repeat with the remaining braids of dough. Place both braided loaves on a greased baking sheet, cover and let rise until doubled in bulk, about 1 hour. Bake in a preheated 350° oven for 30 to 40 minutes.

Makes 2 braided loaves.

Saint Michael's Cooks By Design
Saint Michael's Episcopal Church, Litchfield, Connecticut

$\mathcal{P}$ARKER HOUSE ROLLS

Given the time these rolls need to rise, you may be inclined
to "cheat" and use rapid-rise yeast or to make them only occasionally
for holidays or special affairs. The final product is well worth
waiting for, however, for the rolls are attractively shaped, light
golden brown, very tender and absolutely delicious.

1 **package dry yeast**	¼ **cup butter or margarine,**
¼ **cup lukewarm water**	**melted**
2 **cups milk, scalded**	2 **tablespoons sugar**
6 **cups unbleached flour,**	¾ **teaspoon salt**
divided	1 **tablespoon butter or**
	margarine

In a small bowl, dissolve the yeast in the water. Cool the milk to lukewarm, then pour it into a large bowl and mix with the yeast and 2 cups of
the flour. Beat well. Set in a warm place and let rise until spongy (about
3 hours).

Add the melted butter or margarine, sugar, salt and just enough of the
remaining flour to make a kneadable dough. Knead for 5 minutes, let rest
for 5 minutes and knead for 2 minutes more. Set aside and let rise until
doubled in bulk.

Handling the dough gently, turn it out onto a floured surface and roll
out lightly to a ¼" thickness. Cut the dough into rounds with a 3" biscuit
cutter, dot each with butter or margarine and fold over, pinching the edges
to seal. Place the rolls on baking sheets and let rise until doubled in bulk,
about 2 hours. Bake in a preheated 375° oven for 10 minutes, or until deli-
cately browned. Cool on a wire rack.

Makes 36.

Flavors of Cape Cod
Thornton W. Burgess Society, East Sandwich, Massachusetts

$\int$QUASH DINNER ROLLS

Any winter squash, canned or fresh, will work here. These rolls are a lovely color and taste like a cross between a biscuit and a roll.

2 cups milk, scalded	**½ cup sugar**
½ cup shortening	**1 teaspoon salt**
2 packages dry yeast	**1 egg, beaten**
⅓ cup lukewarm water	**8 cups unbleached flour**
1 cup cooked and mashed	**(approximately), divided**
squash	

In a large bowl, combine the milk and shortening, then cool to lukewarm. In a small bowl, dissolve the yeast in the water and add to the cooled milk mixture. Stir in the squash, sugar, salt and egg, blending well. Add the flour, 1 cup at a time, beating after each addition, until you have a soft dough. Place in a bowl, cover with a dish towel and let rise in a warm place until doubled in bulk, about 1 hour.

Punch down the dough and again let rise until doubled in bulk. Divide into 4 pieces and roll out, 1 piece at a time, on a floured surface to a ½" thickness. Cut out circles with a biscuit cutter and place them on a greased baking sheet. Cover with a dish towel and let rise until doubled in bulk. Bake in a preheated 350° oven for 25 to 30 minutes.

Makes 48.

Bouquet of Recipes
Sherman Garden Club, Sherman, Connecticut

$\mathcal{M}$AINE POPOVERS

These popovers are extremely quick and easy to make if you use a blender or food processor. The hardest part is waiting to eat them!

3 eggs	**3 tablespoons butter or**
1 cup milk	**margarine, melted**
1 cup unbleached flour	**¼ teaspoon salt**

In a blender or food processor, lightly beat the eggs, then add the milk, flour, butter or margarine and salt, blending well after each addition. Pour into 6 greased popover pans or custard cups, filling each ½ full. Bake in a preheated 400° oven for 45 to 50 minutes. Do not open the oven door while baking. Serve immediately.

Makes 6.

The Andover Cookbook II
Phillips Academy: The Ladies' Benevolent Society, Andover, Massachusetts

$\int$KY-HIGH BISCUITS

Large, light and luscious, these moist biscuits
are an impressive addition to any meal.

2	cups unbleached flour	½	teaspoon salt
1	cup whole-wheat flour	¾	cup butter or margarine
2	tablespoons sugar	1	cup milk
4½	teaspoons baking powder	1	egg, beaten
¾	teaspoon cream of tartar		

In a large bowl, combine the unbleached flour, whole-wheat flour, sugar, baking powder, cream of tartar and salt. Cut in the butter or margarine until the mixture resembles coarse cornmeal. Add the milk and egg, stirring quickly and briefly. Knead lightly on a floured surface. Roll or pat gently to a 1" thickness, cut into 1"- to 2"-diameter biscuits and place in a greased pan. Bake in a preheated 400° oven for 12 to 15 minutes.

Makes about 12.

Seasoned with Love
Eastman House, Cranston, Rhode Island

 BLUEBERRY MUFFINS

A lemon-sugar topping is just the right touch
for these lovely, light-textured muffins.

1 **cup blueberries**	1 **cup milk**
2 **cups unbleached flour**	¼ **cup butter or margarine,**
⅓ **cup plus 1 tablespoon sugar,**	**melted and cooled**
divided	1 **egg, well beaten**
3 **teaspoons baking powder**	1 **teaspoon grated lemon rind**
½ **teaspoon salt**	

Rinse and pick over the berries, discarding any stems and leaves. Sift the flour, ⅓ cup of the sugar, baking powder and salt into a large bowl. Combine the milk, butter or margarine and egg in a separate bowl and add to the flour mixture, stirring until the batter is almost mixed. Add the berries while a bit of the flour still shows, folding in gently. Spoon the batter into 12 greased muffin cups, filling each ⅔ full. Mix the lemon rind and remaining 1 tablespoon sugar. Sprinkle over the muffins. Bake in a preheated 425° oven for 20 minutes, or until golden brown.

Makes 12.

Cooking with a Maine Accent
Gorham Woman's Club, Gorham, Maine

GINGER-SPICED MUFFINS

Golden brown and moist, these are like gingerbread cupcakes.
Serve them for breakfast or brunch with softened cream cheese.

1¼ **cups unbleached flour**	½ **teaspoon baking soda**
½ **cup light molasses**	½ **teaspoon ground cinnamon**
½ **cup buttermilk**	½ **teaspoon ground ginger**
½ **cup chopped walnuts**	**Pinch of ground nutmeg**
¼ **cup sugar**	¼ **teaspoon salt**
¼ **cup shortening**	1 **egg**

Hometown Cooking in New England

Combine the flour, molasses, buttermilk, walnuts, sugar, shortening, baking soda, cinnamon, ginger, nutmeg, salt and egg in a medium bowl. Beat at low speed just until blended, constantly scraping the bowl with a rubber spatula. Increase the speed to medium and beat for 2 minutes, occasionally scraping the bowl. Spoon the batter into greased or paper-lined muffin cups and bake in a preheated 375° oven for 20 to 25 minutes, or until a toothpick inserted in the center comes out clean. Cool the muffins in the pan on a wire rack for 10 minutes, then remove and serve warm.

Makes 12.

The Sharing & Caring Cookbook
Big Brothers/Big Sisters of the Monadnock Region, Keene, New Hampshire

*G*RAMMY'S BANANA MUFFINS

ॐ

Nothing beats the flavor and aroma of homemade muffins
fresh from the oven. These are sweet and tender, with an appealing
crunch from walnuts. For a nutritional boost, substitute
1 cup whole-wheat flour for 1 cup unbleached flour.
You also can reduce the sugar based on the sweetness of the bananas.

2 cups unbleached flour	1 cup mashed ripe bananas
1 cup sugar	½ cup buttermilk
1 teaspoon baking powder	1 egg, beaten
1 teaspoon baking soda	1 teaspoon vanilla
⅓ cup butter or margarine	½ cup chopped walnuts

In a large bowl, mix the flour, sugar, baking powder and baking soda. Cut in the butter or margarine, then add the bananas, buttermilk, egg and vanilla. Fold in the walnuts and spoon into 12 greased muffin cups. Bake in a preheated 375° oven for 20 to 25 minutes, or until a toothpick inserted in the center comes out clean.

Makes 12.

Merrymeeting Merry Eating
Mid Coast Hospital/Brunswick Auxiliary, Brunswick, Maine

CRANBERRY MUFFINS

Good cranberries bounce—or so it is said. The early settlers were quick to use the freely available cranberries they found growing wild in New England. By the early 1800s, cranberries were being cultivated in Massachusetts and New Jersey, and the new cranberry industry had been founded. Cranberries freeze well and retain their high vitamin C content.

1 **cup cranberries**	1 **cup milk**
½ **cup sugar, divided**	1 **egg, beaten**
2 **cups unbleached flour**	3 **tablespoons butter or**
4 **teaspoons baking powder**	**margarine, melted and**
½ **teaspoon salt**	**cooled**

Pick over the cranberries and rinse them thoroughly. Then put them through a food chopper or coarsely chop in a blender or food processor. Transfer to a small bowl, mix with ¼ cup of the sugar and set aside.

In a large bowl, sift the remaining ¼ cup sugar, flour, baking powder and salt. Combine the milk, egg and butter or margarine and stir into the dry ingredients, mixing only until moistened. Add the cranberries and fold in lightly. Spoon into greased muffin cups, filling each ⅔ full, and bake in a preheated 425° oven for 20 to 25 minutes, or until a toothpick inserted in the center comes out clean.

Makes 12.

Flavors of Cape Cod
Thornton W. Burgess Society, East Sandwich, Massachusetts

$\mathcal{P}$UMPKIN MUFFINS

High in flavor and vitamin A, these muffins fill the kitchen with
an alluring aroma that will pull even the sleepiest heads from their beds.
Because oven temperatures can vary, check the muffins after they have
been in the oven for 15 minutes to make sure they don't overbake.

1 cup unbleached flour	2 eggs
1 cup whole-wheat flour	1/4 cup butter or margarine,
2 teaspoons baking powder	melted and cooled
1 teaspoon baking soda	1 cup canned or fresh mashed
1 teaspoon ground cinnamon	pumpkin
1 teaspoon ground allspice	1/2 cup buttermilk
1/4 teaspoon ground cloves	1/2 cup broken walnuts
1/2 teaspoon salt	1/2 cup raisins or chopped dates
1/2 cup firmly packed brown sugar	

In a medium bowl, combine the unbleached flour, whole-wheat flour,
baking powder, baking soda, cinnamon, allspice, cloves and salt. In a large
bowl, beat together the brown sugar, eggs and butter or margarine until
light and frothy. Blend in the pumpkin and buttermilk. Add the dry ingredients and stir just until moistened. Fold in the walnuts and raisins or
dates, but do not overmix. Spoon into greased muffin cups and bake in a
preheated 400° oven for 15 to 20 minutes, or until lightly brown.

Makes 12.

Rumsey Rare Bites
Rumsey Circle: Rumsey Hall, Washington, Connecticut

HONEY-TOPPED WHOLE-WHEAT DATE MUFFINS

✣

A "honey bear" or other type of squeezable container
works best when drizzling on the sweet topping,
but a honey server or a spoon also is effective. Kids love these
chewy-topped muffins, which make an excellent dessert.

1 egg	½ cup sugar
½ cup milk	2 teaspoons baking powder
¼ cup oil	½ teaspoon salt
¾ cup whole-wheat flour	¾ cup chopped dates
¾ cup unbleached flour	Honey
2 tablespoons bran (optional)	

In a small bowl, beat the egg, milk and oil. In a large bowl, combine the
whole-wheat flour, unbleached flour, bran (if using), sugar, baking powder
and salt. Make a well in the center, add the wet ingredients and dates and
mix until just moistened. Spoon into 8 greased muffin cups and bake in a
preheated 400° oven for 20 to 25 minutes, or until golden. Remove from
the oven and immediately top with a liberal drizzling of honey.

Makes 8.

The Kosher Yankee II
Sisterhood of the Rutland Jewish Center, Rutland, Vermont

FORESIDE BRAN MUFFINS

✣

"My husband loved these, and he is suspicious of any recipe
containing whole-wheat flour," wrote the recipe tester for these muffins.
When there's no time for the morning meal, take one or two along
for a quick and nutritious breakfast-on-the-run.

1 cup molasses	1 egg
1 cup bran	2 cups whole-wheat flour
1 cup raisins or chopped figs	1 tablespoon baking soda

In a medium bowl, beat together the molasses, bran, raisins or figs and egg. In a large bowl, combine the flour and baking soda. Make a well in the center, add the molasses mixture and stir until just moistened. Spoon into greased muffin cups and bake in a preheated 350° oven for 20 to 30 minutes, or until a toothpick inserted in the center comes out clean.

Makes 18.

The Maine Ingredient
Planned Parenthood of Northern New England, Portland, Maine

*T*HREE-GRAIN PEAR MUFFINS

Packed with nutritious ingredients, these portable treats are a
terrific way to provide kids with a healthful snack.

1–2 **medium pears, peeled, cored and chopped (about 1½ cups)**	¾ **cup cornmeal**
½ **cup milk**	½ **cup rolled oats**
⅓ **cup oil**	⅓ **cup sugar**
1 **egg, beaten**	2 **teaspoons baking powder**
¾ **cup unbleached flour**	¼ **teaspoon salt**
½ **cup whole-wheat flour**	**Pinch of ground nutmeg**
	¼ **cup golden raisins**

In a medium bowl, combine the pears, milk, oil and egg, stirring well. In a large bowl, combine the unbleached flour, whole-wheat flour, cornmeal, oats, sugar, baking powder, salt, nutmeg and raisins. Add the wet ingredients and stir just until blended. Spoon the batter into greased or paper-lined muffin cups. Bake in a preheated 375° oven for 25 to 35 minutes, or until browned and a toothpick inserted in the center comes out clean. Cool on a wire rack and serve warm.

Makes 12.

The Mystic Seaport All Seasons Cookbook
Mystic Seaport Museum Stores, Mystic, Connecticut

APPETIZERS & RELISHES

ᘒAGE & CHEDDAR QUACKERS

A welcome change from holiday sweets, these savory crackers can
accompany soups, serve as a snack or carry a dip or spread.

¾ **cup unbleached flour**
1 **teaspoon dried sage**
¼ **teaspoon salt**
   Pinch of ground red pepper
¼ **cup finely ground walnuts or
   pecans**

¼ **cup butter or margarine, cut
   into chunks**
1 **cup shredded extra-sharp
   Cheddar cheese**

Sift the flour, sage, salt and red pepper into a medium bowl. Transfer to
the bowl of a food processor and add the walnuts or pecans. Process until
blended. With the motor running, drop in the butter or margarine and then
the cheese, processing until the dough forms a ball.

Roll out the dough on a lightly floured surface to a ¼″ thickness. Cut
into duck shapes, arrange on ungreased baking sheets and bake in a preheated 350° oven for 10 to 12 minutes, or until the edges turn golden
brown. Cool thoroughly on a wire rack and store in an airtight container.

Makes 24.

Mystic Seaport's Moveable Feasts Cookbook
Mystic Seaport Museum Stores, Mystic, Connecticut

CHEESE TEASERS

These are very rich and filling, and more appropriate as party fare
than an everyday snack. The pecans add a fancy touch.

¼ cup butter or margarine, softened	¼ cup grated Parmesan cheese
¼ cup shortening	1½ cups unbleached flour
1½ cups shredded sharp Cheddar cheese	1 teaspoon paprika
	24 pecan halves

In a large bowl, cream the butter or margarine and shortening until
fluffy. Add the Cheddar cheese and Parmesan cheese, blending well.

Sift the flour and paprika and add to the creamed mixture, blending
well. Form the dough into 24 balls about 1" in diameter, place on ungreased baking sheets about 1" apart and press a pecan half on the top of
each, flattening the balls slightly. Bake in a preheated 350° oven for 12 to
15 minutes, or a little longer, but do not brown. Cool on a wire rack covered with paper towels.

Makes 24.

Stowe Community Church Cookbook
Stowe Community Church: United Ladies Aid, Stowe, Vermont

TYKE TILDEN'S SPICED NUTS

These sweet treats are great for parties and
make a nifty holiday gift, packaged in a fancy tin.

1 egg white	½ teaspoon ground nutmeg
1 tablespoon water	½ teaspoon ground cloves
½ cup sugar	2 cups whole walnuts
1 tablespoon ground cinnamon	

In a medium bowl, beat the egg white and water until frothy. Stir in the sugar, cinnamon, nutmeg and cloves, then fold in the walnuts until thoroughly coated. Spread in a greased 13" × 9" pan and bake in a preheated 300° oven for 30 minutes, stirring every 10 minutes. Transfer to a sheet of aluminum foil to cool.

Makes 2 cups.

Marshfield's Overdue Cookbook
Cliff Rodgers Free Library, Marshfield Hills, Massachusetts

$\mathcal{P}$UMPKIN DIP

This dip is easy to make, and kids love it!
Scoop it up with assorted fruits (such as bananas, apples
or pears) or animal crackers for a snack or dessert.

2   **packages (3 ounces each) cream cheese, softened**
⅓   **cup firmly packed light brown sugar**

½   **cup mashed cooked pumpkin**
2   **teaspoons maple syrup**
½   **teaspoon ground cinnamon**

In a medium bowl, beat the cream cheese and brown sugar until well blended. Add the pumpkin, maple syrup and cinnamon and beat until smooth. Refrigerate until ready to serve.

Makes about 1½ cups.

Derry Community Playground Cookbook
Derry Playground Committee, East Derry, New Hampshire

$\mathcal{Y}$OGURT, CUCUMBER & GARLIC DIP

This is not a spur-of-the-moment preparation unless you already have the drained yogurt (referred to as yogurt cheese) on hand. Serve it with raw vegetables or crackers.

32 ounces nonfat plain yogurt
(*see Note below*)
2 cucumbers
3 cloves garlic, minced

2 tablespoons white wine vinegar
1 tablespoon minced fresh dill
Ground black pepper

Line a colander or strainer with cheesecloth. Spoon in the yogurt and place over a bowl. Let sit overnight, refrigerated.

Peel, seed and shred the cucumbers. In a medium bowl, combine the drained yogurt, cucumbers, garlic, vinegar, dill and pepper. Serve immediately or refrigerate for an hour or so to let the flavors meld.

Note: Do not use yogurt that contains gelatin as a stabilizer, as it won't drain properly.

Makes 4 cups.

St. John's Episcopal Church Cookbook
St. John's Episcopal Church, Barrington, Rhode Island

$\int$LOW-BALL DIP

A tasty dip with an unusual presentation, this is appropriate
for a large dinner party or wedding reception. It takes at least
an hour for the dip to heat through, so you might want to
stir it after the first 30 minutes to ensure even heating.

1 **small round loaf French,
Italian or other unsliced
crusty bread (about
6″ diameter)**

1 **can (10 ounces) chopped
clams, drained (reserve
2 tablespoons juice)**

1 **package (8 ounces) cream
cheese, softened**

1 **tablespoon grated onions**

1 **clove garlic, minced**

1 **tablespoon beer**

1 **teaspoon Worcestershire
sauce**

1 **teaspoon lemon juice**

1 **teaspoon hot-pepper sauce**

⅛ **teaspoon salt**

**Chopped fresh parsley for
garnish**

Crudités for dipping

Cut the top off the bread and set aside. Hollow out the loaf, leaving a
1½″ to 2″ shell. Cut the hollowed-out bread into cubes and toast them.

In a small bowl, beat the clams, cream cheese, onions, garlic, beer,
Worcestershire sauce, lemon juice, hot-pepper sauce, salt and reserved clam
juice. Make a cross of foil on a baking sheet and place the bottom half of
the bread in the center. Pour the clam dip into the bread, cover with the
bread top and wrap in the foil. Bake in a 300° oven for 1 hour. Remove the
top of the bread and sprinkle the dip with the parsley. Serve with the crudités and toasted bread cubes.

Serves 8 to 10.

The Hammersmith Farm Cookbook
Hammersmith Farm, Newport, Rhode Island

LOBSTER WHIP

A little bit of this rich and creamy spread goes a long way.
Serve it directly from the baking dish with crackers.

½ **pound cooked lobster meat, cut up**	¼ **teaspoon Worcestershire sauce**
1 **package (8 ounces) cream cheese, softened**	**Salt and pepper**
2 **tablespoons sour cream**	**Celery salt**
2 **tablespoons minced onions**	¼ **cup slivered almonds**

Place the lobster, cream cheese, sour cream, onions, Worcestershire sauce, salt and pepper to taste and celery salt to taste in a blender or food processor. Mix well. Pour into a greased 2-cup ovenproof dish, sprinkle with the almonds and bake in a preheated 375° oven for 15 minutes. Serve warm.

Makes about 2 cups.

The Taste of Gloucester
The Fishermen's Wives of Gloucester and The Cape Ann League of Women Voters,
Gloucester, Massachusetts

VERY SPECIAL CHEESE RING

For a smoother, firmer texture, use a food processor,
which also cuts down on the preparation time, but decrease the
mayonnaise to ½ cup plus 2 tablespoons. Serve with crackers.

1 **pound sharp Cheddar cheese, shredded**	**Cracked black pepper**
1 **cup chopped nuts**	**Pinch of ground red pepper**
1 **cup mayonnaise**	1 **jar (16 ounces) strawberry preserves (optional)**
1 **small onion, grated**	

In a medium bowl, combine the cheese, nuts, mayonnaise, onions, black pepper to taste and red pepper. Using your hands, carefully mold the mixture into a long, sausagelike shape. Place it on a serving dish, forming it into a ring. Cover with plastic wrap and refrigerate until thoroughly chilled. When ready to serve, fill the center with strawberry preserves (if using).

Serves 15 to 20.

Merrymeeting Merry Eating
Mid Coast Hospital/ Brunswick Auxiliary, Brunswick, Maine

ℋERBED RICOTTA SPREAD
ॐॐ

With so many people these days watching their fat intake or counting calories, it can be difficult deciding what to offer as an appetizer. Here's a tasty way to deal with the dilemma. If you can't find part-skim ricotta, use low-fat cottage cheese, but try your best to locate fresh herbs. Serve with raw vegetables, crackers or dark rye bread.

½ **cup part-skim ricotta cheese**
2 **tablespoons low-fat plain yogurt**
1 **tablespoon minced fresh parsley**

1 **tablespoon minced fresh chives, or 1 teaspoon dried**
1 **tablespoon minced scallions**
1 **tablespoon minced fresh dill, or 2 teaspoons dried**
  Ground black pepper

Combine the ricotta, yogurt, parsley, chives, scallions, dill and pepper in a small bowl. Taste for seasonings, then chill for at least 1 hour.

Makes about ½ cup.

Marblehead Cooks
Tower School, Marblehead, Massachusetts

MARINATED BRUSSELS SPROUTS
🌿

A surprisingly wonderful accompaniment to cocktails—
pretty to look at, healthy to eat, easy to do.
The marinade also is good with mushrooms.

2 **packages (10 ounces each)**
   frozen brussels sprouts
½ **cup tarragon vinegar**
½ **cup oil (half olive oil, half**
   other)
1 **clove garlic, minced (or to**
   taste)

1 **tablespoon sugar**
   Salt
2 **dashes of hot-pepper sauce**
1 **tablespoon sliced scallions**
½ **teaspoon dried tarragon**
   (or to taste)

In a saucepan, cook the brussels sprouts according to the package directions but only until just tender. Remove from the heat, drain and plunge into cold water to preserve their green color.

Combine the vinegar, oil, garlic, sugar, salt to taste, hot-pepper sauce, scallions and tarragon in a bowl, mixing well. Combine the marinade and brussels sprouts in a large, shallow dish and refrigerate for at least 8 hours, stirring often.

Serves 8 to 10.

Vermont Kitchens Revisited
The Women of the Cathedral Church of St. Paul, Burlington, Vermont

MUSHROOM CAPS STUFFED WITH SAUSAGE
🌿

If desired, the removed mushroom stems also can be finely
chopped and added to the stuffing. Any leftover sausage mixture
can be made into patties and fried for breakfast the next day.

1 **pound mild bulk sausage (the**
   milder the better)
½ **cup chopped fresh parsley**

¼ **cup brandy or chicken stock**
24–32 **large mushrooms, depending**
   on size, cleaned and stemmed

In a large bowl, thoroughly mix the sausage, parsley and brandy or stock with your hands. Stuff the mushroom caps with the sausage mixture so that there is about as much sausage mounded above as there is mushroom cap below. Arrange in a greased shallow baking dish and bake in a preheated 350° oven for 40 minutes. If desired, place under the broiler for 3 minutes to brown. Remove to a warm platter and serve hot.

Makes 24 to 32.

Liberal Portions
Unitarian Universalist Church, Nashua, New Hampshire

$\mathcal{R}$ED PEPPER BOATS
❧

Even those who are not fond of anchovies will find these appealing.
The red peppers add a festive touch, and their presentation
makes a unique contribution to a holiday buffet.

2½–3 **medium red bell peppers**
1 **small onion, chopped**
1 **small tomato, peeled, seeded and chopped**
1 **clove garlic, minced**
1 **tablespoon capers**

2 **anchovy fillets, chopped**
½ **teaspoon salt**
¼ **teaspoon ground black pepper**
2 **tablespoons olive oil**

Cut the bell peppers into quarters and remove and discard the seeds and pulp. Set the peppers aside.

In a bowl, combine the onions, tomatoes, garlic, capers, anchovies, salt and pepper, mixing well. Spoon the mixture into the red pepper quarters and set inside a baking dish that is large enough to hold the peppers snugly together. Drizzle the oil over the tops. Bake in a preheated 375° oven for 20 minutes. Serve warm or at room temperature.

Makes 10 to 12.

Marblehead Cooks
Tower School, Marblehead, Massachusetts

SPINACH SQUARES

Cut into bite-size pieces, these terrific cheesy squares
are ideal finger food for parties. Served in larger portions
and accompanied with broiled tomatoes, they also are great
for Sunday brunch, lunch or a light supper.

2 tablespoons butter or margarine	1 pound mild Cheddar cheese, shredded
3 eggs	2 packages (10 ounces each) frozen chopped spinach, cooked and well drained
1 cup unbleached flour	
1 cup milk	
1 teaspoon baking powder	1 tablespoon chopped onions (optional)
½ teaspoon salt	Seasoned salt (optional)

Put the butter or margarine in a 13" × 9" baking dish and melt in a 350°
oven. In a large bowl, beat the eggs. Add the flour, milk, baking powder
and salt and mix well. Add the cheese, spinach and onions (if using) and
mix well. Spoon into the baking dish and smooth the top. Sprinkle with
seasoned salt (if using) and bake in a preheated 350° oven for 35 minutes.
Let cool for 45 minutes before serving.

Serves 4 to 6.

Our Daily Bread
St. Patrick's Church: Our Lady's Guild, Bennington, New Hampshire

CHICKEN PUFFS

Slightly crisp on the outside and moist on the inside,
these puffs are best accompanied with a sweet-and-sour sauce
or hot mustard—and with toothpicks for dipping. They may be
frozen in an airtight container. To thaw and crisp, put them on
a baking sheet in a preheated 250° oven for 10 to 15 minutes.

¾ cup finely chopped cooked chicken	1 tablespoon dried parsley
⅓ cup chopped toasted almonds	¾ teaspoon celery seeds
1 cup chicken stock	½ teaspoon salt
¼ cup oil	⅛ teaspoon ground red pepper (or to taste)
4 teaspoons Worcestershire sauce	1 cup sifted unbleached flour
	4 eggs

In a small bowl, mix the chicken and almonds and set aside. Combine
the stock, oil, Worcestershire sauce, parsley, celery seeds, salt and red
pepper in a saucepan and bring to a boil. Add the flour all at once and cook
over low heat, stirring vigorously, until the mixture leaves the sides of the
pan and forms a smooth ball.

Remove from the heat. Add the eggs, 1 at a time, beating hard after each
addition until the mixture is shiny. (Use a wooden spoon for best results.)
Stir in the chicken mixture.

Drop by rounded teaspoonfuls (about 1″ diameter) onto greased baking
sheets and bake in a preheated 400° oven for 12 to 18 minutes, or until
browned. Do not overbake. Serve warm.

Makes about 40.

A Taste of Glocester
Glocester Heritage Society, Chepachet, Rhode Island

JOHN HANCOCK BRANDIED MEATBALLS

Although John Hancock's signature didn't actually accompany
this recipe, we're sure he would have willingly put his name on it.
These deserve to be front and center on the buffet table.
The meatballs are moist and tender with just a hint of spice,
and the peachy sauce is fragrant, sweet and delectable.

SAUCE
- 1 jar (18 ounces) peach preserves
- ¾ cup firmly packed light brown sugar
- ½ cup brandy
- ½ cup peach brandy or peach nectar
- ¼ teaspoon ground nutmeg

MEATBALLS
- 2 pounds lean ground beef
- ¾ cup milk
- ½ cup dry bread crumbs
- 1 tablespoon Worcestershire sauce
- 1 teaspoon garlic powder
- ½ teaspoon salt
- ¼ teaspoon ground nutmeg
- ¼ teaspoon ground ginger
- ⅛ teaspoon ground black pepper
- 2 dashes of hot-pepper sauce
- 2 tablespoons shortening or oil
- 1 tablespoon cornstarch, combined with 1 tablespoon water (if needed)

To make the sauce: In a medium bowl, combine the preserves, brown sugar, brandy, peach brandy or peach nectar and nutmeg, stirring until thoroughly blended. Set aside.

To make the meatballs: In a large bowl, combine the ground beef, milk, bread crumbs, Worcestershire sauce, garlic powder, salt, nutmeg, ginger, pepper and hot-pepper sauce. Shape the mixture into 1½" to 2" balls.

Heat the shortening or oil in a large skillet and brown the meatballs. Remove with a slotted spoon and set aside.

Lower the heat, pour off all but 1 tablespoon of the meat drippings and blend in the sauce. Simmer for 10 minutes. Add the meatballs to the sauce and coat them thoroughly. Cover and simmer for 45 to 60 minutes. If needed, add the cornstarch and water mixture, stirring constantly, and cook over low heat until thickened. Transfer to a chafing dish for serving.

Makes about 40.

Bulfinch's Boston Faire
Doric Dames, Boston, Massachusetts

MEATBALLS IN RED WINE SAUCE

Whether these meatballs are served as an appetizer or a main dish, they are sure to be a hit with any age group.

2 pounds lean ground beef
1 cup fine dry bread crumbs
3 eggs
1 onion, finely chopped
¼ cup grated Parmesan cheese
½ teaspoon Worcestershire sauce
¾ teaspoon curry powder
¼ teaspoon ground black pepper

2 cloves garlic, minced and divided
1 cup unbleached flour
2 tablespoons oil
2 cans (8 ounces each) tomato sauce
1 cup red wine
½ cup beef consommé
⅛ teaspoon dried oregano

In a large bowl, mix the ground beef, bread crumbs, eggs, onions, Parmesan cheese, Worcestershire sauce, curry powder, pepper and half the garlic. Form the mixture into 1½" meatballs and roll lightly in the flour. Put the oil and remaining garlic in a large skillet, add the meatballs and brown on all sides (about 8 minutes).

Meanwhile, combine the tomato sauce, wine, consommé and oregano in a large saucepan and bring to a simmer. Add the meatballs and simmer for 25 to 35 minutes. Place in a chafing dish and serve with large toothpicks.

Makes about 80.

Cooking to Beat the Band
Contoocook Valley Regional High School Band, Peterborough, New Hampshire

CRAB-STUFFED CHERRY TOMATOES

A table knife works well when scooping the pulp from the tomatoes and when filling them as well. If you want a fancier presentation, pipe the filling in with a pastry bag, using a medium tip.

36 cherry tomatoes	½ teaspoon prepared
¼ cup low-fat cottage cheese	horseradish
½ pound cooked fresh crab-	Pinch of garlic salt
meat, drained and flaked	¼ cup minced celery
1½ teaspoons minced onions	1 tablespoon minced green bell
1½ teaspoons lemon juice	peppers

Cut off about ⅓ of each tomato from the stem end and scoop out the pulp. Invert the tomatoes on paper towels to drain.

Blend the cottage cheese in a blender or food processor until smooth, add the crabmeat and process briefly. Add the onions, lemon juice, horseradish and garlic salt and blend well. Transfer to a bowl and stir in the celery and bell peppers. Spoon the crabmeat mixture into the tomatoes and chill before serving.

Makes 3 dozen.

A Taste of New England
Junior League of Worcester, Massachusetts

FISH SANDWICH LOAF
🌿

The choice of bread for this is important; otherwise, the loaf
will be difficult to slice and serve. This is good finger food for a party.

1 **pound fish fillets (such as cod, haddock or pollack)**	1 **cup shredded Cheddar cheese**
1 **cup boiling water**	½ **cup mayonnaise**
1 **onion slice**	½ **cup chili sauce**
2 **tablespoons lemon juice**	¼ **cup chopped dill pickles**
½ **teaspoon salt, divided**	¼ **cup sliced scallions**
1 **loaf Vienna bread, about 14" long**	1 **tablespoon prepared horseradish**

Place the fish in a 10" skillet. Add the water, onion slice, lemon juice and
¼ teaspoon of the salt. Cover and simmer for 5 to 10 minutes, or until the
fish flakes easily. Remove the fish from the liquid, drain and chill.

Flake the fish and set aside. Cut the loaf of bread in half horizontally.
Hollow out the top and bottom halves, leaving an outside shell ¾" thick.
Tear the bread removed from the center into small pieces.

In a medium bowl, combine the cheese, mayonnaise, chili sauce, pickles,
scallions, horseradish, flaked fish, bread pieces and remaining ¼ teaspoon
salt, mixing well. Pile the mixture into the bottom shell, mounding it
slightly, and place the top shell over the filling. Wrap the loaf securely in
foil and bake in a preheated 400° oven for 40 minutes, or until the loaf is
hot. Cut in thick chunks or slices.

Serves 6.

The Taste of Gloucester
The Fishermen's Wives of Gloucester and The Cape Ann League of Women Voters,
Gloucester, Massachusetts

MARINATED SHRIMP

This special-occasion dish couldn't be simpler.
The only difficulty is waiting until you can eat it.

1 clove garlic, halved
2 pounds shrimp, cooked, peeled and deveined
1/2 cup chopped celery
1 scallion, chopped
1 tablespoon chopped chives
1/4 cup plus 2 tablespoons olive oil
1/4 teaspoon paprika
3/4 teaspoon salt
3 tablespoons lemon juice
1/4 teaspoon hot-pepper sauce
2 tablespoons chili sauce
2 tablespoons ketchup
2 tablespoons prepared horseradish
1 tablespoon Dijon mustard

Rub a large bowl with the garlic, then discard. Add the shrimp, celery, scallions, chives, oil, paprika, salt, lemon juice, hot-pepper sauce, chili sauce, ketchup, horseradish and mustard. Mix thoroughly and refrigerate for 6 to 12 hours, stirring occasionally. Drain and serve chilled.

Serves 8 to 10.

A Taste of New England
Junior League of Worcester, Massachusetts

COQUILLES ST. JACQUES

This dish can be prepared ahead, up to the point when the
shells are filled, and refrigerated until you're ready to serve it.
Then let the mixture stand at room temperature for 15 minutes,
fill the shells and proceed as directed. One-half pound shrimp
can be substituted for the scallops or crabmeat if you wish.

1/3 cup minced onions	1 1/3 cups milk
1 clove garlic, minced	2/3 cup sauternes or other white wine
1/4 cup butter or margarine	1 pound bay scallops
1/4 cup unbleached flour	1/2 pound crabmeat, drained and flaked
1/2 teaspoon salt	Grated Parmesan cheese
1/4 teaspoon ground black pepper	

In a saucepan, sauté the onions and garlic in the butter or margarine
over medium-low heat until softened. Blend in the flour, salt and pepper
and cook, stirring, until bubbly. Mix in the milk and bring to a boil, stirring
constantly. Add the wine and bring to a boil again. Cook, stirring, for
1 minute. Add the scallops and crabmeat and cook, stirring, for 1 minute.

Spoon the mixture into 6 to 8 individual small scallop shells or other
shape ramekins. Sprinkle the tops with the Parmesan cheese and broil
6" to 8" from the heat for 2 to 4 minutes, or until bubbly and lightly
browned.

Serves 6 to 8.

Off the Hook
The Junior League of Stamford-Norwalk, Darien, Connecticut

SCALLOPS WITH GREEN SAUCE

This is a fine alternative to the usual bacon-wrapped scallops that are frequently served as an appetizer. For even less fat and more zest, substitute ½ cup plain yogurt for ½ cup of the mayonnaise.

SCALLOPS
- 1½ pounds scallops
- 1 cup dry vermouth
- 1 bay leaf
- 1 onion, chopped
- 1 teaspoon minced fresh dill
- Salt and pepper

SAUCE
- 1 cup mayonnaise
- ½ cup minced fresh spinach
- ¼ cup minced fresh parsley
- ¼ cup minced fresh chives
- 1 teaspoon minced fresh dill

To make the scallops: Cut the scallops into bite-size pieces and remove and discard the tough "muscle" that attaches the scallop to its shell. Put the scallops in a saucepan along with the vermouth, bay leaf and onions. Add the dill and salt and pepper to taste. Cook until the scallops are white and tender, about 3 to 5 minutes. Drain, saving the cooking liquid, and cool the scallops and liquid separately. When cool, return the scallops to the liquid and refrigerate overnight.

To make the sauce: Combine the mayonnaise, spinach, parsley, chives and dill in a small bowl, mixing well. Refrigerate until ready to use.

At serving time, drain and pat dry the scallops with paper towels. Serve on toothpicks, accompanied with the sauce as a dip.

Serves 8 to 10.

Saint Gabriel's Horn of Plenty
Saint Gabriel's Episcopal Church, Marion, Massachusetts

CLAMS WITH SAUSAGE, TOMATOES & LINGUINE

An elegant appetizer for an intimate dinner party, this also can be served as the entrée, with loaves of crusty bread to soak up the sauce. If desired, mussels may be used in place of clams.

2 tablespoons extra-virgin olive oil

1/4 pound kielbasa, cut into 1/2" slices

1/4 cup chopped onions

3 cloves garlic, chopped

36 littleneck clams, scrubbed

1 cup chopped fresh plum tomatoes

1/2 cup dry white wine

1 pound linguine

1 tablespoon chopped fresh Italian parsley

1 tablespoon finely shredded fresh basil

Heat the oil in a heavy-bottomed pot. Add the kielbasa, onions and garlic. Sauté over low heat until the onions are tender. Stir in the clams, tomatoes and wine, cover the pot and cook over medium-low heat until the clams open.

Cook the linguine in a large pot until just tender. Drain. Serve the clams in their shells along with the sauce over the linguine. Sprinkle with the parsley and basil.

Serves 6.

Watch Hill Cooks
Watch Hill Improvement Society, Watch Hill, Rhode Island

$\mathcal{S}$TEAMED GRAPE LEAVES

If you have a grape arbor, you can pick your own leaves for this recipe. Be sure to select younger ones, which are not as thick veined as the older leaves. Otherwise, look in your grocery or specialty food store for preserved ones.

4 **tablespoons olive oil, divided**	¹/₂ **teaspoon salt**
1 **cup finely chopped onions**	**Ground black pepper**
¹/₃ **cup uncooked long-grain**	2 **tablespoons pine nuts**
white rice	2 **tablespoons dried currants**
³/₄ **cup plus 2 tablespoons water,**	40 **grape leaves**
divided	**Lemon wedges**
¹/₂ **teaspoon ground allspice**	**Plain yogurt**
(optional)	

Heat 2 tablespoons of the oil in a large skillet over medium heat until a haze forms. Add the onions and cook until transparent. Stir in the rice and coat with the oil. Add the ³/₄ cup water, allspice (if using), salt and pepper to taste. Bring to a boil. Cover tightly, reduce the heat and simmer until all the liquid is absorbed, about 15 minutes.

Meanwhile, toast the pine nuts in a 350° oven for 4 to 5 minutes, or until browned. Add them along with the currants to the rice.

If you use fresh grape leaves, bring 2 quarts water to a boil in a large pot. Drop in the leaves and immediately turn off the heat. Let soak for 1 minute, then drain and plunge into ice water. Spread on paper towels to dry.

If you use preserved grape leaves, drain, rinse well in cold water and dry on paper towels.

Reserve 10 leaves. Working on a flat surface, put 1 tablespoon of the filling on the dull side of each remaining leaf and, starting with the stem end, fold over each of the 4 sides. Line the bottom of a heavy 3-quart casserole with the 10 reserved leaves and stack the stuffed leaves, seam side down, on top in layers. Sprinkle with the remaining 2 tablespoons oil and the remaining 2 tablespoons water. Place the casserole over high heat for 3 minutes. Reduce the heat to low and simmer, tightly covered, for 50 minutes. Uncover and cool to room temperature. Garnish with the lemon wedges and serve with the yogurt for dipping.

Makes about 30.

Vermont Kitchens Revisited
The Women of the Cathedral Church of St. Paul, Burlington, Vermont

MAPLE MCINTOSH APPLESAUCE

Maple syrup adds a subtle sweetness and smoothness to this sauce, which freezes beautifully, with no noticeable loss of taste or texture.

5 pounds (about 15) large **McIntosh apples**	2 tablespoons maple syrup
1 cup water	¹/₂ teaspoon ground cinnamon

Wash the apples, then core and cut them into eighths. Do not peel. Put the apples and water into a large pot. Bring to a boil, then reduce the heat and simmer, stirring frequently to prevent the apples from sticking. Continue cooking for 40 minutes, or until the skins soften and fall off. Remove from the heat, let cool and put through a food mill or press through a sieve to remove the skins from the sauce. Add the maple syrup and cinnamon and blend thoroughly.

Makes 2 quarts.

RRMC Family Favorites
Rutland Regional Medical Center Auxiliary, Rutland, Vermont

HARVESTTIME CRANBERRY-APPLE RELISH

Although this keeps very well stored in the refrigerator,
it probably won't last long enough to put it to the test.

2 cups cranberries	**1 orange**
2 apples, peeled, cored and	**½ lemon**
quartered	**1¼ cups sugar**

Pick over the cranberries and rinse them thoroughly. Chop the apples
and cranberries in a food processor or blender, being careful not to process
too fine or puree. Transfer to a medium bowl.

Quarter the orange and lemon, rind and all. Remove the seeds and finely
chop in the food processor or blender. Combine with the cranberries and
apples, add the sugar and blend thoroughly. Cover tightly and chill.

Makes about 3 cups.

Our Daily Bread
St. Patrick's Church: Our Lady's Guild, Bennington, New Hampshire

CRANBERRY-PEAR RELISH

The sweet-tart flavor of this relish is in perfect balance, making it suitable for many foods and occasions. Guests are certain to request the recipe, so make sure to have some extra copies on hand to send home with them.

4 cups cranberries	1 cup orange juice
3 pears, peeled, cored and diced	2 tablespoons grated orange rind
2 apples, peeled, cored and diced	2 tablespoons ground cinnamon
2 cups golden raisins	¼ teaspoon ground nutmeg
1½ cups sugar	½ cup orange liqueur (optional)

Pick over the cranberries and rinse thoroughly. Put them in a 3½-quart saucepan along with the pears, apples, raisins, sugar, orange juice, orange rind, cinnamon and nutmeg. Bring to a boil, stirring, then reduce the heat. Simmer, stirring frequently, until the mixture thickens, about 45 minutes.

Remove the pan from the heat and stir in the orange liqueur (if using). Refrigerate, covered, for at least 4 hours. Serve slightly chilled.

Makes 8 cups.

Mystic Seaport's Seafood Secrets Cookbook
Mystic Seaport Museum Stores, Mystic, Connecticut

CRAN-DATE RELISH

Freeze this relish in small amounts so that you can take it
out as needed. It's divine with ham and poultry.

2 cups cranberries	1 package (8 ounces) pitted
2 cups orange juice	dates, chopped
¼ cup sugar	¼ teaspoon grated orange rind
¾ teaspoon ground ginger	2 heaping tablespoons ginger
	preserves

Pick over the cranberries and rinse them thoroughly. Combine the cranberries, orange juice, sugar and ground ginger in a saucepan and bring to a boil. Simmer for 5 minutes, add the dates and simmer for 5 to 10 minutes more, depending on the consistency you desire. Cool, then stir in the orange rind and ginger preserves. Refrigerate or freeze until ready to serve.

Makes about 4 cups.

Sounds Delicious
Cape Ann Symphony Association, Gloucester, Massachusetts

HOLIDAY CORN RELISH

This quick and easy dish can be made ahead and stored in the
refrigerator for up to a month. It also makes a great hostess gift.

3 ears fresh corn or 1½ cups frozen	⅛ teaspoon ground black pepper
¼ cup water	1 tablespoon chopped green bell peppers
1 small onion, sliced into rings	1 tablespoon chopped pimentos
½ cup thinly sliced celery	⅛ teaspoon ground turmeric
¼ cup white vinegar	½ teaspoon celery seeds
¼ cup firmly packed brown sugar	½ teaspoon salt (optional)
1/16 teaspoon ground red pepper	

If using fresh corn, scrape the kernels from the ears. If using frozen corn, chop it finely using a food processor to approximate the texture of fresh corn scraped from the cob.

Place the corn, water, onions, celery, vinegar, brown sugar, red pepper, black pepper, bell peppers, pimentos, turmeric, celery seeds and salt (if using) in a 1½-quart saucepan. Bring to a boil and simmer, uncovered, for 5 minutes. Remove from the heat, cool, transfer to a covered dish and refrigerate until ready to serve.

Makes 2½ cups.

The Sharing & Caring Cookbook
Big Brothers/Big Sisters of the Monadnock Region, Keene, New Hampshire

$\mathcal{T}$HE WAYBURY INN KIDNEY BEAN RELISH

The flavors in this attractive relish need time to meld,
so it's best to make it at least a day before serving.

2 **cups cooked kidney beans, drained**	2 **tablespoons mayonnaise**
3 **stalks celery, chopped**	2 **teaspoons Dijon mustard**
2 **hard-cooked eggs, chopped**	1 **teaspoon curry powder**
1 **small onion, chopped**	½ **teaspoon salt**

Combine the beans, celery, eggs and onions in a small bowl. Add the mayonnaise, mustard, curry powder and salt and mix well. Refrigerate, covered, for at least 1 hour, preferably overnight.

Makes about 2½ cups.

A Taste of Glocester
Glocester Heritage Society, Chepachet, Rhode Island

*A*PPLE–GREEN TOMATO CHUTNEY
❧

This chutney is fantastic poured over chicken before it is baked.
If you use a food processor instead of a grinder, process briefly
and in small batches so that the ingredients don't turn to mush.
For a more colorful chutney, leave the bell peppers in larger pieces.

1½	pounds green tomatoes (5 or 6 medium)	1	cup distilled white vinegar
2	medium red bell peppers	¾	teaspoon ground cinnamon
2	medium onions	½	teaspoon ground cloves
2	medium red cooking apples	½	teaspoon salt
1¼	cups sugar	½	teaspoon ground black pepper

Wash, trim and quarter the tomatoes, bell peppers and onions. Quarter
and core the apples but do not peel them. Put the tomatoes, bell peppers,
onions and apples through a food grinder with a medium attachment or
chop in a food processor. Drain, discarding the liquid.

In a saucepan, combine the sugar, vinegar, cinnamon, cloves, salt and
pepper and heat to boiling. Add the processed vegetables and apples and
simmer for 30 minutes, stirring occasionally. Freeze until ready to use.

Makes about 6 cups.

Cooking with a Maine Accent
Gorham Woman's Club, Gorham, Maine

*S*WEET TOMATO CHUTNEY
❧

This chutney will keep in the refrigerator for up to 6 weeks.

1	tablespoon oil	¼	teaspoon ground turmeric
1	cinnamon stick	1	pound fresh tomatoes, chopped, or 1 can (16 ounces) tomatoes, drained and chopped
1	bay leaf		
6	whole cloves		
1	teaspoon mustard seeds		
¼	cup sugar	½	cup raisins
1	teaspoon chili powder	½	teaspoon salt

Pour the oil into a 1½-quart saucepan and place over low heat. Add the cinnamon stick, bay leaf and cloves and stir for 1 minute. Add the mustard seeds, and when they begin to crackle, add the sugar, chili powder and turmeric, mixing well. Stir in the tomatoes, raisins and salt. Cover and simmer for 8 to 10 minutes. Add a little water if the liquid thickens too much; tomato chutney should have a medium consistency. Serve hot or cold.

Makes 2 cups.

Celebrities Serve
International Tennis Hall of Fame, Newport, Rhode Island

$\mathcal{G}$REEN TOMATO MINCEMEAT
❧

This mincemeat keeps well canned or frozen. In addition to being used for pies, it is delicious spread on biscuits or corn bread or served with omelets or soufflés. A few drops of brandy added just before baking will enhance the flavor of a mincemeat pie.

3 **cups chopped green tomatoes**	1½ **cups raisins**
3 **cups peeled, cored and chopped apples**	½ **teaspoon ground cinnamon**
	½ **teaspoon ground cloves**
2 **cups firmly packed brown sugar**	¼ **teaspoon ground nutmeg**
	½ **teaspoon salt**
½ **cup vinegar**	¼ **cup butter or margarine**

Place the tomatoes in a colander to drain, then discard the juice. In a large saucepan, combine the tomatoes, apples, brown sugar and vinegar. Add the raisins, cinnamon, cloves, nutmeg and salt. Bring slowly to a boil, stirring often. Reduce the heat and simmer, stirring occasionally, for 2 to 3 hours, or until the mixture thickens. Stir in the butter or margarine and remove from the heat. Allow to cool before using for a pie filling.

Makes about 8 cups.

Vermont II: Kitchen Memories
Montpelier, Vermont

CRANBERRY-HORSERADISH SAUCE FOR SHRIMP

❧

A unique variation on an old theme, this sauce doesn't
have to be limited to shrimp; try it with other seafood and fish as well.

1 cup whole-berry cranberry sauce	2 tablespoons prepared horseradish
½ cup ketchup	1 tablespoon Dijon mustard
¼ cup lemon juice	⅛ teaspoon celery seeds
2 scallions, chopped	

Combine the cranberry sauce, ketchup, lemon juice, scallions, horseradish, mustard and celery seeds in a blender or food processor and process
until smooth. Refrigerate until ready to serve.

Makes about 2 cups.

The Mystic Seaport All Seasons Cookbook
Mystic Seaport Museum Stores, Mystic, Connecticut

SQUASH PICKLES

❧

Neither sweet nor sour, these pickles fall somewhere
in between and offer another opportunity to use up some
of those zucchini that keep multiplying in the garden.

4 cups sliced yellow summer squash or zucchini, or a combination of both	1 teaspoon salt
	1 cup white vinegar
1 large onion, sliced	¾ cup sugar
1 green bell pepper, sliced	1 teaspoon mustard seeds
	1 teaspoon celery seeds

Combine the squash, onions and bell peppers in a large bowl, sprinkle
with the salt and let stand for 1 hour. Press the water out of the vegetables
and set aside while preparing the brine.

In a large saucepan, bring the vinegar, sugar, mustard seeds and celery seeds to a boil. Add the vegetables and bring just to a boil, then reduce the heat and simmer for 7 to 8 minutes, or until the vegetables are soft. Set aside to cool. Pour into plastic containers and freeze until ready to serve.

Serves 10.

Crossroads Cookbook
Somers Congregational Church, Somers, Connecticut

$\mathscr{M}$ELBA'S REFRIGERATOR PICKLES

Here is an easy way always to have sweet pickles on hand.
The brine requires no cooking and can be kept in the refrigerator for months, so you can make a pint or two whenever you wish.

2 **cups sugar**	³/₄ **teaspoon mustard seeds**
2 **cups cider vinegar**	³/₄ **teaspoon ground turmeric**
¹/₄ **cup salt**	1–2 **onions, thinly sliced**
³/₄ **teaspoon celery seeds**	**Cucumbers**

Mix the sugar, vinegar, salt, celery seeds, mustard seeds and turmeric in a medium bowl. Wash and sterilize 3 pint or 6 half-pint jars.

Divide the onions among the jars. Scrub and slice the cucumbers and fill the jars. Stir the brine well and pour it over the cucumbers and onions, filling the jars. Put the lids on the jars and refrigerate for at least 7 days before using. These pickles will keep for months but must be stored in the refrigerator.

Makes 3 pints.

Saint Gabriel's Horn of Plenty
Saint Gabriel's Episcopal Church, Marion, Massachusetts

FRESH REFRIGERATOR PICKLES

For the best results, try to use cucumbers
that do not have a waxy coating on their skins.

3 large cucumbers	2 teaspoons celery seeds
1 green bell pepper	¼ cup sugar
1 onion	½ cup white vinegar
1 tablespoon salt	

Scrub the unpeeled cucumbers and cut them into ⅛" slices. Finely chop the bell pepper and onion and combine with the cucumbers in a large bowl. Sprinkle with salt and celery seeds, mix well and let stand for at least 1 hour. Dissolve the sugar in the vinegar and pour over the vegetables, stirring to blend. Cover and refrigerate for at least 1 day before serving.

Serves 8.

A Hancock Community Collection
First Congregational Church: The Guild, Hancock, New Hampshire

$\mathcal{P}$ICKLED CARROTS

These are great to have on hand to serve with
cocktails or simply as a snack to nibble on.

Carrot sticks
1 **teaspoon salt**
½ **teaspoon sugar**
1 **large clove garlic, sliced**

1 **teaspoon dill seeds or dill weed**
½ **medium onion, sliced**
½ **cup water**
½ **cup vinegar**

Fill a pint jar with carrot sticks and add the salt, sugar, garlic, dill and
onions. In a small saucepan, bring the water and vinegar to a boil and pour
over the carrots. Cool, cover and refrigerate for at least 24 hours before
serving.

Makes 1 pint.

The Andover Cookbook II
Phillips Academy: The Ladies' Benevolent Society, Andover, Massachusetts

Salads
&
Dressings

$\mathcal{A}$PRICOT-DATE SALAD
❧

Crunchy walnuts complement the chewy dried fruits
in this hearty mixture, which is dressed with honey-sweetened
yogurt. Serve on a bed of greens or red cabbage leaves.

½ **cup chopped dried apricots**	1 **teaspoon lemon juice**
¼ **cup chopped dates**	½ **teaspoon ground cinnamon**
2 **cups plain yogurt**	½ **cup chopped walnuts**
2 **tablespoons honey**	

In a medium bowl combine the apricots, dates, yogurt, honey, lemon
juice and cinnamon, mixing until well blended. Chill until ready to serve,
then top with the walnuts.

Makes about 3 cups.

The Charlotte Central Cooks' Book
Charlotte Central PTO, Charlotte, Vermont

$\mathcal{F}$RUIT SALAD

Use only the freshest fruits in this elegant combination of melons, strawberries and blueberries. Serve with an assortment of tea breads for lunch or as a refreshing dessert on a sultry summer evening.

2 **cups honeydew melon cubes or balls**	**Juice of** 1/2 **lime**
2 **cups watermelon cubes or balls**	1/4 **cup apple juice**
	1 **tablespoon honey**
2 **cups sliced strawberries**	1/2 **teaspoon vanilla**
1 **cup cantaloupe cubes or balls**	1/4 **cup blueberries**
	Orange sherbet

In a large, chilled bowl, toss the honeydew, watermelon, strawberries and cantaloupe. Combine the lime juice, apple juice, honey and vanilla in a separate bowl and pour over the fruit, mixing well. Garnish with the blueberries and serve with the sherbet.

Serves 4 to 6.

The Haystack Cookbook
Haystack Mountain School of Crafts, Deer Isle, Maine

$\mathcal{P}$EAR & APPLE SLAW

For an attractive garnish, place thin slices
of orange over the top of the salad.

2 **ripe pears**	1/3 **cup orange juice**
2 **large apples**	4 **cups shredded cabbage**
1/2 **cup mayonnaise or plain yogurt**	1/2 **cup chopped walnuts**
	1/2 **cup raisins**

Peel, quarter, core and dice the pears and place in a small bowl. Peel, quarter, core and dice the apples and place in a second small bowl. Combine the mayonnaise or yogurt and orange juice in another small bowl and drizzle a few tablespoons of this dressing over both bowls of fruit and toss to coat. Cover both bowls of fruit with plastic wrap and refrigerate for at least 1 hour. Cover and refrigerate the dressing also.

At serving time, layer the cabbage in the bottom of a salad bowl. Toss the walnuts with the apples and spoon into the center of the bowl. Spoon the pears around the edge and sprinkle the top of the salad with the raisins. Accompany with the remaining dressing.

Serves 4 to 6.

Family Recipe Cookbook
Habitat for Humanity, Providence, Rhode Island

𝒯HANKSGIVING SALAD
꽃

There's a lot of color and crunch in this slawlike salad,
a fancy combination of fruits and vegetables.
Give it some time to chill in the refrigerator before serving.

1¼ **cups cranberries**	1 **bunch broccoli**
⅔ **cup sugar, divided**	4 **cups finely shredded cabbage**
1 **cup mayonnaise or plain yogurt**	1 **cup coarsely broken walnuts**
	1 **small onion, finely minced**
2 **teaspoons cider vinegar**	½ **cup raisins**

Pick over the cranberries and rinse them thoroughly. In a medium bowl, mix the cranberries and ⅓ cup of the sugar and set aside.

In a small bowl, mix the mayonnaise or yogurt, remaining ⅓ cup sugar and vinegar, stirring until the sugar dissolves. Set aside.

Break the broccoli into florets and reserve the stems and stalk for another use. Combine the broccoli florets, cabbage, walnuts, onions and raisins in a large bowl. Add the cranberry mixture and toss lightly. Pour in the mayonnaise mixture and combine thoroughly. Cover the bowl with plastic wrap and chill until serving, stirring occasionally.

Serves 8 to 10.

The Morrison House Museum Cookbook
Londonderry Historical Society, Londonderry, New Hampshire

HOLIDAY GREEN SALAD

Rather than reserve this for holidays, you'll want to make
it year-round—and can, for the ingredients are always available.

1　small head Boston lettuce	¼　teaspoon dry mustard
1　large or 2 small ripe pears	Salt and pepper
4　ounces Jarlsberg cheese, cubed	Pinch of dried marjoram
	Pinch of ground cloves
½　cup walnut halves	½　package (4-ounce size) alfalfa sprouts
3　tablespoons olive oil	
1　tablespoon white wine vinegar	

A few hours before serving, wash and dry the lettuce. Tear into bite-size
pieces, place in a plastic bag and chill. Chill the pears.

Remove the cheese from the refrigerator and allow it to come to room
temperature. Toast the walnuts in a 350° oven for 10 minutes.

Shortly before serving, whisk the oil, vinegar, mustard, salt and pepper
to taste, marjoram and cloves in a small bowl.

Place the lettuce and sprouts in a large salad bowl. Thinly slice the pears
and add them along with the cheese and walnuts to the salad bowl. Drizzle
on the dressing, toss gently and serve.

Serves 4.

Vermont Kitchens Revisited
The Women of the Cathedral Church of St. Paul, Burlington, Vermont

RAZZLEBERRY SALAD

You *must* make this salad! If you cannot find raspberry mustard, substitute a good-quality Dijon or fruity mustard—but the full flavor comes out only with raspberry mustard. Although romaine lettuce will work, it may be too bitter for this salad. Boston, Bibb or leaf lettuce is better.

SALAD

- 1 **pound fresh asparagus**
- 1 **small cucumber**
- ½ **pint strawberries**
- 4 **cups lettuce torn into bite-size pieces**

DRESSING

- ½ **cup oil**
- ½ **cup raspberry vinegar**
- 1 **tablespoon raspberry mustard**
  Ground black pepper

To make the salad: Cook the asparagus until just tender. Run it under cold water to stop the cooking and set the color. Drain thoroughly and cut into 1" pieces. Peel the cucumber and cut in half lengthwise. Scoop out and discard the seeds and slice the cucumber into half-moons. Thinly slice the strawberries. Place the lettuce in a large salad bowl. Add the asparagus, cucumbers and strawberries and toss.

To make the dressing: Shake the oil, vinegar, mustard and pepper to taste in a jar until well mixed. Pour over the salad, toss to coat and serve.

Serves 4.

Sounds Delicious
Cape Ann Symphony Association, Gloucester, Massachusetts

$\mathcal{S}$TRAWBERRY & ONION SALAD WITH POPPY SEED DRESSING

❧

Substitute different fruits to fit the season or a particular color scheme.
This will keep in the refrigerator for several days.

DRESSING
- ¼ **cup mayonnaise**
- 3 **tablespoons sugar**
- 2 **tablespoons milk**
- 1 **tablespoon vinegar**
- 1 **tablespoon poppy seeds**

SALAD
- 1 **small head romaine lettuce**
- ½ **pint strawberries, sliced**
- ½ **Bermuda onion, sliced**

To make the dressing: Place the mayonnaise, sugar, milk, vinegar and
poppy seeds in a jar. Cover and shake until blended, then refrigerate.

To make the salad: Wash the lettuce, pat dry and refrigerate until serving
time. Place the greens in a large salad bowl. Add the strawberries and
onions, drizzle the dressing over the salad and toss.

Serves 4.

Saint Gabriel's Horn of Plenty
Saint Gabriel's Episcopal Church, Marion, Massachusetts

$\mathcal{P}$ICKLED BEETS SALAD

❧

A tasty addition to meat, poultry or fish, this salad needs
to be refrigerated overnight before serving. Be sure to use a
glass or other nonreactive container while it chills.

- 1 **bunch fresh beets, scrubbed and trimmed**
- ⅓ **cup white or red wine vinegar**
- ¼ **cup firmly packed light brown sugar**
- ½ **teaspoon ground cinnamon**
- ¼ **teaspoon ground allspice**
- ¼ **teaspoon ground cloves**
- ¼ **teaspoon salt**
- **Lettuce**
- **Thinly sliced red onions**
- **Sour cream**

Place the beets in a medium saucepan, cover with cold water and cook until tender. Drain, reserving ¼ cup of the cooking water. When the beets are cool enough to handle, slip off the skins and slice the beets thinly.

Combine the reserved cooking water, vinegar, brown sugar, cinnamon, allspice, cloves and salt in a small saucepan and bring to a boil. Add the beets, cover and simmer for 5 minutes, stirring occasionally. Remove from the heat, transfer to a covered container and chill overnight.

To serve, drain the beets, place on a bed of lettuce and top with the onions and a dollop of sour cream.

Serves 4.

Mystic Seaport's Seafood Secrets Cookbook
Mystic Seaport Museum Stores, Mystic, Connecticut

𝒯ANGY SPINACH SALAD
❧

For extra crunch, serve this salad with toasted whole-wheat pita slices or garlic croutons. Sliced, chilled beets as a garnish add a beautiful touch.

3 cloves garlic, thinly sliced	Salt and pepper
¼ cup olive oil	¼ cup chopped dates
¼ cup balsamic vinegar	2 tablespoons chopped red bell
1½ teaspoons firmly packed brown sugar	peppers
1½ teaspoons dried basil	6 cups fresh spinach torn into bite-size pieces
¾ teaspoon dried thyme	

In a small skillet, sauté the garlic in the oil until lightly browned. In a large bowl, combine the garlic and oil mixture with the vinegar, brown sugar, basil and thyme, mixing well. Add the salt and pepper to taste, dates and bell peppers and toss. Chill for 1 hour. Add the spinach at serving time and combine thoroughly.

Serves 4.

Rhode Island Cooks
American Cancer Society: Rhode Island Division, Pawtucket, Rhode Island

$\mathcal{S}$PINACH & SPROUTS SALAD

Those who prefer a less-sweet dressing may want to reduce the sugar to only 1 or 2 tablespoons, depending on the acidity of the vinegar.

SALAD

- 1½ pounds fresh spinach
- 8 ounces fresh bean sprouts
- 1 can (8 ounces) sliced water chestnuts, drained
- 2–4 slices cooked bacon, crumbled

DRESSING

- ⅔ cup oil
- ⅓ cup sugar
- ⅓ cup ketchup
- ⅓ cup red wine vinegar
- ⅓ cup finely minced onions
- 2 teaspoons Worcestershire sauce
- 2 hard-cooked eggs, sliced or chopped

To make the salad: Rinse the spinach, discarding any tough stems and imperfect leaves. Pat dry or spin dry thoroughly, break the leaves into bite-size pieces and put in a large salad bowl. Toss with the bean sprouts, water chestnuts and bacon.

To make the dressing: In a large jar with a tight-fitting lid, combine the oil, sugar, ketchup, vinegar, onions and Worcestershire sauce. Add the eggs and shake well. Pour over the salad ingredients and toss. Serve immediately.

Serves 6 to 8.

Doorway to Healthy Eating
Trinity Church on the Green: Episcopal Church Women, Branford, Connecticut

CORN SALAD

This change-of-pace salad can be made in a jiffy and kept in the refrigerator until ready to serve. Use fresh corn right off the cob when it's available.

2 cans (17 ounces each) whole-kernel corn, drained
¾ cup diced cucumbers
¼ cup diced onions
2 small tomatoes, coarsely chopped
¼ cup sour cream

2 tablespoons mayonnaise
1 tablespoon vinegar
½ teaspoon salt
¼ teaspoon dry mustard
¼ teaspoon celery seeds
   Lettuce

Combine the corn, cucumbers, onions and tomatoes in a medium bowl. In another bowl, blend the sour cream, mayonnaise, vinegar, salt, mustard and celery seeds. Add to the vegetable mixture and toss gently just until the vegetables are coated. Chill and serve on the lettuce.

Serves 6 to 8.

A Taste of Glocester
Glocester Heritage Society, Chepachet, Rhode Island

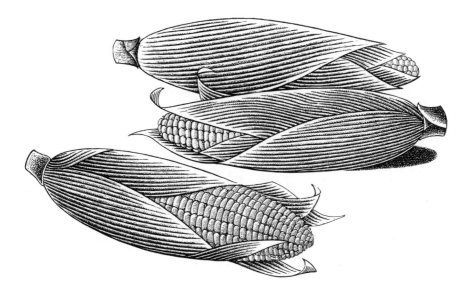

TOSSED ZUCCHINI SALAD

Festive and unusual, this salad makes a great lunch
accompanied with cheese and crusty wheat rolls.

DRESSING
- 1/3 **cup olive oil**
- 2 **tablespoons lemon juice**
- 2 **tablespoons red or white wine vinegar**
- 2 **teaspoons chopped fresh parsley**
- 1 **teaspoon sugar**
- 1/2 **teaspoon salt**
- 1/4 **teaspoon ground black pepper**

SALAD
- 1 **medium zucchini**
- 1 **large red Delicious apple**
- 1/2 **cup sliced red onions**
- 1/2 **cup coarsely chopped green bell peppers**
- 1/2 **cup thinly sliced celery (cut on the diagonal)**
- 1/4 **cup sliced radishes**

To make the dressing: In a large salad bowl, combine the oil, lemon juice, vinegar, parsley, sugar, salt and pepper and mix well.

To make the salad: Cut the zucchini lengthwise into quarters, then crosswise into 1/2"-thick pieces. Quarter and core the apple but do not peel it, then cut into 1/2"-thick pieces. Add the zucchini, apples, onions, bell peppers, celery and radishes to the dressing in the bowl and mix well. Cover and refrigerate for 1 to 2 hours, tossing at 30-minute intervals to distribute the dressing.

Serves 4 to 6.

Liberal Portions
Unitarian Universalist Church, Nashua, New Hampshire

CAESAR SALAD WITHOUT EGG

With the latest data recommending against the use of raw eggs,
certain foods are no longer acceptable. This longtime favorite, however,
doesn't have to be given up entirely—just the eggs.When made
in this fashion, you'll never know they are missing.

<table>
<tr><td>¾</td><td>cup olive oil</td><td>1</td><td>teaspoon ground white pepper</td></tr>
<tr><td>¼</td><td>cup red wine vinegar</td><td>1</td><td>cup grated Parmesan cheese</td></tr>
<tr><td>5–6</td><td>anchovy fillets</td><td></td><td>Salt</td></tr>
<tr><td>4</td><td>cloves garlic</td><td>1</td><td>head romaine lettuce, washed and spun dry</td></tr>
<tr><td>1</td><td>tablespoon Dijon mustard</td><td></td><td>Croutons (optional)</td></tr>
<tr><td>1</td><td>tablespoon lemon juice</td><td></td><td></td></tr>
</table>

Combine the oil, vinegar, anchovies, garlic, mustard, lemon juice and
white pepper in a food processor or blender. Add the Parmesan cheese and
pulse until combined. Season with salt to taste. Store in an airtight container in the refrigerator for up to 3 days and bring to room temperature
before serving.

Break up the romaine leaves and place in a large salad bowl. Add enough
dressing to coat, toss with the croutons (if using) and serve.

Serves 6 to 8.

The Andover Cookbook II
Phillips Academy: The Ladies' Benevolent Society, Andover, Massachusetts

HARVEST SALAD

This is a refreshing and unusual salad; it travels well and can be carried to a church supper—just be sure to bring along the recipe. When trying this for the first time, you might want to use the juice of only ½ lemon to see if that provides adequate tartness.

2 large carrots	Juice of 1 orange
1 zucchini	¼ cup oil
½ cup golden raisins	¼ cup chopped fresh mint
Juice of 1 lemon	Pinch of ground black pepper

Coarsely shred the carrots and zucchini into a medium bowl. Add the raisins, lemon juice, orange juice, oil, mint and pepper and toss to combine. Cover and refrigerate for several hours. Serve very cold.

Serves 8.

Bulfinch's Boston Faire
Doric Dames, Boston, Massachusetts

MUSHROOM SALAD

To spruce up the appearance of these delicious marinated mushrooms, serve them on a bed of greens and garnish with sprigs of fresh parsley or chopped pimento. An easy way to marinate something like this is to pour everything into a large, self-seal plastic bag, seal securely and set inside the refrigerator. Each time you open the refrigerator, turn the bag over. Transfer the contents to an attractive bowl when you're ready to serve the salad.

½ cup olive oil	¼ teaspoon ground black pepper
1½ tablespoons red or white wine vinegar	3 tablespoons thinly sliced scallions
1 tablespoon Dijon mustard	1 pound mushrooms, thinly sliced
1 teaspoon sugar	
1 teaspoon garlic powder	
½ teaspoon salt	

In a small bowl, whisk the oil, vinegar, mustard, sugar, garlic powder, salt and pepper until slightly thickened. Stir in the scallions. Pour the dressing over the mushrooms and chill until ready to serve, stirring from time to time.

Serves 4 to 6.

Mystic Seaport's Moveable Feasts Cookbook
Mystic Seaport Museum Stores, Mystic, Connecticut

No-MAYONNAISE POTATO SALAD

This salad is a crowd pleaser and an
excellent choice for parties, picnics and family reunions.

SALAD

- 2 **pounds red potatoes, unpeeled and cooked**
- 1 **small red onion, thinly sliced**
- ½ **cup sliced black olives**
- 2 **scallions, sliced**

DRESSING

- ¼ **cup plus 2 tablespoons olive oil**
- 2 **tablespoons red wine vinegar**
- 1 **tablespoon Dijon mustard**
- ½ **teaspoon salt**
- ¼ **teaspoon ground black pepper**
- 1 **clove garlic, minced**

To make the salad: Cut the potatoes into uniform chunks. Combine with the onions, olives and scallions in a salad bowl, tossing to mix.

To make the dressing: In a small bowl, whisk together the oil, vinegar, mustard, salt, pepper and garlic. Pour over the salad, mixing well. Serve at room temperature.

Serves 6 to 8.

The Kinderhaus Cookbook
Kinderhaus Children's Center, Williston, Vermont

QUILTER'S POTATO SALAD

This requires a bit more time than a traditional potato salad,
but it's so delicious that you won't regret having made the effort.

DRESSING
- 2 eggs, lightly beaten
- 1/3 cup vinegar
- 1/3 cup sugar
- 1 teaspoon Dijon mustard
- 1 teaspoon salt
- 1/4 teaspoon ground black pepper
- 1/2 cup mayonnaise
- 1/2–1 teaspoon chopped fresh chives (optional)
- 1/2 teaspoon celery seeds (optional)

SALAD
- 2 1/2 pounds red potatoes, scrubbed
- 1 cup diced celery
- 1 cup chopped onions
- Salt and pepper
- Paprika
- Parsley sprigs

To make the dressing: Combine the eggs, vinegar, sugar, mustard, salt and pepper in a small saucepan and cook over low heat, stirring constantly, until thickened. Cool, then blend with the mayonnaise, stirring until smooth. Add the chives (if using) and celery seeds (if using). Store in the refrigerator until ready to use.

To make the salad: Cook the potatoes in salted water to cover for 30 to 40 minutes, or until tender. Drain and place in cold water to cool. Refrigerate until cold. Peel the potatoes and cut into 1" chunks. Add the celery, onions, salad dressing and salt and pepper to taste, blending thoroughly. Spoon into a serving bowl and sprinkle with paprika. Garnish with parsley sprigs.

Serves 6 to 8.

The Kinderhaus Cookbook
Kinderhaus Children's Center, Williston, Vermont

WARM POTATO & GREEN BEAN SALAD

Because this salad is served at room temperature,
it's ideal for picnics and other occasions for dining outdoors.

SALAD

1 pound small red potatoes, scrubbed

¼ pound fresh green beans, trimmed and halved crosswise

½ small red onion, cut into thin wedges

½ red bell pepper, chopped (optional)

DRESSING

3 tablespoons olive oil

2 tablespoons dry white wine

2 teaspoons white wine vinegar

½ teaspoon salt

½ teaspoon ground black pepper

2 teaspoons chopped fresh parsley

½ teaspoon dried oregano

½ teaspoon dried thyme

⅛ teaspoon dried basil

To make the salad: Place the potatoes in a saucepan and cover with cold water. Bring to a boil and cook for about 15 minutes, or until easily pierced with a fork but not mushy. Meanwhile, in a small saucepan, bring 1" of water to a boil, add the beans and cook for about 5 minutes, or until crisp-tender.

Drain the potatoes and beans and let cool slightly. Cut the potatoes into halves or quarters, depending on their size. Place the potatoes, beans, onions and bell peppers in a large bowl, mixing gently.

To make the dressing: In a small bowl, whisk the oil, wine, vinegar, salt, pepper, parsley, oregano, thyme and basil, blending thoroughly. Pour over the vegetables, tossing gently to coat. Let stand for at least 1 hour at room temperature before serving.

Serves 4.

Saint Michael's Cooks By Design
Saint Michael's Episcopal Church, Litchfield, Connecticut

$\mathcal{H}$OT CRAB & GREEN BEAN SALAD

Instead of using individual dishes, the mixture can be transferred
to a shallow casserole and baked for 25 minutes.

1 **pound fresh or thawed frozen crabmeat**	1 **small clove garlic, minced**
2 **pounds green beans, cut into 1" pieces**	¼ **cup finely chopped onions**
¾ **cup mayonnaise**	¼ **teaspoon salt**
2 **tablespoons lemon juice**	**Ground black pepper**
½ **teaspoon dry mustard**	¼–½ **cup fine dry bread crumbs**
	2 **tablespoons butter or margarine, melted**

Drain the crabmeat and pick it over carefully, breaking up any large
pieces. Cook the green beans in boiling salted water for about 15 minutes,
or until crisp-tender, then drain.

Combine the mayonnaise, lemon juice, mustard, garlic, onions, salt and
pepper in a large bowl, blending well. Carefully stir in the beans and then
the crabmeat. Spoon the mixture into greased baking shells or ramekins.
Top each dish with a sprinkling of bread crumbs, drizzle with the butter
or margarine and bake, uncovered, in a preheated 400° oven for about
15 minutes, or until the salads are hot and the crumbs browned.

Serves 4.

A Century of Good Cooking
Waldoboro Woman's Club, Waldoboro, Maine

WHITE BEAN SALAD

A fine accompaniment to an Italian meal, this is a simple, colorful dish.
For the best flavor, use a high-quality extra-virgin olive oil.

2 cups cooked white beans, drained	**2 tablespoons chopped fresh oregano, or 2 teaspoons dried**
2 large tomatoes, peeled, seeded and diced	**¼ cup chopped black olives**
¼ cup diced red onions	**3 tablespoons olive oil** **Salt and pepper**

In a salad bowl, toss the beans, tomatoes, onions, oregano and black
olives. Drizzle on the oil, add salt and pepper to taste and toss again. Adjust
the seasonings, if necessary, and serve at room temperature.

Serves 4.

Celebrities Serve
International Tennis Hall of Fame, Newport, Rhode Island

TORTELLINI SALAD WITH CHESTNUTS

Colorful, flavorful and unusual, this salad can be prepared in advance and kept in the refrigerator. If so, don't add the basil or parsley until the very end, and let the salad sit at room temperature for 1 hour before serving.

DRESSING
- ½ cup olive oil
- ⅓ cup balsamic vinegar
- 1 tablespoon Dijon mustard
- 1 clove garlic, minced
- 1 tablespoon lemon juice
- ⅛ teaspoon salt
- ⅛ teaspoon ground black pepper

SALAD
- 1 package (15-ounce size) cheese tortellini
- ½ package (15-ounce size) spinach tortellini
- ½ pound green beans, fresh or frozen, cut into 1" pieces
- 1 package (6–8 ounces) frozen chestnuts or 1 jar (8 ounces) roasted chestnuts, quartered
- 1 red bell pepper, diced
- 1 bunch scallions, chopped
- ¼ cup chopped fresh basil or parsley

To make the dressing: In a small bowl, whisk the oil, vinegar, mustard, garlic, lemon juice, salt and pepper.

To make the salad: Cook the tortellini in boiling salted water until just tender and drain. Add the dressing to the pasta while it is still hot.

Cook the beans for 5 to 7 minutes, or until crisp-tender. Drain and rinse under cold running water. Drain well.

Mix the beans, chestnuts, bell peppers and scallions with the tortellini and toss well. Cool to room temperature. Just before serving, add the basil or parsley and toss again.

Serves 8 to 10.

A Collection of Favorite Italian Recipes
St. Anthony's Church: The Women's Guild, Woonsocket, Rhode Island

ℒAMB, PASTA & GREEN BEAN SALAD

Distinctive in appearance and taste, this substantial salad can be prepared in no time, but it needs to chill for at least 1 hour before serving.

1 **cup orzo (rice-shaped pasta)**	½ **pound cooked (preferably**
3 **tablespoons Dijon mustard**	**rare) lamb, cut into slivers**
1½ **tablespoons boiling water**	¼ **pound green beans, blanched**
1½ **tablespoons lemon juice**	**and cut into julienne strips**
1 **clove garlic, minced**	1 **small red onion, sliced into**
½ **cup olive oil**	**thin rings**
1 **tablespoon heavy cream**	1 **small red bell pepper, thinly**
Salt and pepper	**sliced**
	¼ **cup minced fresh parsley**

In a large saucepan of boiling water, cook the orzo for 6 to 8 minutes, or until just tender. Drain.

In a large salad bowl, combine the mustard, boiling water, lemon juice and garlic. Add the olive oil in a stream, whisking until well combined, then whisk in the heavy cream. Add salt and pepper to taste. Stir in the orzo, lamb, green beans, onions, bell peppers and parsley. Chill for at least 1 hour, tossing occasionally.

Serves 4.

Marblehead Cooks
Tower School, Marblehead, Massachusetts

$\mathcal{L}$AMB WALDORF SALAD

Lamb transforms this salad from something that is more
often served on the sidelines into the focal point of the meal.

2	cups chopped cooked lamb	$\frac{1}{2}$	teaspoon salt
$1\frac{1}{2}$	cups diced apples	$\frac{1}{4}$	teaspoon ground black
$1\frac{1}{2}$	cups grapes cut into halves		pepper
1	cup chopped walnuts	$\frac{1}{4}$	teaspoon paprika
$\frac{1}{2}$	cup sour cream or plain	$\frac{1}{8}$	teaspoon ground red pepper
	yogurt		Whole lettuce leaves
$\frac{1}{2}$	cup mayonnaise		Parsley sprigs
2	tablespoons red or white wine		
	vinegar		

Combine the lamb, apples, grapes and walnuts in a large bowl. In a
small bowl, mix the sour cream or yogurt, mayonnaise, vinegar, salt, black
pepper, paprika and red pepper. Pour over the lamb mixture and toss to
coat.

Line a salad bowl or individual salad bowls with lettuce, fill with the
salad and garnish with a few sprigs of parsley.

Serves 4.

Community Rescue Squad Cookbook
Rescue Squads of Deering, Hillsboro and Washington, New Hampshire

$\mathcal{S}$UMMER CHICKEN SALAD

To preserve the color and freshness of the blueberries,
serve this soon after it is made.

$1\frac{1}{2}$	cups diced cooked chicken	$\frac{1}{4}$	cup chopped walnuts
	breast	$\frac{1}{4}$	cup raisins
2–3	apples, cored and diced		Mayonnaise
$\frac{1}{3}$	cup blueberries	$\frac{1}{2}$	teaspoon salt (optional)

In a large bowl, combine the chicken, apples, blueberries, walnuts and raisins. Add just enough mayonnaise to moisten the mixture and stir in the salt (if using). Serve immediately.

Serves 4.

Crossroads Cookbook
Somers Congregational Church, Somers, Connecticut

$\mathcal{D}$UCKTRAP FARM SMOKED TROUT & RICE SALAD

This needs an hour to marinate, so keep that in mind when planning your menu. If desired, the vegetables may be marinated in the dressing before they are combined with the trout and rice.

DRESSING
- 3 cloves garlic, minced
- ½ cup olive oil
- Juice of ½ lemon
- 1 teaspoon cider vinegar
- 1 teaspoon dry mustard
- Salt and pepper

SALAD
- 4 cups cooked rice, cooled
- 2 cups chopped celery
- 2 cups finely chopped carrots
- ½ cup chopped black olives
- ½ cup chopped fresh parsley
- 1 medium onion, chopped
- 3–4 smoked trout fillets

To make the dressing: Place the garlic, oil, lemon juice, vinegar, mustard and salt and pepper to taste in a jar and shake. Set aside.

To make the salad: In a large bowl, combine the rice, celery, carrots, olives, parsley and onions. Flake the trout fillets into the bowl but don't break them up too finely. Dress the salad at least 1 hour before serving and toss gently. Chill until ready to serve.

Serves 4 as a main dish, 8 as a dinner salad.

The Maine Collection
Portland Museum of Art, Portland, Maine

ABNAKI DRESSING

We wish we could trace the origins of this recipe to the people for whom it is named (Native Americans of Maine, New Brunswick and southern Quebec), but we can't vouch for that. What we can confirm is that it is a cinch to make and a deliciously substantial addition to any green salad.

2	hard-cooked egg yolks	1	tablespoon finely chopped pimentos
½	cup oil	1	tablespoon finely chopped green bell peppers
2	tablespoons tarragon vinegar	1	tablespoon finely chopped pickled beets
1	tablespoon lemon juice	1	tablespoon chopped walnuts
1	teaspoon confectioners' sugar	1	teaspoon minced fresh parsley
⅛	teaspoon paprika		
⅛	teaspoon ground red pepper		
⅛	teaspoon ground white pepper		
⅛	teaspoon salt		

Press the egg yolks through a fine sieve and transfer to a jar. Add the oil, vinegar, lemon juice, confectioners' sugar, paprika, red pepper, white pepper and salt and shake vigorously. Add the pimentos, bell peppers, beets, walnuts and parsley and shake again. Chill until serving time.

Makes about ¾ cup.

Portland Symphony Cookbook
Portland Symphony Orchestra Women's Committee, Portland, Maine

NEWBURY STREET DRESSING

Sweet yet tangy, this dressing can be used immediately.
Store any that is left over in the refrigerator.

⅓	cup confectioners' sugar	1	teaspoon celery seeds
¾	cup cider or wine vinegar	½	teaspoon salt
3	tablespoons tomato sauce	¾	cup olive oil
1	teaspoon grated onions		

Sift the confectioners' sugar into a medium bowl, add the vinegar and whisk until the sugar dissolves. Stir in the tomato sauce, onions, celery seeds and salt. Add the oil, whisking until well blended. Pour the dressing into a jar with a tight-fitting lid and shake well before using.

Makes about 1½ cups.

Cooking Favorites of the St. James Nursery School
St. James Nursery School, Laconia, New Hampshire

ANNA'S POPPY SEED DRESSING

Make this the day before you plan to use it so that the flavors have time to mingle. It can be stored, covered, in the refrigerator for up to 1 month. The best salad combinations to use it with are lettuce, sliced apples, chopped walnuts and shredded Cheddar cheese, or lettuce, orange and grapefruit sections, sliced avocado and almond slivers.

¼ **cup sugar**
½ **cup cider vinegar**
1 **teaspoon dry mustard**
1 **cup oil**

2 **tablespoons molasses**
2 **scallions, sliced**
1 **tablespoon poppy seeds**

In a glass jar with a tight-fitting lid, dissolve the sugar in the vinegar. Add the mustard and mix well. Add the oil, molasses, scallions and poppy seeds and shake vigorously.

Makes 1½ cups.

Crossroads Cookbook
Somers Congregational Church, Somers, Connecticut

MAPLE DRESSING

This versatile dressing is scrumptious on tossed greens as
well as fruit salads like Waldorf. As an alternative to mayonnaise,
try it with carrot and raisin salad or even coleslaw.

¾ cup oil	1 teaspoon dry mustard
¼ cup cider vinegar	½ teaspoon salt
¼ cup maple syrup	½ teaspoon paprika

In a small bowl, whisk the oil, vinegar, maple syrup, mustard, salt and
paprika. Serve immediately or refrigerate until ready to use.

Makes 1¼ cups.

College Street Congregational Church 125th Anniversary Cookbook
College Street Congregational Church, Burlington, Vermont

MAPLE–CELERY SEED SALAD DRESSING

This recipe is subject to many variations. Fresh mint is a nice
addition in the summer. The salt can be eliminated altogether,
the amount of sugar decreased, other spices added, honey substituted
for maple syrup and so on. Try it on fruit salads as well as greens.

1 small onion, chopped	1 teaspoon paprika
⅓ cup sugar	1 teaspoon celery seeds
⅓ cup maple syrup	¼ teaspoon salt
1 tablespoon lemon juice	1 cup oil, divided
1 teaspoon dry mustard	⅓ cup vinegar

Blend the onions and sugar in a food processor or blender. Add the maple syrup, lemon juice, mustard, paprika, celery seeds and salt. Blend until thoroughly combined. With the processor or blender running, add $\frac{1}{2}$ cup of the oil and the vinegar, then slowly add the remaining $\frac{1}{2}$ cup oil.

Makes about 2 cups.

Northeast Kingdom Cookbook
Caledonia Home Health Care, St. Johnsbury, Vermont

$\mathcal{B}$LENDER FRENCH DRESSING
❧

Preparing this dressing is much easier than traveling to the market for a bottle of the commercial product—and far superior as well. It enhances just about any type of salad—from simple greens to fancier fare like lobster.

1 **cup ketchup**	$\frac{1}{2}$ **teaspoon ground ginger**
$\frac{3}{4}$ **cup oil**	$\frac{1}{2}$ **teaspoon salt**
$\frac{1}{2}$ **cup maple syrup**	$\frac{1}{4}$ **teaspoon ground black**
$\frac{1}{2}$ **cup cider vinegar**	**pepper**
$\frac{1}{2}$ **teaspoon dry mustard**	

Put the ketchup, oil, maple syrup, vinegar, mustard, ginger, salt and pepper in a blender or food processor and blend on high speed for 20 seconds. Pour into a bowl, jar or bottle and refrigerate until ready to use.

Makes 2$\frac{3}{4}$ cups.

A Collection of Maple Recipes
New Hampshire Maple Producers Association, Londonderry, New Hampshire

Garlic lovers as well as health-conscious consumers
will adore this dressing—not only because it's loaded
with garlic but also because it's low in fat.

½ **cup vinegar**	½ **teaspoon salt**
½ **cup tomato juice**	¼ **teaspoon ground black**
¼ **cup oil**	**pepper**
1 **teaspoon paprika**	4 **cloves garlic, minced**

In a glass bottle or jar with a tight-fitting lid, combine the vinegar,
tomato juice, oil, paprika, salt, pepper and garlic. Shake vigorously to
blend. Refrigerate until ready to use and store any leftover dressing in the
refrigerator.

Makes 1¼ cups.

The Harvard Cookbook
Harvard Unitarian Church, Harvard, Massachusetts

PEPPER DRESSING

This dressing works wonders with tuna fish, spruces up the most ordinary salads and is a marvelous dip for crudités.

¼ cup water
1½ teaspoons lemon juice
2 dashes of hot-pepper sauce
½ teaspoon Worcestershire sauce
½ teaspoon steak sauce
¾ teaspoon dry mustard
¾ teaspoon sugar

¾ teaspoon garlic powder
2–4 tablespoons grated Parmesan cheese
½ teaspoon salt
2 tablespoons ground black pepper
2 cups mayonnaise

In a blender or food processor running at high speed, mix the water, lemon juice, hot-pepper sauce, Worcestershire sauce, steak sauce, mustard, sugar, garlic powder, cheese, salt and pepper. Pour into a bowl and blend in the mayonnaise by hand. Cover and refrigerate until ready to use.

Makes about 2½ cups.

The Andover Cookbook II
Phillips Academy: The Ladies' Benevolent Society, Andover, Massachusetts

WOODRUFF FAMILY SALAD DRESSING

This keeps very well, for the oil isn't added until right
before you dress the salad. Try it without the oil as a zesty, fat-free
herb-vinegar dressing drizzled over steamed fresh vegetables.

1	cup cider vinegar	½	teaspoon dried oregano
⅓	cup sugar	¼	teaspoon dried tarragon
½	teaspoon salt	¼	teaspoon dried rosemary
	Pinch of garlic powder		Ground black pepper
½	teaspoon dried basil		Oil

In a small bowl, combine the vinegar, sugar, salt and garlic powder, stirring to dissolve the sugar and salt. Using a mortar and pestle, grind together the basil, oregano, tarragon and rosemary. Add the herbs and pepper to taste to the vinegar mixture and blend well. Set aside for the flavors to meld.

To use, mix 1 part of the vinegar mixture with 2 parts oil.

Makes 1½ cups.

Liberal Portions
Unitarian Universalist Church, Nashua, New Hamsphire

$\mathcal{H}$ARTWELL FARM SALAD DRESSING
※

Just about any blue cheese will work fine here.
Use more or less depending on personal preference.

1 cup mayonnaise
2 tablespoons cider vinegar
1 tablespoon dried parsley

½ cup crumbled Roquefort
cheese

Mix the mayonnaise, vinegar and parsley in a blender or whisk them together. Stir in the cheese, transfer to a bottle and refrigerate until ready to use.

Makes about 1⅔ cups.

Our Daily Bread
St. Patrick's Church: Our Lady's Guild, Bennington, New Hampshire

$\mathcal{Y}$OGURT DRESSING
※

Tightly covered and stored in the refrigerator,
this dressing will keep for about a week.

1¼ cups low-fat plain yogurt
1 tablespoon grated onions
1 tablespoon fresh dill, or
½ teaspoon dried

2 teaspoons lemon juice
¼ teaspoon salt

In a small glass bowl or wide-mouth jar, combine the yogurt, onions, dill, lemon juice and salt. Cover and chill in the refrigerator until the flavors meld.

Makes 1½ cups.

St. John's Episcopal Church Cookbook
St. John's Episcopal Church, Barrington, Rhode Island

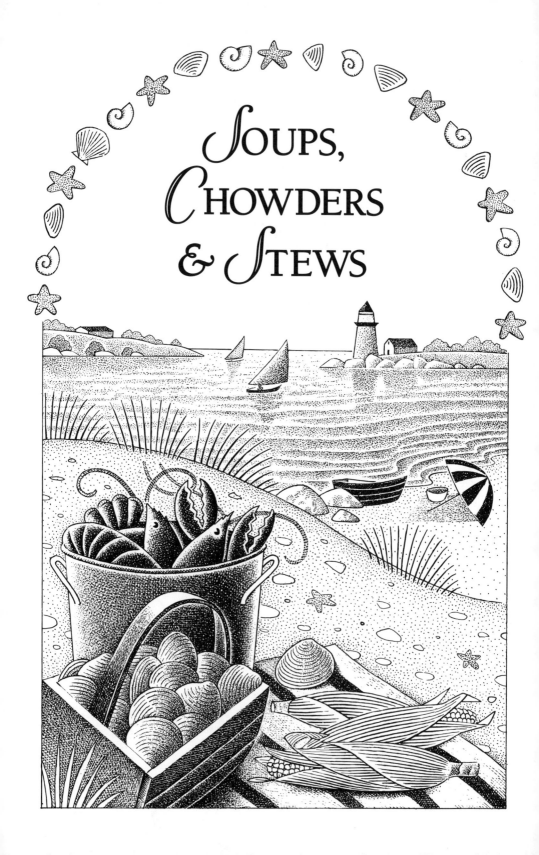

Soups, Chowders & Stews

$\mathcal{C}$OOL STRAWBERRY-WINE SOUP

Light, healthful and refreshing, this lovely soup should
be served soon after it's made. Present it as a first course or as
an accompaniment to a salad or special sandwich.

1 **quart very ripe strawberries**	¼ **cup confectioners' sugar**
3 **tablespoons dry white wine**	**(approximately)**
2 **cups plain yogurt**	

Whirl the strawberries and wine in a blender or food processor. Strain
through a sieve to remove the seeds and whirl the mixture, along with the
yogurt and confectioners' sugar, in the blender or processor. The amount of
sugar will depend on the sweetness of the berries. Chill for 45 minutes and
serve.

Serves 4 to 6.

Cohasset Entertains, Encore
The Community Garden Club, Cohasset, Massachusetts

$\mathcal{G}$INGERED PEACH SOUP

If fresh or frozen peaches are not available, substitute
canned ones. Use their syrup in place of the water, omit the
sugar and eliminate the simmering step.

3 cups sliced fresh or frozen peaches	3 tablespoons bourbon (optional)
1½ cups water	1½ tablespoons cornstarch, combined with 1½ table-
1½ cups dry white wine	spoons water
3 thin, quarter-size slices fresh ginger	¼ cup sour cream or plain yogurt
½ cup sugar	1 tablespoon grated lemon rind

Set aside 4 to 6 peach slices and combine the remaining slices with the
water, wine and ginger in a large saucepan. Bring to a simmer, cover and
cook for 15 minutes. Add the sugar, bourbon (if using) and cornstarch and
water mixture. Bring to a boil, stirring well, and cook until thickened.
Remove from the heat and cool slightly.

In a blender or food processor, combine the peach mixture with the sour
cream or yogurt and lemon rind. Blend until smooth. Refrigerate for at least
4 hours and serve in chilled bowls with a peach slice on each.

Serves 4 to 6.

A Taste of New England
Junior League of Worcester, Massachusetts

$\mathcal{B}$LUEBERRY SOUP

Similar to a cold beet borscht, this fresh berry soup can be made
with plain yogurt instead of sour cream to reduce the fat content.

2 cups water	1 lemon, thinly sliced
1 pint blueberries	1 cinnamon stick
½ cup sugar	1 cup sour cream

Combine the water, blueberries, sugar, lemon slices and cinnamon stick in a saucepan. Bring to a boil, reduce the heat and simmer for 15 minutes.

Discard the cinnamon stick and cool the mixture slightly. Put through a food mill or puree in a blender or food processor. Transfer to a bowl, cool completely and whisk in the sour cream. Chill thoroughly before serving.

Serves 6.

Vermont II: Kitchen Memories
Montpelier, Vermont

CRANBERRY SOUP

Although this isn't a sweet soup, its pretty pink color makes it ideal
for Valentine's Day. Serve it in small cups accompanied with slices of bread
that have been cut out with a heart-shaped cookie cutter and toasted,
or with homemade savory crackers cut in the same shape.

1 **cup cranberries**	1 **cup half-and-half, divided**
2 **tablespoons butter or**	1 **cup milk**
margarine	**Salt and pepper**
3 **large onions, chopped**	

Pick over the cranberries and rinse them thoroughly. In a large saucepan, melt the butter or margarine and sauté the onions and cranberries until the onions are soft. In a blender or food processor, puree half the onion mixture and ½ cup of the half-and-half. Repeat with the remaining onion mixture and ½ cup half-and-half. Return to the saucepan and stir in the milk. Heat until just bubbly. Season to taste with salt and pepper. May be served hot or cold.

Serves 4 to 6.

People Food
Animal Rescue League of Southern Rhode Island, Peacedale, Rhode Island

CRANBERRY-ROSÉ SOUP

The dollop of sour cream or yogurt is important to counterbalance the sweetness of the soup. Serve with Thanksgiving or Christmas dinner.

2 cups cranberries	1 cinnamon stick
2 cups water	1 tablespoon grated lemon rind
1 cup rosé wine	4–6 tablespoons sour cream or
¾ cup sugar	plain yogurt
1½ teaspoons ground allspice	Toasted slivered almonds

Pick over the cranberries and rinse them thoroughly. Bring the water to a boil in a saucepan. Add the cranberries and wine, cover and cook until the berries pop, about 20 minutes. Stir in the sugar, allspice, cinnamon stick and lemon rind and cook, stirring constantly, until the sugar is dissolved.

Remove the cinnamon stick and press the mixture through a sieve or run through a food mill. Return the puree to the saucepan and bring to a boil, stirring constantly. If the soup is too thick, add more wine. Serve hot with 1 tablespoon sour cream or yogurt and a sprinkle of almonds on top.

Serves 4 to 6.

RSVP
Junior League of Portland, Maine

CARROT & ORANGE SOUP

Beat the heat with this refreshing chilled soup for lunch or supper.

1 medium onion, chopped	1 tablespoon unbleached flour
1 tablespoon butter or	¼ cup loosely packed mint
margarine	leaves
2½ cups sliced carrots	1 clove garlic, chopped
1½ cups chicken stock	½ teaspoon chopped shallots
⅛ teaspoon ground cloves	1 cup orange juice
⅛ teaspoon ground white	Juice of ¼ lemon
pepper	Orange slices or mint sprigs

In a large saucepan, sauté the onions in the butter or margarine until tender. Add the carrots, stock, cloves and pepper. Simmer, covered, over medium heat for 15 minutes, or until the carrots are crisp-tender.

In a small bowl, blend the flour into 2 tablespoons of the soup stock, then stir the mixture into the soup. Simmer, stirring constantly, for 5 minutes, or until thickened. Cool for 15 to 20 minutes.

Add the mint, garlic and shallots to the cooled soup. Puree in several small batches in a food processor or blender. Combine in a large bowl with the orange juice and lemon juice, mix well and chill in the refrigerator. Serve in chilled soup bowls, garnished with orange slices or mint sprigs.

Serves 4.

Rhode Island Cooks
American Cancer Society: Rhode Island Division, Pawtucket, Rhode Island

CARROT-CIDER SOUP

Smooth and satisfying, this soup is best served in small portions as a first course to accompany a meal with a hearty entrée.

8–10 carrots, roughly chopped	½ cup apple cider
½ onion, roughly chopped	(approximately)
1 cooking apple, peeled, cored	½ cup milk or light cream
and chopped	¼ teaspoon ground cumin
	Salt and pepper

In a saucepan, cook the carrots and onions in water to cover until tender. Add the apples and continue cooking until the apples are tender. Let cool slightly, then transfer to a blender or food processor and puree.

Return the puree to the saucepan. Add the cider, milk or light cream, cumin and salt and pepper to taste. Heat until hot but not boiling, adding more cider if you want a thinner soup.

Serves 4.

Vermont Kitchens Revisited
The Women of the Cathedral Church of St. Paul, Burlington, Vermont

CURRIED APPLE-ZUCCHINI SOUP

When nothing sounds as appealing as a bowl of homemade soup, turn to this recipe. The ingredients are readily available, preparation time is minimal, and the final product is creamy and flavorful. An appealing way to use the fall harvest, this spicy, creamy soup will be in demand throughout the year.

2	tablespoons butter or margarine	1	quart chicken stock
1	large onion, chopped	2	cups diced zucchini
1	large apple, peeled, cored and chopped	1/4	cup uncooked rice
1-2	teaspoons curry powder	1/2	teaspoon salt
		1	cup milk

In a saucepan, melt the butter or margarine and sauté the onions and apples until soft. Sprinkle with the curry powder and cook, stirring, for about 1 minute. Pour in the stock and bring to a boil. Add the zucchini, rice and salt and cook until the zucchini is tender, about 30 minutes. Cool slightly and pour into a blender or food processor and puree until smooth. Return to the saucepan, add the milk and heat but do not boil.

Serves 4 to 6.

The Maine Collection
Portland Museum of Art, Portland, Maine

APPLE-TURNIP BISQUE

This soup can be served hot or cold. It is unusual, tangy and flavorful but probably better suited to an adult's palate than a child's.

1 tablespoon butter or margarine

1 cup peeled, cored and diced tart apples (Granny Smith if possible)

½ cup diced turnips

½ cup diced potatoes

¼ cup dry white wine

¾ cup apple juice (approximately)

¾ cup chicken stock (approximately)

¼ cup half-and-half

Dash of lemon juice

Salt and pepper

In a heavy-bottomed saucepan, heat the butter or margarine until it foams. Add the apples, turnips and potatoes and sauté until well coated with the butter or margarine. Add the wine and enough apple juice and stock to cover the apples and vegetables. Cover the pan, bring to a boil and lower the heat to a simmer. When the vegetables are very soft (30 to 40 minutes), remove from the heat and let cool slightly.

Puree the soup in a food processor or food mill. Stir in the half-and-half and season to taste with the lemon juice and salt and pepper just before serving.

Serves 4.

Vernon Bicentennial Cookbook
Vernon Bicentennial Cookbook Committee, Vernon, Vermont

ACORN SQUASH & APPLE SOUP

Acorn squash are difficult to peel when raw, so you might want
to cut them in half, remove the seeds and bake in a hot oven until tender.
Scoop out the squash, chop it and add it to the sautéed onions,
continuing with the recipe as directed.

2 **small acorn squash, peeled,
seeded and chopped**
1 **medium onion, chopped**
¼ **cup oil**
3 **cups apple juice**
3 **cups chicken stock**

1 **large apple, peeled, cored and
chopped**
   Salt and white pepper
1 **tablespoon firmly packed
brown sugar**
   Sour cream or plain yogurt
   Chopped fresh parsley

In a soup pot, sauté the squash and onions in the oil for 3 minutes. Add
the apple juice, stock, apples, salt and white pepper to taste and brown
sugar. Cook until the vegetables are tender, about 40 minutes, then puree
in small batches in a blender or food processor. Serve hot or cold with a
dollop of sour cream or yogurt. Garnish with the parsley.

Serves 6.

RRMC Family Favorites
Rutland Regional Medical Center Auxiliary, Rutland, Vermont

CURRIED PUMPKIN SOUP

Don't let this recipe slip by. It combines just the right ingredients in just the right proportions. Serve it as a first course for a fancy dinner or as the main course for lunch or supper.

8 ounces mushrooms, sliced	**3** cups chicken stock
¼ cup chopped onions	**2** cups pureed pumpkin
2 tablespoons butter or margarine	**1** tablespoon honey
	Ground nutmeg
2 tablespoons unbleached flour	Salt and pepper
1 tablespoon curry powder	**1** cup evaporated milk

In a saucepan, sauté the mushrooms and onions in the butter or margarine. Stir in the flour and curry powder. Gradually add the stock and cook, stirring constantly, until thickened. Add the pumpkin, honey, nutmeg to taste and salt and pepper to taste, mixing well. Simmer for 10 to 15 minutes. Add the milk and simmer just until heated through; do not boil.

Serves 4.

Rhode Island Cooks
American Cancer Society: Rhode Island Division, Pawtucket, Rhode Island

FRESH GREEN PEA SOUP

Garden-fresh vegetables are the key to this exquisite soup,
which has the consistency of vichyssoise.

2–3 scallions, chopped
1 tablespoon butter or
  margarine
2 cups water
1½ cups chicken stock
1 large red potato, quartered
2 cups shelled fresh peas

2 cups fresh garden lettuce
  torn into bite-size pieces
2 tablespoons chopped fresh
  mint
  Whipped cream or sour
  cream

In a soup pot, sauté the scallions in the butter or margarine until soft.
Add the water, stock and potatoes. Cook, partially covered, until the potatoes are tender. Add the peas and lettuce, cover, cook for 10 minutes and
add the mint. Cool slightly, then puree in a blender or food processor.
Return to the pot, heat and serve hot with a dollop of whipped cream, or
refrigerate until thoroughly chilled and serve cold with a dollop of sour
cream.

Serves 4.

The Maine Collection
Portland Museum of Art, Portland, Maine

$\mathcal{F}$IDDLEHEAD FERN SOUP

This recipe comes from a native New Englander who hunts the
early spring woods each year for tiny, curled-up fiddleheads.
These delicate little plantlets can be found canned and ready to go
in certain fancy food shops, but the real joy is the search: early spring,
the walk in the woods, the canoe trip down the river along which
the ferns grow. Fiddleheads must be picked at just the right time—when
the heads are just out of the ground and still tightly curled.

2 pounds fiddlehead ferns	**2 chicken bouillon cubes**
1½ quarts water	**Sherry**
Evaporated milk	**Salt and pepper**
Skim milk	

Thoroughly clean the ferns of dirt, grit and last year's growth—the
brown hulls that cling to the new green curlicues. It will take about 4 rinses
in water to be sure they are ready for cooking.

In a saucepan, boil the ferns in the water for 12 minutes, then drain,
reserving the broth. Whirl the fiddleheads in a blender with just enough
broth to make a smooth puree.

In another saucepan, combine equal amounts of fern puree, fern broth,
evaporated milk and skim milk. Add the bouillon cubes and sherry to taste.
Heat through, but do not boil. Add salt and pepper to taste.

Serves 6 to 8.

Vermont Kitchens Revisited
The Women of the Cathedral Church of St. Paul, Burlington, Vermont

RED ONION SOUP WITH APPLE CIDER

This soup can be prepared a day in advance, up to
and including the point where the salt and pepper are added.
Remove it from the heat and let it cool, then cover and refrigerate.
Before serving, reheat it while making the croutons.

2 tablespoons unsalted butter or margarine	½ cup dry white wine (optional)
1¼ pounds red onions, thinly sliced	½ cup apple cider
	1 bay leaf
2 teaspoons unbleached flour	1½ teaspoons dried thyme
1 teaspoon minced garlic	Salt and pepper
3 cups beef stock	1 loaf French bread, sliced ½" thick
3 cups chicken stock	Shredded Cheddar cheese

Melt the butter or margarine in a large, heavy soup pot over medium
heat. Add the onions and cook, stirring frequently, until light golden
brown, about 15 minutes. Add the flour and cook, stirring, for 2 minutes.
Add the garlic and cook for 1 minute. Add the beef stock, chicken stock,
wine (if using), cider and bay leaf. Bring to a boil, skimming the surface
occasionally. Reduce the heat, add the thyme and simmer for 40 minutes.
Season with salt and pepper to taste.

Preheat the broiler. Place the bread on a baking sheet, top with the
cheese and broil until it melts.

Ladle the soup into bowls, top each with a bread-and-cheese crouton
and pass the remaining croutons separately.

Serves 4.

Saint Michael's Cooks By Design
Saint Michael's Episcopal Church, Litchfield, Connecticut

POTATO-CHEESE SOUP

Ready in about 45 minutes from start to finish, this soup tastes as good as many that require lengthy simmering. For extra chunkiness, reserve a cup of the cooked potatoes and add before serving, making sure the pieces get heated through. Serve with dark rye bread and a green salad.

4 cups diced potatoes	2 tablespoons butter or
2 cups water or vegetable stock	margarine
1 leek, sliced	½ teaspoon salt
1 tablespoon oil	¼ teaspoon ground black
5 sprigs parsley	pepper
3 cups milk	Pinch of garlic powder
1 cup shredded Cheddar cheese	

In a large pot, cook the potatoes in the water or stock until tender. Drain, reserving the cooking liquid.

In a skillet, sauté the leeks in the oil until soft. Place a portion of the potatoes and the reserved liquid, leeks and parsley in a blender or food processor. With the blender or processor no more than half full, puree until smooth. Return the potato mixture to the pot and add the milk.

Stirring constantly, add the cheese, butter or margarine, salt, pepper and garlic powder. Heat until the cheese is melted and the soup is hot, but do not boil.

Serves 8 to 10.

Divine Cooking
St. Giles' Church: Episcopal Church Women, Jefferson, Maine

MINESTRONE

Many people shy away from minestrone recipes because they require what seems to be an endless list of ingredients and an interminably long time to prepare. This, however, is a wonderfully easy and richly satisfying soup that can be tossed together in about 20 minutes. While it simmers for an hour on the stove, you can turn your attention to other matters, like enjoying the aroma wafting from the kitchen.

2 tablespoons olive oil	1 package (10 ounces) frozen
2 cloves garlic, minced	peas and carrots
1 cup chopped onions	½ teaspoon dried rosemary
1 cup chopped celery	½ teaspoon salt
2 cans (6 ounces each) tomato	¼ teaspoon ground black
paste	pepper
1 can (10 ounces) beef stock	1 can (16 ounces) kidney
2 quarts water	beans, undrained
1 cup chopped cabbage	1 cup small elbow macaroni
	Grated Parmesan cheese

Heat the oil in a large soup pot and sauté the garlic, onions and celery for 5 minutes. Stir in the tomato paste, stock, water, cabbage, peas and carrots, rosemary, salt and pepper. Bring to a boil. Reduce the heat, cover and simmer for 1 hour.

Add the kidney beans and macaroni and cook for 15 minutes more. Top with the Parmesan cheese just before serving.

Serves 6 to 8.

A Taste of Glocester
Glocester Heritage Society, Chepachet, Rhode Island

HEARTY BEAN SOUP

Dried beans don't always have to be soaked overnight before they can be used. A quicker method is to place them in a pot, cover with water, bring to a boil and cook for 2 minutes. Remove the pot from the heat, cover and let sit for 1 hour. Then proceed with the recipe.

⅔ cup dried Great Northern beans

1 quart water or chicken stock (approximately)

½ pound Spanish or Portuguese sausage (chorizo or linguiça)

1 onion, chopped

4 cloves garlic, chopped

1 teaspoon salt

Ground black pepper (optional)

2 bay leaves

1 teaspoon dried thyme

4 large potatoes, peeled and cut into chunks

6 carrots, peeled and thickly sliced

½ cup uncooked brown rice

Rinse the beans and remove any stones. Put the beans into a soup kettle and cover with 3 times as much cold water. Soak overnight.

Drain the beans and add the water or stock. Bring to a boil and add the sausage, onions, garlic, salt, pepper (if using), bay leaves and thyme. Cover, reduce the heat and simmer for 2 hours, stirring occasionally. Add the potatoes, carrots and rice (and more water or stock if needed) and simmer, covered, for 30 to 40 minutes, or until the vegetables are tender. Remove the bay leaves before serving.

Serves 6 to 8.

Liberal Portions
Unitarian Universalist Church, Nashua, New Hampshire

$\mathcal{L}$ENTIL, SPINACH & SQUASH SOUP

This soup has just a hint of hot spice. If you prefer more, either
increase the amount of ground red pepper or add a dash or two of hot-
pepper sauce to your bowl after the soup is served.

2   tablespoons oil
1   medium onion, chopped
1   slice (about 1½" thick) fresh
     ginger, peeled and minced
3   cloves garlic, minced
1   teaspoon ground cumin
1   teaspoon ground turmeric
½   teaspoon ground coriander
½   teaspoon ground red pepper
1   cup uncooked lentils
¾   pound yellow summer squash
     or zucchini, cut into
     ½" rounds

1   package (10 ounces) frozen
     chopped spinach, thawed and
     squeezed to remove excess
     water
1   quart chicken stock
1   can (16 ounces) whole
     tomatoes, drained and
     chopped (reserve juice)
     Salt and pepper
     Sour cream or plain yogurt

Heat the oil in a large soup pot. Add the onions, ginger, garlic, cumin,
turmeric, coriander and red pepper and cook until the onions are soft. Mix
in the lentils, squash and spinach. Add the stock, tomatoes, tomato juice
and salt and pepper to taste. Bring to a boil, reduce the heat and simmer
for 50 minutes, stirring occasionally. Serve with a dollop of sour cream or
yogurt.

Serves 6 to 8.

The Charlotte Central Cooks' Book
Charlotte Central PTO, Charlotte, Vermont

ITALIAN SAUSAGE SOUP

Here's a soup you can sink your teeth into. It's chunky, flavorful and sustaining—and a great choice for cold-weather cooking. Canned beef stock tends to be salty, so make sure to dilute it if you're using the concentrated kind. You may even want to add an extra can of water.

1	pound hot or sweet Italian sausage	1½	tablespoons minced fresh parsley
2	cloves garlic	½–1	teaspoon dried basil
1	large onion, chopped	1	zucchini, sliced
1	can (28 ounces) Italian-style tomatoes	½	green bell pepper, chopped
1	can beef stock	2	cups uncooked large bow-tie pasta
¾	cup dry red wine		Grated Parmesan cheese

Remove and discard the casings from the sausage and break up the meat into pieces. In a large soup pot, sauté the sausage, garlic and onions until the sausage is browned. Drain off the fat, then add the tomatoes, stock, wine, parsley and basil. Simmer for 30 minutes, stirring occasionally. Add the zucchini and bell peppers and simmer for 15 to 20 minutes. Stir in the pasta and cook for 8 to 10 minutes more, or until the pasta is just tender. Top each serving with Parmesan cheese.

Serves 4 to 6.

350th Guilford, Connecticut, Birthday Cook Book
Leete's Island Garden Club, Guilford, Connecticut

PORCUPINE MEATBALL SOUP WITH DICED CARROTS & POTATOES

❦

"If you get it just right," wrote the contributor of this recipe, "the rice will cook and stick out of the meatballs, making them look like little porcupines. It always intrigued me as a child; I wondered if I'd find any quills in the bottom of my bowl!" This is a thick and hearty soup that really hits the spot on a cold winter night. Serve it with a loaf of sourdough French bread and a good merlot or burgundy wine.

1 **pound ground lamb or beef**	1 **quart beef stock**
1 **medium onion**	2 **medium carrots, diced**
2 **eggs, divided**	2 **medium potatoes, diced**
4–6 **tablespoons uncooked rice**	1 **tablespoon lemon juice**
4–5 **sprigs parsley, finely chopped**	**Chopped fresh parsley for**
Salt and pepper	**garnish**

Place the meat in a large bowl and grate the onion into it. Beat 1 egg and add it to the meat with the rice and parsley. Season with salt and pepper to taste, knead and form into balls the size of a large marble.

Bring the stock to a simmer in a large saucepan. Drop the meatballs into the hot stock, add the carrots and potatoes and cook, partially covered, for about 20 minutes, or until the vegetables are tender.

In a medium bowl, beat the remaining egg with the lemon juice and slowly add 1 cup of the stock from the saucepan, stirring constantly. Pour this mixture back into the saucepan. Remove from the heat and serve immediately, garnished with parsley.

Serves 6 to 8.

The Andover Cookbook II
Phillips Academy: The Ladies' Benevolent Society, Andover, Massachusetts

WINTER WOOLLY SOUP

As with many soups, this one is best if made a day ahead. It requires a lot of chopping, but the end product definitely rewards your efforts.

Meaty bone from a roasted leg of lamb	**2 onions, chopped**
4 quarts water	**1¼ cups dried split peas**
1 cup chopped cooked lamb	**1 teaspoon salt**
6 carrots, sliced	**¼–½ teaspoon ground black pepper**
3 potatoes, peeled and cubed	**½ teaspoon dried thyme**
2 white turnips, peeled and cubed	**½ teaspoon dried rosemary**
2 stalks celery, sliced	**1 bay leaf**

In a large soup pot, simmer the lamb bone in the water for 1 hour. Add the chopped lamb, carrots, potatoes, turnips, celery, onions, split peas, salt, pepper, thyme, rosemary and bay leaf and simmer for 1 hour more. Remove the bone and bay leaf and refrigerate the soup overnight. Reheat gently the next day and serve.

Serves 8 to 10.

RSVP
Junior League of Portland, Maine

ASPARAGUS & LOBSTER SOUP WITH CHIVES

Dinner party fare with a flare, this soup unites two favorite
New England ingredients—lobster and fresh asparagus.

2 quarts water	1½ pounds fresh asparagus, trimmed
1 cup dry white wine	
1 large onion, quartered	2 tablespoons unsalted butter or margarine
2 stalks celery, coarsely chopped	
1 small carrot, coarsely chopped	2 tablespoons unbleached flour
4 sprigs parsley	1 medium onion, coarsely chopped
4 whole peppercorns	1 clove garlic, crushed
2 sprigs thyme	1 cup half-and-half
1 bay leaf	Salt and pepper
2 lobsters (1 pound each)	Snipped fresh chives

Bring the water, wine, onion quarters, celery, carrots, parsley, peppercorns, thyme and bay leaf to a simmer in a large pot. Add the lobsters and
cook until bright red, about 10 to 12 minutes. Remove the lobsters and
cool completely. Reserve the cooking liquid.

Remove the tail and claw meat from the lobsters. Slice the tail meat into
¼" medallions and cut the claw meat into ¼" pieces. Strain the lobster
cooking liquid into a large saucepan and boil until reduced to 6 cups.

Cut off the top 2" of each asparagus spear and blanch in boiling water
until crisp-tender, about 2 minutes. Drain and reserve.

Cut the asparagus stalks into 1" pieces. Melt the butter or margarine
in a heavy skillet over medium-low heat. Add the flour, asparagus stalks,
chopped onions and garlic and cook, stirring constantly, until the onions
are translucent. Do not let the flour brown. Gradually stir in the reduced
cooking liquid and simmer for 20 minutes to blend the flavors.

Puree the soup in small batches in a blender or food processor. Strain
through a fine sieve into a large saucepan. Add the half-and-half and stir
until heated through. Season with salt and pepper to taste. Add the lobster
meat, asparagus tips and chives and heat for about 1 minute. Ladle the
soup into bowls and serve.

Serves 6.

Watch Hill Cooks
Watch Hill Improvement Society, Watch Hill, Rhode Island

$\mathcal{L}$OW-TIDE BISQUE

The thickness and richness of this bisque are determined by the
cream that is used. Half-and-half works perfectly well
but does not provide the same body that light cream does.

12 **mussels**	1 **small onion, sliced**
12 **clams**	4 **tablespoons butter or**
1 **cup dry white wine**	**margarine, divided**
Generous amount of fresh	2 **cups cold water**
basil	2 **tablespoons unbleached flour**
Generous amount of fresh	1 **cup light cream or**
parsley	**half-and-half**
½ **teaspoon salt**	2 **egg yolks**
½ **teaspoon ground black**	**Chopped fresh parsley for**
pepper	**garnish**
2 **cloves garlic, minced**	

Scrub and debeard the mussels and scrub the clams. Place the mussels
and clams in a deep kettle. Add the wine, basil, parsley, salt, pepper, garlic
and onions along with 2 tablespoons of the butter or margarine. Cover,
bring to a boil, reduce the heat and simmer for 2 minutes. Add the cold
water and simmer gently for 5 minutes, or until the clams and mussels
open. (Discard any that do not.) Strain the broth and reserve.

Remove the mussels and clams from their shells and place in a blender
with 2 cups of the reserved broth. Blend at high speed for 2 minutes.

Heat the remaining 2 tablespoons butter or margarine in a saucepan.
Add the flour and stir over low heat until well blended. Gradually add the
blended broth and stir. Cook gently until the bisque begins to thicken.
Slowly add the cream or half-and-half and cook gently until hot but not
boiling.

Beat the egg yolks and add a little of the warm soup, stirring constantly.
Add this mixture to the soup, again stirring constantly, and cook until
thickened and hot but not boiling. Correct the seasonings if necessary.
Serve in hot soup bowls, garnished with the chopped parsley.

Serves 6.

The Fine Arts Cookbook II
Museum of Fine Arts, Boston, Massachusetts

MUSSEL SOUP

Reminiscent of paella, this is a beautiful dish that is fancy
enough for a festive affair. It's not at all difficult to make but
does involve a number of steps and needs the cook's attention.
Serve it in a colorful tureen with loaves of crusty bread.

2 pounds mussels
4 cups water, divided
1 large onion, chopped
1 clove garlic, minced
2 bay leaves
¼ cup olive oil
2 leeks, white parts only,
   cleaned and chopped

1 large tomato, peeled, seeded
   and coarsely chopped
   Salt and pepper
¼ cup plus 2 tablespoons
   uncooked rice
   Pinch of saffron, soaked in a
   small amount of warm water

Scrub and debeard the mussels. In a large saucepan or soup pot, combine 1 cup of the water with the onions, garlic and bay leaves. Add the
mussels, cover the pot and steam until the mussels open, about 5 minutes.
Discard any that do not open. Remove from their shells and keep warm.
Strain all the liquid through a fine muslin cloth into another container, then
strain again.

Clean the soup pot and heat the oil in it. Add the leeks and tomatoes.
Cook for 2 to 3 minutes, then add the strained mussel liquid, the remaining 3 cups water and salt and pepper to taste. Bring the soup to a boil and
simmer for 15 minutes.

Add the rice and drained saffron and cook for 12 to 15 minutes, or
until the rice is tender. Add the reserved mussels, taste for seasonings and
simmer slowly for 5 minutes more. Serve very hot.

Serves 6.

Rumsey Rare Bites
Rumsey Circle: Rumsey Hall, Washington, Connecticut

$\mathscr{E}$LEGANT SCALLOP CHOWDER

Easy to make with impressive results, this chowder is rich, thick and creamy. Serve it in small amounts as a first course.

3 medium potatoes, peeled and diced	8 ounces fresh mushrooms, sliced
1 medium carrot, chopped	1½ tablespoons butter or margarine
2 stalks celery, chopped	
1 medium onion, chopped	1 pound sea scallops, cut into pieces
2 cups chicken stock	
½ teaspoon dried thyme	½ cup dry white wine
½ teaspoon salt	1 cup half-and-half
¼ teaspoon ground black pepper	Chopped fresh parsley
½ bay leaf	Paprika

Put the potatoes, carrots, celery, onions and stock in a large soup pot and bring to a boil. Add the thyme, salt, pepper and bay leaf. Simmer, covered, until the vegetables are tender. Remove the bay leaf, transfer the mixture to a food processor or blender and process until smooth.

In a large skillet, sauté the mushrooms in the butter or margarine, add the scallops and wine and cook for 1 minute. Stir in the half-and-half and combine with the pureed vegetables and stock. Heat slowly without boiling and serve hot, garnished with a sprinkling of parsley and paprika.

Serves 6 to 8.

Merrymeeting Merry Eating
Mid Coast Hospital/Brunswick Auxiliary, Brunswick, Maine

$\mathcal{T}$HE REVEREND HALL'S CLAM CHOWDER

This recipe evolved from the relationship between the Reverend Hall and an old sea captain from Marblehead, Massachusetts. It is a satisfying chowder that has fed the souls of many generations of Halls at Bible meetings and fish fries. If salt pork is unavailable or undesirable, you can use 1 tablespoon oil instead, but you may want to increase the salt.

1½ **cups diced potatoes**	2 **tablespoons unbleached flour**
1 **pint clams**	½ **teaspoon salt**
½ **cup water**	¼ **teaspoon ground black**
1″ **cube salt pork, cut up**	**pepper**
1 **large onion, chopped**	1 **quart milk, scalded**
2 **tablespoons butter or**	**Worcestershire sauce**
margarine	

Parboil the potatoes, drain and set aside. Drain the clams, reserving the juice. Add the water to the reserved clam juice, strain through cheesecloth and bring to a boil in a small saucepan. Set aside.

In a soup pot, cook the salt pork, onions and butter or margarine over low heat for 5 minutes, stirring constantly. Sprinkle with the flour, salt and pepper and cook for 1 minute more.

Slowly stir in the milk. Add the potatoes, clams and hot clam juice, taking care that the juice is not hot enough to curdle the milk. Cook for 2 to 3 minutes, or until heated through, but do not boil. Add Worcestershire sauce to taste and serve.

Serves 4 to 6.

Boston Cooks
Women's Educational & Industrial Union, Boston, Massachusetts

NEW ENGLAND CLAM CHOWDER

How thick clam chowder should be promotes many a discussion around the dinner table. The answer is probably "however thick you like it." Serving salt crackers or biscuits to crumble into the chowder seems to satisfy some "old salts" who insist that a soupspoon stand straight up in the bowl! Quahogs or littleneck clams make the best New England chowder, but canned minced clams also may be used.

3 cups clams	1 teaspoon salt
1 cup water	½ teaspoon ground black pepper
3 medium potatoes, peeled and diced	2 tablespoons unbleached flour (optional)
4 ounces salt pork, diced	2 tablespoons butter or margarine (optional)
½ cup chopped onions	
2 cups milk	
1 cup light cream	

Drain the clams, reserving the juice. Put the reserved juice, water and potatoes in a soup pot and boil until the potatoes are just barely soft.

In a skillet, fry the salt pork until crisp. Remove the pork bits with a slotted spoon and mix with the potatoes. Sauté the onions in the salt pork fat until soft. Add the onions, clams, milk, cream, salt and pepper to the potato mixture and heat almost to boiling. If you like a thicker chowder, mix the flour with a little water to form a thin paste and add to the chowder, stirring until slightly thickened. At serving time, add a small amount of butter or margarine (if using) to each bowl.

Serves 6.

Flavors of Cape Cod
Thornton W. Burgess Society, East Sandwich, Massachusetts

CHOWDER MASTER'S CLAM CHOWDER

As traditional a chowder recipe and technique as you could find for
a creamy New England chowder—with a bit of sage advice for the pot.
Hot cream or milk may be added to the serving bowls according
to individual preference. (It is not added to the chowder itself.)

1 **quart plus 1 pint chowder clams**	1 **medium onion, chopped**
¼ **pound lean salt pork**	4 **medium potatoes, peeled and diced**

Cut up the clams, reserving their juice. An old-fashioned food grinder is
great if available. More modern equipment will work, but overprocessing
will produce granulated clams in the bottom of the chowder. Cutting up
the clams with kitchen shears is not a pleasant job, but the tougher parts
and the softer parts can be cut into proportionate pieces that will cook
evenly. By whatever method, aim for small but recognizable pieces of clam
in the chowder.

Slice the salt pork into thin strips, trimming away the rind. If you plan to
keep the pieces of pork in the chowder when served, cube them instead. In
a heavy soup pot, melt the fat from the salt pork over medium-low heat
and cook until lightly browned. Add the onions and cook until soft and
opaque.

When the pork and onions are ready, add the potatoes and water to
cover. Cook until the potatoes are tender but not soft. Discard the pork if
you do not want to include it in the final chowder.

Add 1 cup water, the chopped clams and the clam juice. Return to a
simmer and cook gently for about 3 minutes, but do not stir. The layer of
potatoes protects the clams from the heat, and the short cooking time keeps
them tender. After 3 minutes, stir and taste, adding more water if the flavor
is too strong. It is easier to dilute a strong chowder than to retrieve a watery
one, so be careful.

Serves 6 to 8.

Mystic Seaport's Seafood Secrets Cookbook
Mystic Seaport Museum Stores, Mystic, Connecticut

SALMON CHOWDER

This soup can be made ahead and kept in the refrigerator until serving time. If you use fresh salmon, simmer the fillet in a pan with a small amount of water and cook until it flakes easily with a fork.

4 **cups peeled and diced potatoes**	¼ **cup butter or margarine**
1 **cup diced carrots**	¼ **cup unbleached flour**
1 **cup chopped celery**	5 **cups milk, divided**
½ **cup chopped green bell peppers**	1 **fresh salmon fillet (1 pound) or 1 can (16 ounces) salmon, undrained and flaked**
1 **teaspoon salt**	1 **teaspoon dried parsley**
1 **package (10 ounces) frozen peas**	½ **teaspoon dried thyme**
1 **onion, chopped**	½ **teaspoon Worcestershire sauce**

Put the potatoes, carrots, celery and bell peppers in a large pot. Add just enough water to cover the vegetables, add the salt and bring to a boil. Lower the heat and simmer until the vegetables are tender, about 15 minutes. Add the peas and simmer for 5 minutes, remove from the heat and set aside.

In a saucepan, sauté the onions in the butter or margarine until tender. Gradually add the flour, stirring until smooth. Cook for 1 minute, then slowly stir in 2½ cups of the milk, stirring constantly over low heat until the mixture is thickened. Add to the potatoes, carrots and peas. Stir in the salmon (with liquid), parsley, thyme and Worcestershire sauce. Add the remaining 2½ cups milk and reheat gently before serving.

Serves 8.

RSVP
Junior League of Portland, Maine

GREEN SPLIT-PEA CHOWDER

Comforting and sustaining, this chunky chowder is a meal in itself. It takes time to chop all the vegetables and needs about an hour to cook, but once everything is in the pot and on the stove, it requires very little tending, other than an occasional stir. Garnish it with herb and garlic croutons.

3 cups diced cooked chicken	1 package (16 ounces) dried
1½ cups finely chopped carrots	green split peas, rinsed and
1 cup finely chopped onions	picked over
¾ cup finely chopped celery	2 quarts chicken stock
2 medium potatoes, peeled and	¼ teaspoon salt
diced	⅛ teaspoon ground black
¼ teaspoon dried thyme	pepper

In a Dutch oven, combine the chicken, carrots, onions, celery, potatoes, thyme, split peas and stock. Bring to a boil, reduce the heat, cover and simmer, stirring occasionally, for 45 to 60 minutes, or until thickened. Add the salt and pepper and serve.

Serves 8.

A Hancock Community Collection
First Congregational Church: The Guild, Hancock, New Hampshire

CABBAGE CHOWDER

A great make-ahead dish for a light supper, this wholesome soup is a cinch to prepare using a food processor to shred the vegetables and cheese.

2 tablespoons butter or	1 cup water
margarine	½ teaspoon salt
½ small cabbage, shredded	Pinch of ground black pepper
1 large potato, grated	4 ounces Swiss cheese,
1 carrot, grated	shredded
2 cups milk	

Melt the butter or margarine in a large soup pot and add the cabbage, potatoes and carrots. Simmer until soft, about 10 minutes, stirring occasionally. Mash with a fork and blend in the milk and water. Cover and simmer for 15 minutes. Add the salt and pepper and stir in the cheese until it melts.

Serves 4.

The Vermont Symphony Cookbook
Vermont Symphony Orchestra, Burlington, Vermont

$\mathcal{E}$XCELLENT CORN CHOWDER

When unexpected company arrives, this spur-of-the-moment chowder will come to your rescue. It's quick and easy, tasty and fulfilling.

3 slices bacon
1 medium onion, thinly sliced and separated into rings
2 medium potatoes, peeled and diced
½ cup water

1 can (17 ounces) cream-style corn
2 cups whole milk
½ teaspoon salt
Pinch of ground black pepper
2 tablespoons butter or margarine (optional)

In a large saucepan, cook the bacon until crisp. Remove the bacon, crumble and set aside. Reserve 2 tablespoons of the bacon drippings in the saucepan and discard the remainder. Add the onions and cook until lightly browned. Add the potatoes and water and cook over medium heat until the potatoes are tender, about 10 to 15 minutes.

Add the corn, milk, salt and pepper and cook until heated through. Do not boil. Pour into warmed bowls and top each serving with the crumbled bacon and a bit of butter or margarine (if using).

Serves 4.

Our Daily Bread
St. Patrick's Church: Our Lady's Guild, Bennington, New Hampshire

CHRISTMAS EVE OYSTER STEW

An easy but somewhat pricey preparation, this creamy stew is
ideal for the holidays or special occasions. The oysters need to be fresh,
and the sherry is a must! It should be eaten soon after preparation,
but if necessary, it can be kept at room temperature for about an hour.
Reheat gently, without allowing it to boil, just before serving.

¼ **cup butter or margarine**
1 **teaspoon Worcestershire**
   sauce
3 **dashes of hot-pepper sauce**
1 **pint oysters, undrained**
1 **quart half-and-half**

¼ **cup dry sherry**
   Salt and white pepper
   Butter or margarine
   Paprika
   Oyster crackers (optional)

In a soup pot, slowly heat the ¼ cup butter or margarine until melted.
Add the Worcestershire sauce and hot-pepper sauce. Over moderate heat,
add the oysters and their liquor. Simmer until the edges of the oysters curl,
about 3 to 4 minutes.

Add the half-and-half and heat until warmed through, but do not boil.
Stir in the sherry and salt and white pepper to taste. Serve in individual
bowls with a bit of butter or margarine and sprinkled with paprika. Accompany with oyster crackers (if using).

Serves 6 to 8.

Off the Hook
The Junior League of Stamford-Norwalk, Darien, Connecticut

MARINER'S STEW

Although this recipe calls for a lot of ingredients, it's easy to prepare, doesn't take long and makes a great meal for company.

2 cups canned tomatoes	¼ teaspoon dry mustard
1 tablespoon unbleached flour	1½ tablespoons grated fresh ginger
1½ cups sliced onions	
2 tablespoons butter or margarine	¼ teaspoon whole allspice berries
1 tablespoon dried parsley	2 pounds haddock or perch fillets, cut up
¾ teaspoon dried oregano	
1 teaspoon salt	2 large eggs, lightly beaten
½ teaspoon ground black pepper	2 tablespoons lime or lemon juice

Put the tomatoes in a large soup pot and break them up with a fork. Add the flour and mix until smooth. Add the onions, butter or margarine, parsley, oregano, salt, pepper and mustard. Tie the ginger and allspice in a bag, add to the pot and cook, covered, for 15 minutes.

Add the fish and cook for 10 minutes, or until flaky. Remove from the heat and discard the spice bag. Stirring constantly, add a small amount of the hot broth to the eggs, then return the mixture to the pot. Add the lime or lemon juice and cook until slightly thickened, 2 to 3 minutes. Serve hot.

Serves 8 to 10.

The Taste of Gloucester
The Fishermen's Wives of Gloucester and The Cape Ann League of Women Voters, Gloucester, Massachusetts

NEW ENGLAND BOUILLABAISSE

It's harder to spell the name of this dish than it is to make it, but it does require some time and a well-organized work space. So try to get someone to help you. The stock can be made in advance (a wise move if you're working alone), or one person can turn to that while the other continues with the bouillabaisse. With or without assistance, this potpourri of fish and shellfish is so appealing, both in appearance and taste, that you'll be inclined to make it more often than imagined.

LOBSTER STOCK
- 2 quarts water
- 3 carrots, sliced
- 2 stalks celery, sliced
- 6 peppercorns
- 2 bay leaves
- 2–3 lobsters (½ per person)

BOUILLABAISSE
- 1 cup chopped leeks
- 1 cup finely chopped onions
- 3 cloves garlic
- 2 tablespoons olive oil
- 2 cups chopped fresh tomatoes
- 1 cup canned tomatoes
- 1½ cups dry white wine
- 1 teaspoon saffron

- ¼ teaspoon fennel seeds
- 1 bay leaf
- 2 tablespoons butter or margarine
- 2 tablespoons unbleached flour
- 1 quart mussels, cleaned and debearded
- 8–10 cherrystone or littleneck clams
- 1–2 pounds fish fillets (haddock, cod or swordfish), cut into large chunks
- ½ pound shrimp, peeled and deveined
- ½ pound scallops
- ¼ cup finely chopped fresh parsley

To make the lobster stock: Place the water, carrots, celery, peppercorns and bay leaves in a large pot and bring to a boil. Add the lobsters, cover and cook for 10 minutes for 1 pounders, 12 minutes for 1¼ pounders or 15 minutes for 1½ pounders.

Strain the cooking liquid and reserve 3 cups for the bouillabaisse; freeze the remainder. Split the lobsters, remove the meat and chop into large chunks. Set aside until ready to use.

To make the bouillabaisse: In a large soup pot, sauté the leeks, onions and garlic in the oil. Stir in the fresh tomatoes, canned tomatoes, wine, saffron, fennel seeds and bay leaf. Bring to a boil, reduce the heat and simmer for 20 minutes, stirring occasionally. Stir in the reserved lobster stock.

In a saucepan, melt the butter or margarine, add the flour and cook for 1 minute, stirring constantly. Add about ½ cup of liquid from the pot to the butter and flour mixture and bring to a boil. Whisk this back into the pot, stirring until well blended. Add the mussels and clams and simmer for 10 minutes. Add the fish and cook for 5 minutes more. Add the shrimp, scallops, reserved lobster meat and parsley. Simmer until the fish flakes easily with a fork. Serve immediately in large, shallow bowls.

Serves 4 to 6.

A Taste of New England
Junior League of Worcester, Massachusetts

ＳPICY SCALLOP & TORTELLINI STEW

Enlivened with herbs and red pepper flakes, this stew is a unique way to serve scallops. Be sure to cook the stew gently after you add the scallops so that they don't toughen.

1 **cup chopped onions**	2 **teaspoons dried basil**
6 **cloves garlic, minced**	¼ **teaspoon red pepper flakes**
1 **tablespoon olive oil**	**(or to taste)**
1 **can (28 ounces) stewed**	1 **pound scallops**
tomatoes	1 **package (9 ounces) cheese**
2 **teaspoons dried parsley**	**tortellini**

In a soup pot, cook the onions and garlic in the oil until tender. Stir in the undrained tomatoes, parsley, basil and red pepper flakes. Bring to a boil, add the scallops, reduce the heat and simmer for 3 to 5 minutes. Stir in the tortellini and simmer, covered, until just tender.

Serves 4 to 6.

The Kinderhaus Cookbook
Kinderhaus Children's Center, Williston, Vermont

BEEF STEW WITH BISCUITS

An excellent stew with or without the biscuits. It can be made ahead of time through the step where it is thickened with flour and water.

STEW

2 pounds stew beef
1 tablespoon oil
1 medium onion, chopped
1 clove garlic, minced
1½ teaspoons salt
1 teaspoon sugar
1 teaspoon Worcestershire sauce
½ teaspoon paprika
¼ teaspoon ground black pepper
3 cups water, divided
6 carrots, sliced or cut into chunks
6 small potatoes, quartered
6–10 small white onions
1 cup fresh or frozen peas
¼ cup unbleached flour

BISCUITS

2 cups unbleached flour
4 teaspoons baking powder
2 teaspoons sugar
½ teaspoon salt
½ teaspoon cream of tartar
½ cup shortening
⅔ cup milk

To make the stew: In a Dutch oven, brown the meat on all sides in the oil over medium-high heat. Add the chopped onions, garlic, salt, sugar, Worcestershire sauce, paprika and pepper. Pour in 2½ cups of the water, cover and simmer for 1½ hours.

Add the carrots, potatoes and white onions. Cover and cook for 30 minutes. Add the peas and cook for 5 minutes, or until the vegetables are tender.

In a jar with a tight-fitting lid, shake the remaining ½ cup water and flour until thoroughly blended. Slowly stir into the stew and cook, stirring, until thickened.

To make the biscuits: In a medium bowl, mix the flour with the baking powder, sugar, salt and cream of tartar. Cut in the shortening until the mixture resembles coarse crumbs. Add the milk all at once and stir only until the dough follows the fork around the bowl.

Knead the dough gently for 30 seconds on a lightly floured surface. Roll out to a ½" thickness and cut with a 1½" biscuit cutter. Place the biscuits in a ring on top of the hot stew and bake in a 450° oven for 12 to 15 minutes.

Serves 8.

The Kinderhaus Cookbook
Kinderhaus Children's Center, Williston, Vermont

RAGOUT OF BEEF WITH CRANBERRIES

This filling and aromatic dish has a superb flavor combination
of sweet and tart. It ages well, although the cranberries are
distinctively red only when first cooked. Serve with noodles.

1 tablespoon unsalted butter or margarine	¾ cup port or red wine
1 tablespoon oil	¾ cup beef stock
2 pounds lean stew beef	2 tablespoons red wine vinegar
2 onions, chopped	1 tablespoon tomato paste
2 cloves garlic, minced	1½ cups cranberries
¼ teaspoon salt	⅓ cup firmly packed light brown sugar
Ground black pepper	2 tablespoons unbleached flour
8 ounces mushrooms, sliced	

Melt the butter or margarine and oil in a Dutch oven and brown the
meat well on all sides. Stir in the onions, garlic, salt and pepper to taste.
Add the mushrooms, port or red wine, stock, vinegar and tomato paste and
bring to a boil. Reduce the heat and simmer, covered, for about 2 hours, or
until the meat is tender.

Meanwhile, pick over the cranberries and rinse them thoroughly.
Coarsely chop them with the brown sugar and flour in a food processor.
Add the mixture to the stew and cook for 10 minutes more.

Serves 6.

Christmas Memories Cookbook
Mystic Seaport Museum Stores, Mystic, Connecticut

DILLY LAMB STEW

This is a great meal to fill you up and warm you up on a cold winter day. The dill flavor is evident but not overpowering. Serve over rice.

1 tablespoon butter or margarine	4–5 carrots, peeled and cut into 2" pieces
1½ pounds lamb stew meat	3–4 stalks celery, cut into 2" pieces
2 cups water	1 cup plain yogurt
1 teaspoon dried dill	2 tablespoons flour
½ teaspoon salt	
4–5 medium potatoes, peeled and quartered	

In a Dutch oven or heavy skillet, melt the butter or margarine and brown the meat on all sides. Stir in the water, dill and salt, cover and simmer for 1 hour, or until the meat is almost tender.

Add the potatoes, carrots and celery and simmer for 30 minutes, or until the vegetables are tender but not mushy.

Remove the meat and vegetables to a warmed serving dish, combine the yogurt and flour in a small bowl and stir into the liquid in the Dutch oven or skillet. Cook over low heat, stirring constantly, until thickened, then cook for 2 minutes more. Pour the gravy over the lamb and vegetables and serve immediately.

Serves 4 to 6.

A Taste of Harrisville
Wells Memorial School PTA, Harrisville, New Hampshire

NORTHEAST KINGDOM LAMB

When company is coming, this recipe fills the bill. It makes a large quantity and can be partially prepared in advance. After the meats have simmered for 30 minutes, remove the pot from the heat and refrigerate the stew for several hours or overnight. About 30 minutes before serving, return it to the stove and proceed with the recipe.

2 tablespoons unsalted butter or margarine	30 dried apricot halves
2 pounds lamb from the leg, cut into 1" cubes	2 cups peeled and cubed butternut squash
1/4 pound pork, cut into 1/2" cubes	2 cups green beans, cut into 1/2" pieces
2 cups chopped onions	1 can (20 ounces) white kidney beans (cannellini), drained
2 tablespoons sugar	1/4 cup coarsely chopped walnuts
1 1/2 cups beef stock	2 tablespoons chopped fresh dill (optional)
1/2 teaspoon salt	
1/2 teaspoon ground black pepper	

In a Dutch oven, melt the butter or margarine over medium-high heat. Add and brown the lamb in several batches, removing each batch with a slotted spoon to another dish. Brown the pork in the same pot. Remove the pork to the same dish.

Add the onions to the drippings and cook until limp but not browned, about 3 minutes. Add the sugar and let it caramelize for a few minutes. Stir in the stock, salt and pepper and bring to a simmer. Add the meats and simmer, covered, for about 30 minutes.

Add the apricots and squash and simmer gently, covered, for 10 minutes. Add the green beans and continue simmering for 5 minutes more. Add the cannellini and walnuts and simmer for 5 minutes. Serve sprinkled with dill (if using).

Serves 8 to 10.

Vermont Kitchens Revisited
The Women of the Cathedral Church of St. Paul, Burlington, Vermont

Main Dishes

$\mathcal{M}$EAT

$\mathcal{Y}$ANKEE POT ROAST

If you enjoy carrots and potatoes with a pot roast, these can be added during the last 30 to 45 minutes of cooking time. If preferred, the roast can be cooked on top of the stove over low heat.

2 **cloves garlic, minced**	12 **whole peppercorns**
1 **tablespoon butter or**	12 **whole allspice berries**
margarine	1 **bay leaf**
1 **pot roast (3–4 pounds)**	1 **tablespoon grated fresh**
Salt and pepper	**horseradish**
Flour	½ **cup rum or dry red wine**
1 **large onion, thinly sliced**	½ **cup water**

In a skillet, sauté the garlic in the butter or margarine until golden. Sprinkle the meat with salt and pepper to taste and with the flour and brown well on all sides in the garlic butter. Spread a layer of onions in a large, heavy-bottomed pot with a tight-fitting lid. Place the meat on top and add the garlic butter, peppercorns, allspice, bay leaf and horseradish. Pour in the rum or wine and water, cover tightly and simmer in a 300° oven for 2 to 3 hours, or until tender.

Remove the meat to a serving platter. Defat the drippings, then heat in the pot and season to taste. Pour over the meat and serve.

Serves 6 to 8.

350th Guilford, Connecticut, Birthday Cook Book
Leete's Island Garden Club, Guilford, Connecticut

$\mathcal{N}$EW ENGLAND BOILED DINNER

One of the many advantages of this dish is its versatility.
Depending on family preferences, some New Englanders eliminate
the beets and turnips and use onions instead.

1 **corned beef brisket (4 pounds)**	1 **small head cabbage, cut into sixths**
3 **turnips, peeled**	6 **small beets, cleaned but with $1/2''$ of tops left on**
6 **carrots, cleaned**	8 **potatoes, peeled**

Place the beef in a deep kettle and cover with cold water. Bring to a boil
and boil gently for 15 minutes, skimming the top. Reduce the heat and
simmer for 4 hours, or until the meat is tender. During the last hour, add
the turnips, carrots, cabbage and beets (or cook the beets separately so they
do not color the other vegetables). Thirty minutes after adding the other
vegetables, add the potatoes and cook until tender.

When you're ready to serve dinner, slip the skins from the beets, place
the meat on a large serving platter and surround with the vegetables. Cool
the cooking liquid, remove the fat and save the stock for Red Flannel Hash
(recipe follows).

Serves 6 to 8.

Our Town Cookbook
Peterborough Historical Society, Peterborough, New Hampshire

$\mathcal{R}$ED FLANNEL HASH

This has an attractive, chunky texture and a rosy hue
from the beets, plus a crusty brown underside. The tradition in some
New England homes is to add a splash of cider vinegar to each serving.
Corn bread is a great accompaniment to this dish.

Meat and vegetables left over from a boiled dinner	**Salt and pepper**
	Stock from boiled dinner

Use all the meat and vegetables left over from the boiled dinner. Cook extra potatoes if necessary: there should be twice as many potatoes as beets. Chop the meat and vegetables coarsely in a wooden bowl or on a cutting board with a chef's knife; do not use a food chopper. Put 1 tablespoon of the meat drippings in a heavy skillet, add the chopped meat and vegetables, and sprinkle with salt and pepper to taste. Moisten with some of the stock left from the boiled dinner. Smooth the hash flat in the skillet, cover and cook slowly until browned and crusted on the bottom. Fold over like an omelet and serve, or turn out upside down on a serving platter.

Number of servings depends on amount of leftovers.

Our Town Cookbook
Peterborough Historical Society, Peterborough, New Hampshire

$\mathcal{G}$RILLED PEPPERED STEAK WITH MAPLE-CIDER GLAZE

This tart and tangy glaze adds zip to the grilled steaks
and can be used with other kinds of red meat, too.

2 cups beef stock	Salt and pepper
1 cup apple cider	4 New York sirloin steaks
1/4 cup maple syrup	(6 ounces each)
1/4 cup balsamic vinegar	Cracked black pepper

Combine the stock, cider and maple syrup in a medium saucepan and mix well. Simmer for 30 to 40 minutes, or until thickened. Stir in the vinegar and simmer for 10 minutes more. Season the glaze with salt and pepper to taste and set aside.

Rub the steaks with cracked pepper, then grill them over medium-high heat for 4 to 5 minutes per side. Place on serving plates, spoon the glaze over each and serve immediately.

Serves 4.

Boston Cooks
Women's Educational & Industrial Union, Boston, Massachusetts

BRISKET OF BEEF WITH FRUIT

The fruit sauce gives this recipe a festive touch and keeps the meat tender and juicy. This is very easy to prepare but does require long, slow cooking.

1 beef brisket, first cut (about 6 pounds)
1 large onion, thinly sliced
1 can (12 ounces) beer or 1½ cups water
1 cup pitted prunes
1 cup dried apricots
3 tablespoons firmly packed brown sugar

2 tablespoons orange marmalade
Juice and grated rind of 1 lemon
1 teaspoon Worcestershire sauce
¾ teaspoon ground ginger
½ teaspoon ground cinnamon
½ teaspoon ground black pepper

Remove some of the external fat from the beef. Arrange half the onion slices on the bottom of a shallow pan large enough to contain the brisket. Set the brisket on the onions and cover with the remaining onions. Bake in a preheated 350° oven for 30 minutes. Remove from the oven and cover the pan tightly with foil. Return the brisket to the oven and roast for 3 hours more.

Put the beer or water, prunes, apricots, brown sugar, marmalade, lemon juice and rind, Worcestershire sauce, ginger, cinnamon and pepper in a large saucepan. Heat to a quick boil and remove from the heat.

Reduce the oven temperature to 300° and remove the brisket from the oven. Uncover the meat, pour the fruit mixture over it and continue roasting for 1 hour more. If the sauce begins to dry up, add more beer or water.

Remove the brisket from the oven and let sit for 10 to 15 minutes. Slice against the grain and serve with the fruited sauce.

Serves 8 to 10.

Hospitality
Salem Hospital Aid Association, Salem, Massachusetts

MAPLE-BARBECUED SPARERIBS

Another use for New England's "liquid gold" is this maple syrup–based barbecue sauce, which is equally luscious on pork and poultry.

3 pounds beef spareribs
1 small onion, minced
1 cup maple syrup
2 tablespoons chili sauce
2 tablespoons vinegar

2 teaspoons Worcestershire sauce
½ teaspoon dry mustard
½ teaspoon salt
⅛ teaspoon ground black pepper

Cut the spareribs into serving-size pieces and place them in a single layer in a baking pan. Combine the onions, maple syrup, chili sauce, vinegar, Worcestershire sauce, mustard, salt and pepper in a small bowl and brush the mixture on all sides of the ribs. Bake in a preheated 375° oven until the ribs are tender, about 1½ to 2 hours, brushing with the sauce often and turning frequently so all portions will be coated.

Serves 4 to 6.

A Collection of Maple Recipes
New Hampshire Maple Producers Association, Londonderry, New Hampshire

SELMA'S STUFFED CABBAGE

These cabbage rolls are the real thing. The sweet-sour sauce and savory meat filling contrast nicely, and the texture is compact yet tender.

CABBAGE ROLLS
- 1 teaspoon shortening or oil
- ¼ cup diced onions
- 2 pounds lean ground beef
- 2 eggs, beaten
- ½ cup water
- ½ cup uncooked rice
- ½ teaspoon salt
- ¼ teaspoon ground black pepper
- 1 large head cabbage

SAUCE
- 1 can (16 ounces) tomatoes
- 1 can (8 ounces) tomato puree
- 1 cup water
- ¼ cup diced onions
- ¼ cup firmly packed brown sugar
- 2 tablespoons honey
- 1–2 tablespoons lemon juice
- 4–5 gingersnaps, crumbled
- ⅓ cup raisins
- ½ teaspoon salt

To make the cabbage rolls: Heat the shortening or oil in a skillet and sauté the onions until golden. Add to the ground beef along with the eggs, water, rice, salt and pepper, mixing well. Set aside.

Core the cabbage and separate into leaves. Place the leaves in a large pot, cover with water and bring to a boil. Reduce the heat and simmer for 5 to 10 minutes. Drain and cool until they can be easily handled.

Cut the large leaves in half, removing the hard core. Place 2 or 3 tablespoons of the meat mixture on a leaf. Fold the edges toward the center and roll up. Repeat until all the leaves are used. Place the rolls in a large pot with the edges down, piling one on top of another and separating them with a few of the small cabbage leaves.

To make the sauce: In a saucepan, combine the tomatoes, tomato puree, water, onions, brown sugar, honey, lemon juice, gingersnaps, raisins and salt. Simmer for 10 minutes, then taste and adjust the sweet and sour to your liking. Pour the sauce over the cabbage rolls, cover and cook gently on top of the stove for 1 to 1½ hours.

Serves 6 to 8.

The Kosher Yankee II
Sisterhood of the Rutland Jewish Center, Rutland, Vermont

BRAISED STUFFED ONIONS

Cinnamon, cloves and raisins are an unexpected but
excellent addition to this delectable dish. Serve it with
scalloped potatoes and steamed fresh spinach.

6 **large sweet onions**	2 **tablespoons tomato paste**
1 **tablespoon oil**	2 **tablespoons red wine vinegar**
1 **clove garlic, minced**	¼ **teaspoon ground cinnamon**
½ **pound lean ground beef**	⅛ **teaspoon ground cloves**
½ **pound ground pork**	**Salt and pepper**
4 **medium tomatoes, peeled and chopped**	12 **pimento-stuffed green olives, chopped**
3 **green chili peppers, finely chopped**	3 **tablespoons grated Parmesan cheese**
¼ **cup raisins**	1 **cup beef stock**

Drop the unpeeled onions into a large pot of boiling salted water. Cook,
uncovered, for 20 minutes. Drain in a colander set under cold running
water. When cool, remove the outer skin and slice off the top and bottom
of each onion. Gently push out the centers, leaving a shell of 2 or 3 layers.
Place the shells in a generously buttered baking dish. Chop ½ cup of the
centers and set aside.

Combine the oil, garlic and reserved chopped onions in a large skillet
and cook until tender. Add the beef and pork and cook, stirring frequently,
until the meat is no longer pink. Add the tomatoes, chili peppers and
raisins and stir to mix. Blend in the tomato paste, vinegar, cinnamon, cloves
and salt and pepper to taste. Simmer, uncovered, for 20 minutes, or until
all the liquid has evaporated.

Remove the mixture from the heat and add the olives. Spoon the stuffing
into the onion shells. Sprinkle with the Parmesan cheese, pour the stock
around the onions, cover with foil and bake in a preheated 350° oven for
45 to 55 minutes, or until the onions are tender.

Serves 6.

The Mark Twain Library Cookbook, Vol. III
Mark Twain Library Association, Redding, Connecticut

$\mathcal{G}$RANDMA MERCURI'S MEATBALLS & SAUCE

This dish is most enjoyable to make when you have some time
to spend in the kitchen. The sauce requires 2½ hours for simmering and
the meatballs take an additional 1½ hours to cook. One of the tricks to
cooking meatballs properly is not to push them around. Instead, place a
fork under the meatball, lift it up and with a quick flip, turn it over.

MEATBALLS

- 8 slices Italian bread
  Milk
- 2 pounds lean ground beef
- 1 teaspoon salt
- ½ teaspoon ground black
  pepper
- ¼ cup grated Parmesan or
  Romano cheese
- 2 cloves garlic, minced
- 2 tablespoons chopped fresh
  Italian parsley
  Chopped fresh basil
- 4 eggs, beaten

SAUCE

- 4 quarts tomato puree
- 2 tablespoons chopped fresh
  Italian parsley
  Salt
- ¼ cup olive oil
- 1 onion, chopped
- 2 cloves garlic, chopped
- 1 can (8 ounces) tomato paste

To make the meatballs: Place the bread in a toaster just long enough to dry
but not brown the slices. Soak the bread in enough milk just to cover the
slices, then set aside.

In a large bowl, mix the beef, salt, pepper, Parmesan or Romano cheese,
garlic, parsley and basil to taste. Squeeze and drain the soaked bread and
crumble into the meat mixture. Add the eggs and mix with your hands.
Roll into balls and refrigerate until ready to cook.

To make the sauce: Put the tomato puree in a large pot and bring to a
rolling boil. Simmer, uncovered, until thick, then cover and cook slowly for
at least 2½ hours. Add the parsley and salt to taste.

Heat the oil in a heavy skillet. Roll each meatball a bit more before
adding it to the oil. Brown well on all sides. Remove the meatballs from the
oil with a slotted spoon and set aside.

Reduce the heat to medium, add the onions and garlic and sauté until
tender. Add the tomato paste and ¾ can of water. Increase the heat to

medium-high and stir in ½ can more water. Reduce the heat to medium and cook just enough to blend. Add to the tomato puree mixture and bring to a boil.

Add the meatballs and cook gently, covered, for at least 1½ hours over medium heat.

Serves 6.

The Community Cooks
Pine Hill Waldorf School, Wilton, New Hampshire

*A*PPLESAUCE BEEF LOAF

This round loaf has a depression in the center for the pungent filling.

BEEF LOAF
- 1 **cup dry bread crumbs**
- ½ **cup applesauce**
- 1 **pound lean ground beef**
- 1 **egg, beaten**
- 2 **tablespoons minced onions**
- 1 **teaspoon dried celery leaves**
- 1 **teaspoon Dijon mustard**
- ½ **teaspoon salt**
- ⅛ **teaspoon ground black pepper**

FILLING
- ½ **cup applesauce**
- 1 **tablespoon firmly packed brown sugar**
- 1 **tablespoon vinegar**
- 1 **teaspoon Dijon mustard**

To make the beef loaf: In a large bowl, combine the bread crumbs and applesauce. Add the meat, egg, onions, celery leaves, mustard, salt and pepper. Blend thoroughly. Shape into a round loaf and place in a 9″ × 9″ pan.

To make the filling: In a small bowl, combine the applesauce, brown sugar, vinegar and mustard. Make a depression in the center of the loaf and spoon in the filling. Bake in a preheated 350° oven for 1 hour.

Serves 4.

Vermont II: Kitchen Memories
Montpelier, Vermont

ORANGE PORK TENDERLOIN

Aromatic and mouthwatering, this dish makes a special treat
for the family or an easy entrée for a small dinner party.

1 **tablespoon butter or margarine, softened**	1 **pork tenderloin (1½–2 pounds)**
¼ **teaspoon dried thyme, crumbled**	¾–1 **cup orange juice**
Pinch of ground red pepper	1 **tablespoon unbleached flour**
	1½ **teaspoons sugar**
	1 **teaspoon aromatic bitters**

In a small bowl, mix the butter or margarine, thyme and red pepper and
spread evenly over the tenderloin. Place the tenderloin in a shallow roasting
pan and pour ¾ cup of the orange juice over the meat. Roast in a 375°
oven for 25 to 30 minutes (155° to 160° on a meat thermometer), basting
occasionally. Remove the meat to a serving platter and keep warm while
finishing the sauce.

Pour the basting liquid into a measuring cup, adding additional orange
juice if necessary to make ¾ cup. Pour into a small pan and quickly whisk
in the flour, sugar and bitters. Cook, stirring constantly, until the mixture
boils and thickens. Cut the tenderloin into 1″ slices and drizzle on the sauce.

Serves 4.

From Our House to Yours
The Hikers, Melvin Village, New Hampshire

HOMETOWN COOKING IN NEW ENGLAND

ROAST LOIN OF PORK

The calvados or applejack is an important ingredient,
even though the amount called for is small.
It may be hard to find in some areas but is worth the search.

PORK

- 3 tablespoons unbleached flour
- 2 teaspoons ground black pepper
- 1 teaspoon salt
- 1 teaspoon dried sage
- ¾ teaspoon dried marjoram
- 1 boneless pork loin (4–5 pounds)
- 1 clove garlic, chopped
- 1 cup beef stock (approximately)
- ½ cup apple cider

SAUCE

- 2 tablespoons unbleached flour
- 1 cup beef stock
- 1 cup water
- 1 cup applesauce
- 1½ tablespoons ketchup
- 2 teaspoons prepared horseradish
- 1 teaspoon Dijon mustard
- ½ teaspoon salt
- 2–4 tablespoons calvados or applejack

To make the pork: Combine the flour, pepper, salt, sage and marjoram in a small bowl and rub over the meat. Place the pork on a wire rack in a roasting pan, add the garlic, stock and cider and bake in a preheated 425° oven for 30 minutes. Reduce the heat to 325° and bake for 1 hour 20 minutes more, basting occasionally and adding additional stock if needed. Remove the roast from the oven, place on a serving platter and let stand for 10 minutes before carving.

To make the sauce: Spoon off and discard the excess fat from the roasting pan, stir in the flour and cook over medium heat for 3 minutes. Add the stock, water, applesauce, ketchup, horseradish, mustard and salt and heat thoroughly. Remove from the heat and stir in the calvados or applejack. Serve in a sauceboat.

Serves 6 to 8.

The Fine Arts Cookbook II
Museum of Fine Arts, Boston, Massachusetts

APPLE-STUFFED PORK CHOPS

These tender chops, with a sweet-savory stuffing, make a fine meal for company. If there's stuffing left over, place it in an ovenproof dish and bake it during the last 10 to 15 minutes that the chops are in the oven.

4–6 thick (about 1½") pork chops
1 tablespoon oil
1 small onion, finely chopped
1 cup unseasoned dry bread crumbs
1 large tart apple, peeled, cored and shredded
¼ cup raisins, plumped in hot water for 10 minutes and drained

1 tablespoon minced fresh parsley
¼ teaspoon salt
¼ teaspoon dried sage
¼ teaspoon dried thyme
Salt and pepper
1 cup apple cider or apple juice, divided
2 tablespoons red currant jelly

Trim the chops of excess fat and cut a pocket in the side of each. Brown in the oil in a large skillet. Remove from the skillet and sauté the onions in the drippings until tender.

In a medium bowl, combine the onions with the bread crumbs, apples, raisins, parsley, ¼ teaspoon salt, sage and thyme. Stuff each chop with the mixture and place them snugly together in a casserole. (This will prevent the stuffing from falling out as they bake.) Season with salt and pepper to taste, add ½ cup of the cider or juice to the casserole, cover and bake in a preheated 350° oven for 30 minutes.

Remove the cover and bake for 20 to 30 minutes more, or until the chops are well-done. Remove to a serving platter, skim the excess fat from the casserole and add the remaining ½ cup cider or juice. Stir in the jelly and simmer until slightly thickened, about 5 minutes. Serve the sauce over the chops.

Serves 4 to 6.

Merrymeeting Merry Eating
Mid Coast Hospital / Brunswick Auxiliary, Brunswick, Maine

VERMONT PORK CHOPS

An alternative method of cooking these tender chops is to dredge them in flour, brown in a skillet and cover with sauce. Cover the skillet and cook on top of the stove for 45 minutes. Either way, basting is an important step.

6	pork chops, trimmed of excess fat	1	tablespoon vinegar
2	teaspoons oil	½	teaspoon chili powder
¼	cup chopped onions	½	teaspoon salt
¼	cup maple syrup	⅛	teaspoon ground black pepper
¼	cup water		Flour
1	tablespoon Worcestershire sauce		

In a skillet, lightly brown the pork chops in the oil, then place in a flat baking dish. Combine the onions, maple syrup, water, Worcestershire sauce, vinegar, chili powder, salt and pepper in a saucepan and cook over low heat until blended. Pour over the chops, cover and bake in a preheated 400° oven for 45 minutes, basting occasionally. Uncover and bake for 15 minutes more.

Place the chops on a warming platter. Thicken the sauce very slightly with flour and serve over the chops.

Serves 4 to 6.

From Our House to Yours
The Hikers, Melvin Village, New Hampshire

PORK CHOPS & PEARS

The richness of pork is complemented by a spicy, fruity sauce.
To keep the meat moist, baste it frequently as it simmers.

4 **pork chops**
1 **cup water**
½ **cup frozen orange juice concentrate**
½ **cup raisins**
2 **tablespoons firmly packed brown sugar**
½ **teaspoon salt**

½ **teaspoon ground cinnamon**
⅛ **teaspoon ground cloves**
3 **pears, peeled, quartered and cored**
1 **tablespoon cornstarch, combined with 2 tablespoons water**

Brown the pork chops in a large skillet and pour off the fat. Combine the water, orange juice concentrate, raisins, brown sugar, salt, cinnamon and cloves in a small bowl and pour over the pork chops. Simmer, covered, for 25 minutes. Add the pears, baste with the juices and simmer, covered, for 15 minutes more.

Remove the chops and pears to a serving platter. Pour the juices from the skillet into a 2-cup measure and add enough water, if necessary, to make 1½ cups liquid. Return to the skillet, stir in the combined cornstarch and water and cook until the liquid thickens. Pour over the pork and pears and serve.

Serves 4.

A Century of Good Cooking
Waldoboro Woman's Club, Waldoboro, Maine

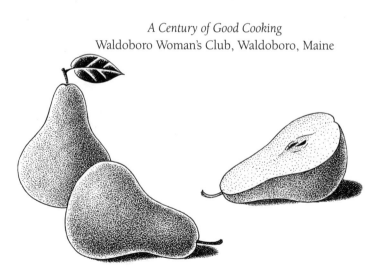

PORK SCHNITZEL

A rich and tangy cream sauce is spooned over the pork cutlets.
Serve on a platter, garnish with fresh dill and
thin slices of lemon and accompany with spaetzle.

6 loin pork cutlets (about
   1½ pounds)
¼ cup plus 1 tablespoon
   unbleached flour, divided
½ teaspoon salt
¼ teaspoon ground black
   pepper
1 cup fine dry bread crumbs

1 teaspoon paprika
¼ cup milk
1 egg, beaten
2 tablespoons oil
¾ cup chicken stock
1 teaspoon minced fresh dill,
   or ¼ teaspoon dried
½ cup sour cream

Pound the pork cutlets to a ¼" thickness. Cut small slits around the
edges to prevent curling. Combine ¼ cup of the flour with the salt and
pepper on a plate. Combine the bread crumbs and paprika on another
plate. Mix the milk and egg in a small bowl. Dredge the meat in the
seasoned flour, dip in the egg mixture and coat with the bread crumbs.

In a large skillet, heat the oil and cook 3 cutlets at a time for 2 to 3
minutes per side. Remove and keep warm.

Pour off the excess oil and add the stock to the skillet, scraping the
bottom as you stir. Blend the remaining 1 tablespoon flour, dill and sour
cream in a small bowl. Slowly stir into the stock and heat, but do not let
boil. Pour over the cutlets and serve.

Serves 6.

Rumsey Rare Bites
Rumsey Circle: Rumsey Hall, Washington, Connecticut

Pork Pie (Tourtière)

This meat-packed pie is robust cold-weather fare.
Serve it hot after skiing or pack it in a basket for a tailgate picnic.

1 onion, finely minced	½ teaspoon ground black
1 tablespoon butter or	pepper
margarine	½ teaspoon dried thyme
1 pound ground pork	½ teaspoon ground nutmeg
1 pound lean ground beef or	¼ teaspoon dried sage
veal	Pinch of ground cloves
¼ cup chopped dried celery	Pastry for double-crust 9" pie
leaves	1 egg, lightly beaten with
½ teaspoon salt	1 tablespoon water

In a large iron skillet, sauté the onions in the butter or margarine. In a large bowl, combine the pork, beef or veal, celery leaves, salt, pepper, thyme, nutmeg, sage and cloves, mixing well. Add to the onions and continue to cook slowly for about 20 minutes, breaking up the meat and stirring to prevent sticking. Drain off the excess fat and set aside to cool.

Line a 9" pie plate with the bottom crust. Fill with the cooked meat mixture and cover with the top crust. Crimp the edges and seal carefully. Slash the top to permit steam to escape and brush with the egg wash. Bake in a preheated 400° oven for about 15 minutes. Reduce the heat to 350° and bake for 15 minutes more, or until golden brown.

Serves 6 to 8.

The Fine Arts Cookbook I
Museum of Fine Arts, Boston, Massachusetts

CRANBERRY MEAT LOAF

This out-of-the-ordinary meat loaf is festive, slightly sweet and lower in fat than the more familiar version made with ground beef and ground pork.

SAUCE
- 2 cups cranberries
- 1 cup sugar
- 1 cup water

MEAT LOAF
- 2 cups ground cooked ham
- 1 pound ground raw turkey breast
- ½ cup dry bread crumbs
- 2 eggs
- 3 tablespoons chopped fresh parsley
- 1 small onion, finely chopped
- ½ teaspoon salt
- ⅛ teaspoon ground black pepper

To make the sauce: Pick over the cranberries and rinse them thoroughly. Boil the sugar and water in a saucepan for 5 minutes. Add the cranberries and boil, without stirring, until all the skins pop, about 5 minutes. Remove from the heat and cool in the pan.

To make the meat loaf: Combine the ham, turkey, bread crumbs, eggs, parsley, onions, salt and pepper. Add ½ cup of the sauce and blend well. Form the mixture into a round loaf, place on a baking sheet and bake in a preheated 375° oven for about 45 minutes. Pour the remaining sauce over the loaf and bake for 15 minutes more.

Serves 6 to 8.

Flavors of Cape Cod
Thornton W. Burgess Society, East Sandwich, Massachusetts

NEW ENGLAND HAM LOAF

Children will enjoy this basic, mild-flavored dish. Baked beans
make a nice accompaniment, and leftovers are great as sandwiches.

1 pound ground smoked ham	1/2 cup firmly packed brown
1 1/2 pounds ground pork	sugar
1 cup unsalted cracker crumbs	1 teaspoon dry mustard
1 cup milk	1/4 cup vinegar
2 eggs, beaten	1/4 cup water

In a large bowl, mix the ham, pork, cracker crumbs, milk and eggs until
well blended. Pack into two 7 3/8" × 3 5/8" loaf pans.

In a small bowl, mix the brown sugar and mustard, then add the vinegar
and water. Spoon some of this mixture over the tops of the loaves and bake
in a preheated 350° oven for about 1 hour, basting from time to time.

Serves 6 to 8.

Saint Michael's Cooks By Design
Saint Michael's Episcopal Church, Litchfield, Connecticut

CHATHAM STUFFED LEG OF LAMB

This lamb is rich and flavorful, with a natural-juice
gravy that is out of this world.

1 leg of lamb (6–7 pounds), trimmed, boned and butterflied	1/2 cup rye bread crumbs
	1 clove garlic, crushed
	1/4 teaspoon salt
1/2 teaspoon dried thyme	1/4 teaspoon ground black
Salt and pepper	pepper
1/4 cup milk	1 1/2–3 tablespoons vermouth
1 egg, beaten	1/2 cup Dijon mustard
1/2 cup chopped fresh parsley	1–2 teaspoons dried rosemary

Rub the inner surface of the lamb with the thyme and salt and pepper to taste. In a small bowl, combine the milk, egg, parsley, bread crumbs, garlic, ¼ teaspoon salt and ¼ teaspoon pepper and mix well. Spread the mixture over the inner surface of the lamb. Tie the lamb evenly with butcher's twine, tucking in the end pieces. Sprinkle with 1½ tablespoons of the vermouth. Lightly coat with the mustard and sprinkle with the rosemary. Place in a roasting pan, cover and bake at 325° for 2 to 2½ hours, basting occasionally with the remaining vermouth.

Serves 10 to 12.

Bulfinch's Boston Faire
Doric Dames, Boston, Massachusetts

$\mathcal{H}$ERBED LAMB CHOPS

A pungent spread of mustard and herbs keeps these chops tender and juicy and complements the full flavor of the lamb. Serve with long-grain and wild rice.

4 **rib lamb chops (1½" thick)**	1 **teaspoon minced fresh**
1 **tablespoon oil**	**parsley, or ½ teaspoon dried**
1 **tablespoon Dijon mustard**	½ **teaspoon dried rosemary**
1 **clove garlic, minced**	**Ground black pepper**

Place the chops on a broiler pan. Combine the oil, mustard, garlic, parsley, rosemary and pepper to taste. Spread half the mixture on top of each chop. Broil about 4" to 5" from the heat source for 4 to 6 minutes. Turn the chops over and spread with the remaining mixture. Broil for another 4 to 6 minutes, or to desired doneness.

Serves 2.

Country Classics
Welcome Wagon Club, Londonderry, New Hampshire

SAUTÉED SPICED LAMB CHOPS WITH GINGER CRISPS

🪶

Golden, crisp curls of fresh ginger not only enliven the flavor
of these chops but also enhance their presentation.
This dish takes less than 45 minutes from start to finish.

8 thick (1"–1½") lamb chops	½ teaspoon salt (optional)
4 teaspoons ground coriander	½ cup peeled, finely julienned
2 teaspoons firmly packed dark	fresh ginger
brown sugar	2 tablespoons oil
1 teaspoon ground black	1 tablespoon butter or
pepper	margarine

Pat the chops dry with paper towels and prick them with a fork. Combine the coriander, brown sugar, pepper and salt (if using) in a small bowl. Rub this mixture on both sides of the chops, then let them sit at room temperature for 15 minutes.

In a skillet, fry the ginger in the oil until it turns a pale golden color, then transfer it to a paper towel to drain. Melt the butter or margarine in the skillet and sauté the chops for about 4 to 6 minutes per side, depending on the degree of doneness you prefer. Transfer to a serving platter and top with the ginger crisps.

Serves 4.

Doorway to Healthy Eating
Trinity Church on the Green: Episcopal Church Women, Branford, Connecticut

POULTRY

APRICOT-ROSEMARY CHICKEN

This moist, succulent and fragrant dish is special enough
for company and requires very little time in the kitchen.
Serve it with rice or boiled new potatoes.

8–10	dried apricots	2	onions, sliced
	Salt and pepper	¼	cup orange juice
2	whole boneless, skinless chicken breasts, halved	1	teaspoon dried rosemary

Soak the apricots in hot water in a small bowl for 15 minutes. Drain and
slice into strips. Sprinkle salt and pepper to taste on the chicken breasts
and place each on a separate piece of foil. Top with the apricots and onions,
drizzle with the orange juice and sprinkle with the rosemary. Seal the foil,
making loose but airtight packages. Place on a baking sheet and bake in a
preheated 450° oven for 20 to 25 minutes.

Serves 4.

The Kosher Yankee II
Sisterhood of the Rutland Jewish Center, Rutland, Vermont

GRILLED CHICKEN BREASTS

Don't let this recipe slip by. Although its title doesn't knock
your socks off, the finished dish will. Marinated overnight in a
combination of citrus juice, cider, mustard, brown sugar and oil,
the chicken absorbs the piquant sauce and is tenderized by it as well.
Serve to the family or to company any time of the year.

3–4 cloves garlic, crushed
½ cup firmly packed light
brown sugar
3 tablespoons whole-grain
mustard
2 tablespoons apple cider or
dry white wine
Juice of 1 lime

Juice of ½ large lemon
½ teaspoon salt
¼ cup plus 2 tablespoons olive
oil
Ground black pepper
6 whole boneless, skinless
chicken breasts

In a small bowl, combine the garlic, brown sugar, mustard, cider or
wine, lime juice, lemon juice and salt. Whisk in the oil and pepper to taste.
Place the chicken in a shallow nonreactive dish and cover with the marinade. Refrigerate for at least 8 hours, turning once.

Remove the chicken from the refrigerator and let stand at room temperature for 15 minutes. Grill over hot coals or broil for 4 minutes per side, or
until the juices run clear.

Serves 6.

A Taste of New England
Junior League of Worcester, Massachusetts

HOMETOWN COOKING IN NEW ENGLAND

ℒEMON-MUSTARD CHICKEN

These tender cutlets are topped with a zesty sauce. Serve them with plain rice and a green salad tossed with a simple vinaigrette.

½ cup unbleached flour
½ teaspoon salt
½ teaspoon ground black pepper
4 chicken breast cutlets
1 tablespoon olive oil
1½ cups chicken stock
1 small red bell pepper, diced

4 scallions, thinly sliced
2 teaspoons Dijon mustard
2 tablespoons lemon juice
1 teaspoon grated lemon rind
1 tablespoon cornstarch
1 teaspoon dried tarragon
Lemon slices
Chopped fresh tarragon

Combine the flour, salt and pepper in a shallow dish and coat the chicken with the mixture. Heat the oil in a skillet, add the chicken and sauté until golden on both sides. Transfer to a plate and keep warm.

Add the stock, bell peppers and scallions to the skillet and cook for 2 minutes. In a small bowl, combine the mustard, lemon juice, lemon rind and cornstarch, blending well. Whisk the mixture into the stock, add the dried tarragon and cook until thick.

Add the cutlets and heat for about 10 minutes. Remove the chicken to a serving platter, cover with the sauce and garnish with the lemon slices and fresh tarragon.

Serves 4.

St. John's Episcopal Church Cookbook
St. John's Episcopal Church, Barrington, Rhode Island

RUM-RAISIN CHICKEN

The flavor from the rum-raisin mixture is very subtle,
not at all sweet, and provides an unexpected and appealing
contrast to the cream sauce. The simple preparation and attractive
presentation make this a good choice for easy entertaining.

3 tablespoons raisins	2 whole boneless, skinless
3 tablespoons rum	chicken breasts, halved
¼ cup sliced almonds	1 cup chicken stock
3 teaspoons margarine or oil	2 teaspoons cornstarch
(approximately), divided	¼ cup light cream or
	half-and-half

In a small bowl, soak the raisins in the rum for at least 1 hour. In a
skillet, sauté the almonds in 1 teaspoon of the margarine or oil until lightly
browned, then remove from the skillet and set aside.

In the same skillet, melt the remaining 2 teaspoons margarine or oil and
sauté the chicken, turning often until browned and cooked through. Add
more margarine or oil if needed. Remove the chicken and keep warm.

Add the stock to the skillet, mix the cornstarch with the cream and add
it to the stock. Cook, stirring constantly, until thickened. Add the rum and
raisins, return the chicken to the skillet and reheat. Transfer the chicken to
a serving platter, spoon the sauce over all and sprinkle with the almonds.
Serve at once.

Serves 4.

Anniversary Celebration Cookbook
Trinity Lutheran Church, Chelmsford, Massachusetts

$\mathcal{P}$ENNY'S CHICKEN BREASTS

Although canned peaches work fine, fresh ones are definitely
superior in taste and appearance. This dish is simple enough to
serve as a family meal but also well suited for company.

2 **whole boneless, skinless
   chicken breasts, halved**
   Salt and pepper
2 **tablespoons butter or oil**
¼ **cup minced onions or shallots**
1 **clove garlic, minced**
1 **teaspoon paprika**

1 **bunch broccoli**
4 **fresh or canned peach halves**
1 **cup plain yogurt or sour
   cream**
¼ **cup mayonnaise**
¼ **cup grated Parmesan cheese**

Season the chicken with salt and pepper to taste. In a small skillet, heat
the butter or oil and sauté the onions or shallots and garlic. Stir in the
paprika and add the chicken, turning it in the mixture until well coated.
Put the chicken in a shallow broiler-proof pan, cover loosely with foil and
bake in a preheated 375° oven for 30 to 35 minutes.

Meanwhile, steam the broccoli until crisp-tender. After the chicken has
baked, place the broccoli and peaches in the pan beside it. Mix the yogurt
or sour cream and mayonnaise in a small bowl and spoon it over all.
Sprinkle with the Parmesan cheese and broil for 6 to 8 minutes. Serve
immediately.

Serves 4.

RSVP
Junior League of Portland, Maine

CHICKEN DIVINE

A superb sauce spooned over the chicken not only adds flavor
but also prevents the meat from drying out while baking.

¼ cup unbleached flour	½ cup nonfat plain yogurt
½ teaspoon salt	⅓–½ cup apricot preserves
2 whole boneless, skinless chicken breasts, halved	1 tablespoon Dijon mustard
	2 tablespoons slivered almonds

Grease the bottom of a shallow baking pan. Put the flour and salt in a
large plastic bag and shake the chicken until coated. Place in a single layer
in the pan and bake in a preheated 375° oven for 15 minutes.

Meanwhile, in a small bowl, combine the yogurt, apricot preserves and
mustard. Remove the chicken from the oven, turn the pieces over and
spread with the yogurt mixture. Return to the oven and bake for 20 minutes more. Serve garnished with almonds.

Serves 4.

Doorway to Healthy Eating
Trinity Church on the Green: Episcopal Church Women, Branford, Connecticut

MAINE MAPLE CHICKEN

This maple syrup–sweetened sauce is similar to a
barbecue sauce. If there's any left over, bring it to a boil in a
small saucepan and serve it with the chicken.

1 can (6 ounces) tomato paste	4–6 chicken breast quarters, or 1 whole chicken, cut up
½ cup maple syrup	
¼ cup white vinegar	1 large onion, sliced
2 tablespoons Dijon mustard	Salt and pepper
2 tablespoons oil	½ cup water
	Parsley sprigs

In a medium bowl, whisk the tomato paste, maple syrup, vinegar, mustard and oil, blending well. Place the chicken pieces in a casserole, arrange the onions on top of and in between the chicken and sprinkle with salt and pepper to taste. Add the water to the bottom of the casserole and bake in a preheated 375° oven for 30 minutes. Remove from the oven, spoon the sauce over the chicken and return to the oven for 15 to 20 minutes more, watching closely so that the sauce doesn't burn. Garnish with the parsley and serve.

Serves 4 to 6.

The Maine Collection
Portland Museum of Art, Portland, Maine

$\mathcal{P}$OKER HILL'S SAVORY BAKED CHICKEN

Moist on the inside and crisp on the outside, this is similar to fried chicken but without the frying and high fat content.

¾ **cup plain yogurt**	⅛ **teaspoon garlic powder**
1 **tablespoon lemon juice**	1¼ **cups fine dry bread crumbs**
1 **teaspoon paprika**	1 **broiler-fryer chicken**
½ **teaspoon salt**	**(2½–3 pounds), cut up**
½ **teaspoon Worcestershire**	2 **tablespoons butter or oil**
sauce	

In a large, shallow bowl, combine the yogurt, lemon juice, paprika, salt, Worcestershire sauce and garlic powder. Spread the bread crumbs on a plate. Dip the chicken in the yogurt mixture and roll in the crumbs. Place in a broad, shallow baking dish and dot with the butter or drizzle with the oil. Cover and bake in a preheated 350° oven for 45 minutes. Remove the cover and bake for 30 to 35 minutes more.

Serves 4.

Poker Hill Cookbook
Poker Hill School, Underhill, Vermont

CURRIED CHICKEN & VEGETABLES

For a lower-fat and even simpler version, use skinned
chicken breasts. Place them in a baking dish, add the partially cooked
potatoes and carrots, pour the sauce over the chicken and
vegetables and bake for 30 to 35 minutes, basting occasionally.

½	cup honey	¼	teaspoon red pepper flakes
¼	cup Dijon mustard	1	broiler-fryer chicken
1	tablespoon butter or		(2½–3 pounds)
	margarine		Oil or melted butter
2	tablespoons minced onions	2	large potatoes, peeled and
2	tablespoons water		quartered
1	clove garlic, minced	6	medium carrots, chopped
2	teaspoons curry powder	2	medium apples, peeled, cored
½	teaspoon salt		and cut into chunks
¼	teaspoon ground ginger		

In a small saucepan, combine the honey, mustard, butter or margarine,
onions, water, garlic, curry powder, salt, ginger and red pepper flakes.
Bring to a boil, stirring constantly, then remove from the heat and set aside.

Rinse the chicken and pat dry with paper towels. Place breast side up in
a shallow roasting pan. Brush with oil or melted butter and roast in a preheated 375° oven for 1¼ to 1½ hours, basting occasionally with the honey-
mustard sauce.

Meanwhile, in a large saucepan, cook the potatoes and carrots in boiling
water for 20 to 25 minutes, or until nearly tender, then drain.

About 20 minutes before the chicken is done, drain off any fat in the
roasting pan and add the potatoes, carrots and apples. Continue roasting
until a meat thermometer registers 185° and the vegetables and apples are
tender. Baste occasionally with the honey-mustard sauce during roasting
and again just before serving.

Serves 6.

Crossroads Cookbook
Somers Congregational Church, Somers, Connecticut

CHICKEN RUBY

Children love this dish, which is easy and attractive.
The chicken can be cooked with or without its skin—the latter being
lower in fat—but either way, be sure to baste it every 10 minutes or so.

⅓ cup unbleached flour	1½ cups cranberries
½ teaspoon salt	¾ cup sugar
Ground black pepper	¼ cup chopped onions
1 broiler-fryer chicken	¾ cup orange juice
(2½–3 pounds), cut up	1 teaspoon grated orange rind
2 tablespoons butter or	¼ teaspoon ground cinnamon
margarine	¼ teaspoon ground ginger

In a shallow dish, combine the flour, salt and pepper to taste and coat
the chicken pieces with the mixture. Melt the butter or margarine in a large
skillet and brown the chicken on all sides. Meanwhile, pick over the cranberries and rinse them thoroughly. In a large saucepan, combine the cranberries, sugar, onions, orange juice, orange rind, cinnamon and ginger.
Bring to a boil, stirring constantly, then remove from the heat.

Place the chicken in a shallow baking dish and pour the sauce on top.
Bake in a preheated 350° oven for 35 to 40 minutes, or until the chicken is
tender and the juices run clear when the chicken is pricked with a fork.

Serves 4 to 6.

Cape Cod Kitchen Secrets
Cape Cod Hospital Auxiliary, Chatham, Massachusetts

VERMONT SPRING CHICKEN

A simple, succulent dish with just the right amount of sweetness.
This works equally well with boneless, skinless chicken breasts,
just reduce the baking time to 25 to 30 minutes.

1 **broiler-fryer chicken** **(2½–3 pounds), cut up**	¼ **cup chopped almonds** 2 **teaspoons lemon juice**
2 **tablespoons butter or** **margarine, melted**	½ **teaspoon grated lemon rind** ½ **teaspoon salt**
½ **cup maple syrup**	**Pinch of ground black pepper**

Place the chicken in a casserole. Mix the butter, maple syrup, almonds, lemon juice, lemon rind, salt and pepper and pour over the chicken. Bake in a preheated 350° oven for 50 to 60 minutes, basting occasionally.

Serves 4.

College Street Congregational Church 125th Anniversary Cookbook
College Street Congregational Church, Burlington, Vermont

CHICKEN PRUNELLA

If desired, you may finish this dish on a grill.
Depending on the size of the pieces, remove the chicken from the
oven after 30 to 45 minutes. Keep the sauce warm and grill the
chicken over low coals for the last 15 minutes. Serve as below.

3 cloves garlic, minced
¼–½ cup pitted prunes cut into
halves
8 Spanish olives
2 tablespoons capers with juice
2 tablespoons olive oil
2 tablespoons red wine vinegar
2 bay leaves
1 tablespoon dried oregano

Salt and pepper
1 broiler-fryer chicken
(2½ pounds), quartered
¼ cup firmly packed light
brown sugar
¼ cup white wine
2 tablespoons chopped fresh
parsley

In a large, shallow dish, combine the garlic, prunes, olives, capers, oil,
vinegar, bay leaves, oregano and salt and pepper to taste. Add the chicken
and turn to coat. Cover and refrigerate overnight.

Arrange the chicken in a baking dish and pour the marinade over the
pieces. Sprinkle the brown sugar on top and pour the wine around the
chicken. Bake in a preheated 350° oven for 45 to 60 minutes.

To serve, arrange the chicken on a platter, spoon the juices over the top
and sprinkle with the parsley.

Serves 4.

Hospitality
Salem Hospital Aid Association, Salem, Massachusetts

CHICKEN BREASTS FLORENTINE

This is a fancy way to serve chicken breasts—
rolled up with a spinach, mushroom and cheese filling.

½ cup diced onions
½ cup chopped mushrooms
1 clove garlic, minced
2 teaspoons oil
½ cup cooked, chopped and
  thoroughly drained spinach
½ cup part-skim ricotta cheese
¼ teaspoon dried oregano

2 whole boneless, skinless
  chicken breasts, halved and
  pounded to a ¼" thickness
Oil
2 tablespoons dry bread
  crumbs
3 tablespoons dry white wine

In a skillet, sauté the onions, mushrooms and garlic in the 2 teaspoons oil until tender. Remove from the heat and stir in the spinach, cheese and oregano. Spread the mixture evenly over each breast, leaving a ½" border on all sides. Carefully roll up the breasts to enclose the filling. Place them seam side down in a 10" × 6" baking pan coated with a no-stick spray or lightly greased. Brush the tops of the rolled breasts with oil, sprinkle with the bread crumbs and add the wine to the bottom of the dish. Bake, covered with foil, in a preheated 350° oven for 35 minutes. Remove the foil and bake for 15 minutes more. Serve immediately.

Serves 4.

From Our House to Yours
The Hikers, Melvin Village, New Hampshire

COUNTRY CHICKEN PIE

Tender chunks of chicken with diced vegetables in a creamy,
herb-flavored sauce create an ideal casserole for a party.
The browned lattice crust turns this classic into classy fare.

2	cups diced onions	¼	teaspoon ground black pepper
1	cup diced celery		
1	tablespoon oil	½	teaspoon dried thyme, crumbled
4	cups diced carrots		
6–8	chicken breast halves, or 2 broiler-fryer chickens, cut up	¼	teaspoon dried rosemary, crumbled
⅓	cup butter or margarine	1	cup light cream or milk
⅓	cup unbleached flour		Pastry to make lattice crust
1	teaspoon salt		for 13" × 9" casserole

In a skillet, sauté the onions and celery in the oil for 2 to 3 minutes.
Steam the carrots for 3 minutes, then set the partially cooked vegetables
aside.

In a large soup pot, simmer the chicken in water to cover for 45 minutes,
or until tender. Remove from the heat and pull the meat off the bones, discarding the skin and bones. Measure out 2 cups of the stock; reserve the
remainder for another use. Cut the meat into bite-size pieces.

Melt the butter or margarine in a saucepan. Stir in the flour, salt, pepper,
thyme and rosemary. Gradually add the 2 cups stock and cream or milk.
Cook, stirring, over medium heat until thickened and bubbly; set aside but
keep warm.

Roll out the pastry dough into a 13" × 9" rectangle and cut into strips.

Add the chicken, carrots, celery and onions to the warm sauce and heat
until hot. Pour into a 13" × 9" baking dish and arrange the dough strips in
a lattice design on top. Bake in a preheated 450° oven for 15 minutes, or
until the crust is golden.

Serves 8.

Portland Symphony Cookbook
Portland Symphony Orchestra Women's Committee, Portland, Maine

$\mathcal{C}$HICKEN & BROCCOLI CRÊPES

For the best results, make the crêpe batter a day in advance.

CRÊPES
- 4 eggs
- ½ teaspoon salt
- 2 cups unbleached flour
- 2¼ cups milk
- ¼ cup butter or margarine, melted and cooled

FILLING
- ¼ cup butter or margarine
- ¼ cup unbleached flour
- 2 cups chicken stock
- 2 teaspoons Worcestershire sauce
- 2 cups shredded Cheddar cheese, divided
- 1 cup sour cream or plain yogurt
- 1½ pounds fresh broccoli or 2 packages (10 ounces each) frozen broccoli, cooked, drained and chopped
- 2 cups cubed cooked chicken

To make the crêpes: Combine the eggs and salt in a large bowl. Gradually add the flour alternately with the milk, beating well. Beat in the butter or margarine, then refrigerate the batter for at least 1 hour.

Heat a lightly greased 6" skillet and pour in enough batter to thinly coat the bottom, tilting the skillet to spread the batter evenly. Cook until lightly browned on the bottom, turn over and cook the other side.

Set aside 12 crêpes. Place the remaining 20 to 24 crêpes between pieces of waxed paper and stored in the freezer for later use.

To make the filling: Melt the butter or margarine in a saucepan, add the flour and cook, stirring, until bubbly. Add the stock slowly, then add the Worcestershire sauce. Cook, stirring constantly, until the mixture is smooth and thick. Stir in 1½ cups of the cheese.

Put the sour cream or yogurt in a medium bowl and slowly add the hot cheese sauce, stirring constantly.

Divide the broccoli and chicken evenly among the crêpes, spoon on 1 tablespoon of the sauce, fold over the sides of the crêpe and place in a greased 13" × 9" baking dish. Pour the remaining sauce over the crêpes, sprinkle with the remaining ½ cup cheese, cover and bake in a preheated 350° oven for 20 to 30 minutes.

Serves 6.

Flavors of a Vermont Village
West Newbury Women's Fellowship, West Newbury, Vermont

SKI-DAY CHICKEN CASSEROLE

Because this dish can be made a day in advance, it is ideal after a
full day of skiing, when everyone is exhausted and ravenous.

¼ **cup plus 2 tablespoons butter**
 or margarine, divided
¼ **cup unbleached flour**
1½ **cups chicken stock**
1 **cup sour cream**
¼ **cup white wine or dry sherry**
⅛ **teaspoon ground nutmeg**
⅛ **teaspoon ground black**
 pepper

 Salt
½ **pound cooked flat egg**
 noodles
4½ **cups cut-up cooked chicken**
8 **ounces mushrooms, sliced**
 and sautéed
1 **cup soft bread crumbs**
½ **cup grated Parmesan cheese**

Melt ¼ cup of the butter or margarine in a saucepan. Stir in the flour
and cook over medium heat until bubbly, stirring constantly. Add the
stock, sour cream and wine or sherry. Cook until thickened, again stirring
constantly. Add the nutmeg, pepper and salt to taste, blending well.

Arrange the noodles in a 13" × 9" baking dish. Layer the chicken, mushrooms and sauce on top. Melt the remaining 2 tablespoons butter or margarine and mix with the bread crumbs. Top the casserole with the buttered
crumbs and sprinkle with the cheese. Bake in a preheated 350° oven for
30 minutes, or until hot and bubbly.

Serves 6 to 8.

Merrymeeting Merry Eating
Mid Coast Hospital/Brunswick Auxiliary, Brunswick, Maine

$\mathcal{B}$AKED MACARONI, CHEESE & CHICKEN CASSEROLE

Colorful and substantial, this familiar dish gets a nutritious boost from the chicken and visual appeal from the pimentos and bell peppers.

2	quarts water	¼	cup chopped pimentos
1	teaspoon salt, divided	¼	cup chopped green bell
2	cups elbow macaroni		peppers
¼	cup butter or margarine	2	cups shredded Cheddar
¼	cup unbleached flour		cheese, divided
1	teaspoon dry mustard	1	cup slivered cooked chicken
⅛	teaspoon ground black	1	large ripe tomato, cored and
	pepper		cut into wedges (optional)
2	cups milk		

In a large pot, bring the water and ½ teaspoon of the salt to a rolling boil over high heat. Add the macaroni all at once and stir. Return to a boil, reduce the heat to medium-low and simmer for 4 to 5 minutes, or until the macaroni is barely tender. Do not overcook. Drain and set aside.

Melt the butter or margarine in a medium saucepan, remove from the heat and stir in the flour, mustard, remaining ½ teaspoon salt and pepper. When the mixture is smooth, gradually add the milk, stirring until no longer lumpy.

Return the saucepan to the heat and cook, stirring constantly, until the mixture comes to a boil and thickens slightly. Add the pimentos and bell peppers and simmer for 1 minute more. Stir 1½ cups of the cheese, the macaroni and the chicken into the milk mixture. Pour into a shallow 2-quart baking dish and sprinkle the remaining ½ cup cheese on top. The casserole can be prepared up to this point 1 to 2 days before you plan to bake and serve it. Cover it tightly with plastic wrap or aluminum foil and keep it in the refrigerator until you are ready to proceed.

Bake the casserole in a preheated 375° oven for 20 minutes (longer if the casserole has been chilled), or until the sauce is hot and bubbly and the cheese is melted. Remove from the oven, arrange the tomato wedges (if using) on top and serve.

Serves 6.

Derry Community Playground Cookbook
Derry Playground Committee, East Derry, New Hampshire

HOMETOWN COOKING IN NEW ENGLAND

$\mathcal{B}$LUE RIBBON NEW ENGLAND PIE

A prize of a pie, this has everything: clams, chicken and vegetables
bound together in a creamy sauce and topped with a flaky crust.
It can easily be doubled or baked as individual pies.

4 tablespoons butter or margarine, divided	2 whole boneless, skinless chicken breasts, cooked and cubed
18 small white onions, peeled	1 package (8 ounces) frozen corn, thawed
½ cup chopped celery	2 hard-cooked eggs, quartered
½ cup unbleached flour	Pastry to cover 13″ × 9″ casserole
1 teaspoon dried thyme	
1½ cups chicken stock	1 egg yolk, lightly beaten with 1 teaspoon water
1½ cups light cream or milk	
Salt and pepper	
2 cups quahogs, coarsely chopped, or cherrystones, cut in half	

Melt 1 tablespoon of the butter or margarine in a medium saucepan. Add
the onions and celery, cover and cook gently for 10 minutes, stirring frequently. Do not brown the vegetables.

Add the remaining 3 tablespoons butter or margarine, flour and thyme.
Cook for about 1 minute, stirring constantly. Whisk in the stock and light
cream or milk. Cook until the sauce thickens, then season with salt and
pepper to taste.

Add the quahogs or cherrystones, chicken and corn, mixing thoroughly.
Gently fold in the eggs and pour into a buttered 13″ × 9″ casserole.

Roll out the pastry to a 13″ × 9″ rectangle, place on top of the casserole
and seal the edges. Brush the top generously with the egg wash and make
several slits in the top. Bake in a preheated 400° oven for 30 minutes, or
until browned.

Serves 6.

Mystic Seaport's Seafood Secrets Cookbook
Mystic Seaport Museum Stores, Mystic, Connecticut

ROAST FRESH TURKEY & DRESSING

This recipe recommends roasting the turkey breast side down for
the first 2 hours, then turning it breast side up for the duration of the
roasting time. Those who prefer not to wrestle with the bird can simply
roast it breast side up the entire time (4 to 5 hours), basting periodically.
Either way, the turkey will be moist, tender and tantalizing.

1	fresh turkey (10–12 pounds)	1	teaspoon poultry seasoning
1	small onion, chopped		(approximately)
	Salt		Ground black pepper
2	peppercorns	½	pound ground sausage
1	bay leaf	¼	cup cooked wild rice
¼	cup butter or margarine	¼	cup cooked brown rice
2	cups chopped celery	1½	cups crumbled corn bread
1	cup chopped onions	4	cups crumbled Swedish limpa
½	medium red or green bell		bread
	pepper, chopped	¼	cup butter or margarine,
1¼	teaspoons dried sage		melted
		2–3	tablespoons jelly

Remove the giblets from the turkey. Wash the turkey and pat dry, then
return it to the refrigerator. Place the heart, neck and gizzard in a small
saucepan and cover with water. Add the small chopped onion, salt to taste,
peppercorns and bay leaf. Heat to boiling, reduce the heat and simmer for
1 hour, or until the gizzard is tender. Add the liver for the last 10 minutes.
Drain the giblets, reserving the broth. Chop the giblets, place in a large
bowl and set aside for the dressing.

Melt the ¼ cup butter or margarine in a skillet over medium-high heat
and sauté the celery, 1 cup chopped onions and bell peppers until tender.
Add to the bowl containing the giblets. Stir in the sage, poultry seasoning
(adjust amount to taste) and salt and pepper to taste.

Brown the sausage in the skillet, drain and crumble into the bowl with
the giblets. Add the wild rice and brown rice and toss lightly. Combine the
corn bread and limpa with the giblet mixture and moisten with some of the
reserved giblet broth, stirring well. At this point, cool the dressing or refrigerate overnight.

Stuff the turkey cavity loosely. Any leftover dressing can be baked in a
casserole during the last hour of roasting time. Skewer and truss the turkey
to seal in the stuffing. Secure the legs and wings with string. Place the bird

breast side down on a rack. Combine the melted butter and jelly, stirring until smooth. Brush on the turkey, then use it to baste the turkey every 45 minutes or so. Roast in a preheated 325° oven for 2 hours, then turn the turkey breast side up and continue roasting for 2 to 3 hours more, or until the skin is a nice deep brown or the juices run clear when the skin of the thigh is pricked with a fork.

Serves 6 to 8.

Vermont II: Kitchen Memories
Montpelier, Vermont

♪URE SUCCESS TURKEY BREAST

Turkey with taste! This is so easy to prepare and there's so little waste that it is destined to become a frequently made meal. It's economical, too!

1 tablespoon paprika	Sliced onions
1 teaspoon garlic powder	Sliced celery
½ teaspoon salt	¼ cup sauternes
¼ teaspoon ground black pepper	¼ cup cold water
1 turkey breast (4–5 pounds)	2 tablespoons butter or margarine, melted

In a small bowl, combine the paprika, garlic powder, salt and pepper. Add enough water to make a thick paste. Rub the paste on the turkey inside and out, using all of it. Place the turkey in a large roasting pan, cover securely with foil and refrigerate for several hours or overnight.

When you're ready to bake the turkey, remove it from the refrigerator and take off the foil. Place the onions and celery in the cavity. Combine the sauternes, water and butter or margarine and pour over the turkey. Cover with the foil and bake in a preheated 350° oven for 2½ hours, basting frequently.

Serves 6 to 8.

Poker Hill Cookbook
Poker Hill School, Underhill, Vermont

TURKEY & SPINACH MEAT LOAF

Green flecks of spinach make this an attractive as well as a tasty dish. Take the time to remove as much water from the spinach as possible; otherwise, it will make the loaf too moist and crumbly. This loaf freezes well.

1 pound ground turkey
1 package (10 ounces) frozen chopped spinach, thawed and pressed to remove excess water
1 egg
¾ cup dry bread crumbs
½ cup chopped onions or 2 tablespoons dried onion flakes

1 tablespoon chopped fresh parsley
3 tablespoons ketchup
2 teaspoons lemon juice
½ teaspoon salt or 1 teaspoon soy sauce
¼ teaspoon ground black pepper
2 tablespoons skim milk

In a large bowl, mix the turkey, spinach, egg, bread crumbs, onions or onion flakes, parsley, ketchup, lemon juice, salt or soy sauce and pepper. Moisten with the skim milk.

Put in a 9″ × 5″ loaf pan and cover loosely with foil. Bake in a preheated 350° oven for 30 minutes, remove the foil and bake for 30 minutes more. Remove from the oven and cool for 5 to 10 minutes before slicing.

Serves 4 to 6.

Mystic Seaport's Moveable Feasts Cookbook
Mystic Seaport Museum Stores, Mystic, Connecticut

TURKEY SHORTCAKE

Here's another way to use up the holiday turkey—
with only a few ingredients and even fewer steps.

3 cups dry bread crumbs	¼ cup chopped onions
2 cups milk	½ teaspoon salt
2 eggs, beaten	1 can (8 ounces) whole-berry
3 cups chopped cooked turkey	cranberry sauce

In a large bowl, soak the bread crumbs in the milk. Stir in the eggs and add the turkey, onions and salt, mixing well. Transfer to a greased 13" × 9" pan. Bake in a preheated 350° oven for 25 minutes. Remove from the oven, spread the cranberry sauce evenly over the top and bake for 10 minutes more. Serve hot.

Serves 4 to 6.

Community Rescue Squad Cookbook
Rescue Squads of Deering, Hillsboro and Washington, New Hampshire

$\mathcal{S}$MOKED TURKEY

❧

A smokehouse used to be an essential part of the country homestead, where meat or fish would be cured by the use of dense smoke. A similar effect can be achieved today using a covered barbecue or smoker. Here's a fun recipe for turkey.

1 turkey (16–18 pounds)	2 tablespoons ground black
6 quarts water	pepper
3 cups salt	1 tablespoon ground allspice
1½ cups sugar	1 quart apple juice
1 clove garlic	¼ cup butter or margarine, melted

Place the turkey in a large, deep roasting pan. In a small bowl, combine the water, salt, sugar, garlic, pepper and allspice. Pour over the turkey and marinate for at least 10 hours, turning every 2 hours.

About an hour before the turkey has finished marinating, prepare the barbecue or smoker. Soak hickory chips in water for 1 hour. Punch about 6 holes in the bottom and sides of a coffee can. Remove the turkey from the marinade and rinse thoroughly. Put 2 lit charcoal briquets in the bottom of the coffee can and the hickory chips on top of them. (You may need to add more lit coals and chips.) Put the can in the barbecue or smoker with the marinated turkey, close the lid and open the vents slightly. The object is to smoke-smolder without producing a lot of heat. The more smoke and the less heat the better. Smoke for 3 hours, basting frequently with the apple juice. Preheat the oven to 275°.

Remove the turkey from the barbecue or smoker, place in a roasting pan and brush generously with the butter or margarine. Soak a piece of cheese-cloth in apple juice and lay it over the turkey. Cover the turkey loosely and roast in a preheated 275° oven for 1¾ hours, basting frequently with apple juice.

Serves 8 to 10.

Marblehead Cooks
Tower School, Marblehead, Massachusetts

HOMETOWN COOKING IN NEW ENGLAND

GRILLED GAME HENS IN BLUEBERRY MARINADE

꙳

This recipe requires some advance planning.
For an elegant picnic, transport the marinating birds in self-seal
plastic bags, packed in a cooler, and grill on a boat or beach.

4 **Cornish game hens (about 1 pound each), split**	²/₃ **cup olive oil**
1 **pint fresh or frozen blueberries**	3 **small bay leaves**
1 **cup blueberry vinegar (available at specialty shops)**	2 **teaspoons chopped fresh thyme, or 1 teaspoon dried**
	Salt and pepper

One day before serving, rinse the hens, pat dry and place them in a shallow baking dish. Combine the blueberries and blueberry vinegar in a saucepan, heat to boiling and boil for 1 minute. Remove from the heat. Stir in the oil, bay leaves, thyme and salt and pepper to taste. Cool to room temperature. Pour the marinade over the hens and marinate in the refrigerator overnight, turning several times.

Prepare the grill. When the coals are hot, grill the hens a few inches above the coals, basting often with the marinade. The birds are cooked when juices from a cut made in the thickest part of the thighs run clear. Game hens also may be roasted in a preheated 400° oven for 45 minutes, basting occasionally with the marinade.

Serves 4.

The Mystic Seaport All Seasons Cookbook
Mystic Seaport Museum Stores, Mystic, Connecticut

CRANBERRY DUCK

Here is a foolproof recipe for anyone who has shied away
from making duck. It promises excellent results with little effort.
The sweet-tart sauce, which complements the rich flavor of the duckling,
also could be used with roast chicken or turkey.

1 **duckling (4 pounds), with giblets**
1 **can (10½ ounces) condensed beef stock**
¾ **cup cranberry juice**
2 **tablespoons butter or margarine**

2 **tablespoons sugar**
2 **tablespoons vinegar**
1 **tablespoon cornstarch, combined with 1 tablespoon cranberry juice**

Remove the giblets from the bird and set them aside. Rinse the duckling,
pat dry and place breast side up on a rack in a roasting pan. Roast in a preheated 375° oven for 1½ hours. While the bird roasts, place the neck and
giblets in a saucepan. Add the stock and simmer, covered, for 1 hour. Strain
the stock, return to the saucepan and add the cranberry juice. Cook until
reduced to 1 cup.

After the duck has cooked for 1½ hours, increase the heat to 425° and
roast for 15 minutes more.

Meanwhile, melt the butter or margarine and blend in the sugar. Cook,
stirring constantly, until golden brown. Add the vinegar and reduced stock
and stir to blend.

Remove the duck from the roasting pan and place on a serving platter.
Skim the fat from the juices in the roasting pan and add about 1½ tablespoons of the juices to the stock mixture. Add the combined cornstarch
and cranberry juice and cook, stirring, until the sauce boils. Simmer for
1 to 2 minutes. Transfer to a gravy boat and pass along with the duck.

Serves 4 to 6.

Family Recipe Cookbook
Habitat for Humanity, Providence, Rhode Island

FISH & SHELLFISH

SIMPLY SAVORY BAKED FISH

When time is of the essence and unexpected guests are on the way, this dish will get you off the hook. To ensure that the bread crumbs adhere to the fillets, you may want to dip the fish in milk first and then the crumbs.

1 cup bread crumbs, preferably homemade	1 tablespoon cider vinegar
1½ pounds white fish fillets (sole, flounder or haddock), rinsed and patted dry	1 tablespoon Worcestershire sauce
¼ cup plus 2 tablespoons butter or margarine	1 tablespoon lemon juice
	1 teaspoon Dijon mustard (or to taste)

Place the bread crumbs on a plate, dredge the fish in the crumbs and arrange the fillets in a single layer in a 13" × 9" baking dish.

In a small saucepan, melt the butter or margarine, then stir in the vinegar, Worcestershire sauce, lemon juice and mustard. Pour the sauce evenly over the fish. Bake in a preheated 350° oven for 20 minutes, basting every 5 minutes or so. Serve directly from the baking dish.

Serves 4.

Off the Hook
The Junior League of Stamford-Norwalk, Darien, Connecticut

COD SUPREME
❧

If cod isn't available, you may substitute haddock, pollack or hake.

2 tablespoons butter or margarine
1 large onion, thinly sliced
1 clove garlic, crushed
1 can (16 ounces) stewed tomatoes, drained
½ teaspoon hot-pepper sauce
1 tablespoon chopped fresh oregano, or 1 teaspoon dried
1 teaspoon salt

¼ teaspoon ground black pepper
1½ pounds cod fillets, cut into 4–6 pieces
⅔ cup plain yogurt
1 cup fresh or dry bread crumbs
2 tablespoons grated Parmesan cheese

Melt the butter or margarine in a skillet, add the onions and garlic and cook over low heat until soft but not browned. Add the tomatoes, hot-pepper sauce, oregano, salt and pepper.

Spread half the sauce on the bottom of a shallow 11" × 7" baking dish. Place the cod on top and cover with the remaining sauce. Stir the yogurt until smooth and pour over the cod. Sprinkle with the bread crumbs and Parmesan cheese. Bake in a preheated 375° oven for 20 to 30 minutes, or until the fish flakes easily and the top is browned.

Serves 4 to 6.

1717 Meetinghouse Cookbook II
West Parish of Barnstable: Women's Guild, West Barnstable, Massachusetts

CLAY-POT COD

A clay pot is perfect for this recipe, for the food remains moist but requires very little fat. It also can be made in a covered casserole, but bake at 375° instead. Serve with coleslaw, rye bread and fruit compote.

1½ **pounds cod fillets**	2 **green bell peppers, sliced**
2 **onions, sliced**	**Salt and pepper**
4 **potatoes, peeled and thinly**	1 **bay leaf**
sliced	1 **tablespoon oil**
3 **tomatoes, sliced**	

Soak the clay pot in cold water for 10 minutes. Meanwhile, remove the skin and any bones from the cod and cut it into several pieces.

Arrange 5 layers in the pot, starting with the onions, then the potatoes, cod, tomatoes and bell peppers. Season each layer with some of the salt and pepper to taste. Bury the bay leaf among the ingredients and sprinkle the oil on top. Cover and place in a cold oven. Turn the heat to 450° and bake for 1 hour.

Serves 4.

Rumsey Rare Bites
Rumsey Circle: Rumsey Hall, Washington, Connecticut

$\mathcal{B}$LOCK ISLAND "TURKEY"

This flavorfully seasoned turkey-of-the-sea is rich
and satisfying and comes together quickly and easily.

1 **pound cod fillets**
1 **cup dry bread crumbs**
2 **eggs**
1 **heaping teaspoon dried**
  rosemary
¼ **teaspoon dried basil**
¼ **teaspoon dried thyme**

3 **tablespoons butter or**
  margarine
1 **cup half-and-half**
  Salt and pepper
12 **small new potatoes, boiled**
  and quartered

Cut the cod into serving portions. Put the bread crumbs in a shallow
dish. In another dish, beat the eggs, rosemary, basil and thyme. Dip the cod
first in the egg mixture and then in the crumbs.

Melt the butter or margarine in a large, heavy skillet. Brown the cod on
both sides just until golden. Add the half-and-half and simmer over low
heat for 10 minutes. Add salt and pepper to taste.

Serve the fish and potatoes on a plate covered with the cream "gravy"
from the pan.

Serves 2 to 3.

Mystic Seaport's Seafood Secrets Cookbook
Mystic Seaport Museum Stores, Mystic, Connecticut

$\mathcal{B}$ROILED SCROD

The word *scrod* does not denote a particular species of fish but
instead refers to the size. A scrod can be a small cod, haddock or
pollack, any of which is suitable for this simple preparation.

2 **pounds scrod fillets**
¼ **cup butter or margarine,**
  melted
2 **tablespoons lemon juice**

½ **teaspoon paprika**
  Salt and pepper
¼ **cup dry bread crumbs**

Place the scrod fillets in a single layer in a greased shallow baking dish. In a small bowl, mix the butter or margarine, lemon juice and paprika. Spread the mixture over the fillets and sprinkle with salt and pepper to taste. Place under a preheated broiler for 5 minutes. Brush the fillets with the butter mixture from the baking dish, scatter the bread crumbs over the top and broil for 2 to 3 minutes more, or until golden brown and the fish flakes easily when tested with a fork.

Serves 4.

Smith Neck Friends Meeting Cookbook
Smith Neck Friends Meeting of Dartmouth Monthly Meeting,
South Dartmouth, Massachusetts

*H*ADDOCK STUFFED WITH OYSTERS

Though somewhat pricey, this luscious dish has a
tendency to win friends and influence people.

3 **pounds haddock or cod fillets**	2 **tablespoons butter or**
2 **teaspoons lemon juice**	**margarine, melted**
Salt	**Paprika**
½–1 **pint oysters**	**Lemon wedges**
1 **egg, lightly beaten**	**Parsley sprigs**
1 **cup dry bread crumbs**	

Brush the fish with the lemon juice, sprinkle lightly with salt to taste and place half the fish in a buttered baking dish. Cover with the oysters and top with the remaining fish. Brush the tops of the fillets with some of the beaten egg.

Mix the bread crumbs with the butter or margarine and a generous pinch of the paprika and distribute over the fish. Bake in a preheated 350° oven for 30 to 35 minutes. Garnish with the lemon wedges and parsley.

Serves 6.

The Fine Arts Cookbook II
Museum of Fine Arts, Boston, Massachusetts

BAKED FISH IN FOIL

Fish seems to intimidate a lot of people, but this recipe is not only hassle free but also guaranteed to please. The moist fish flakes perfectly, and the sauce looks, tastes and smells fantastic.

2	tablespoons olive oil	1	teaspoon Worcestershire sauce
1	cup chopped onions		
1/3	cup chopped green bell peppers	2	dashes of hot-pepper sauce
		3	tablespoons capers
2	cloves garlic, crushed	1/2	teaspoon salt
1	tablespoon unbleached flour	1	teaspoon ground black pepper
1/2	cup bottled clam juice		
1/2	cup tomato juice	6	haddock, flounder or other white fish fillets

Heat the oil in a large skillet. Add the onions, bell peppers and garlic and sauté until tender. Add the flour and blend until smooth. Stir in the clam juice, tomato juice, Worcestershire sauce and hot-pepper sauce and simmer for about 5 minutes. Add the capers, salt and pepper.

Lay the fillets on generous-size foil squares and turn up the edges. Spoon the sauce over each fillet, pull up two opposite sides of foil and fold them down together until the foil fits loosely around the fish. Crimp the ends to seal. Put the wrapped fish in a pan or on a baking sheet and bake in a preheated 350° oven for 45 minutes.

Serves 6.

Our Town Cookbook
Peterborough Historical Society, Peterborough, New Hampshire

SEAFOOD-STUFFED POTATOES

Comfort food par excellence, this dish needs only a salad to
complete the meal. Serve for brunch, lunch or supper.

4 **large baking potatoes**	1 **cup milk, heated**
2 **tablespoons butter or**	**Salt and pepper**
margarine	1 **pound flaked cooked fish**
2 **tablespoons minced onions**	⅔ **cup shredded Cheddar cheese**

Bake the potatoes until soft. Slice off the tops and carefully scoop out
the pulp from the skins. Mash the potatoes with the butter or margarine,
onions, milk and salt and pepper to taste. Stir in the fish and stuff back into
the shells. Sprinkle with the cheese and bake in a preheated 375° oven for
25 to 30 minutes.

Serves 4.

The Kosher Yankee II
Sisterhood of the Rutland Jewish Center, Rutland, Vermont

FISH ROLLS WITH BREAD-CARROT STUFFING

Colorful, healthful and flavorful, these stuffed
fish rolls can be served with a simple garnish or jazzed up
for company with tomato sauce drizzled on top.

3 tablespoons butter or margarine, preferably unsalted, divided	1 egg, lightly beaten
1 cup minced onions	1/2 cup water
1/2 cup minced pimentos (optional)	1/4 cup grated Parmesan cheese
2 tablespoons minced fresh parsley	1 teaspoon celery seeds
1 cup fresh bread crumbs	4 large (or 8 small) flounder fillets (about 1 1/2 pounds total)
3/4 cup finely shredded carrots	Lemon slices
	Parsley sprigs

In a large skillet, melt 2 tablespoons of the butter or margarine and sauté the onions, pimentos (if using) and parsley for 3 minutes. Remove from the heat and add the bread crumbs, carrots, egg, water, Parmesan cheese and celery seeds, mixing well.

Spread the mixture on the fillets, roll up and place seam side down in a greased shallow 13" × 9" baking dish. Melt the remaining 1 tablespoon butter or margarine and brush over the fish. Bake in a preheated 350° oven for 25 to 35 minutes, or until the fish flakes easily with a fork. Remove to a serving platter and garnish with lemon slices and parsley.

Serves 4 to 6.

The Hammersmith Farm Cookbook
Hammersmith Farm, Newport, Rhode Island

$\mathcal{B}$LUEFISH WITH MUSTARD GLAZE

A tangy glaze cuts the oily flavor of the bluefish and
transforms it into what some might think is swordfish.

3 tablespoons mustard seeds	**⅓ cup whole-grain mustard**
3 tablespoons dry white wine	**⅓ cup mayonnaise or plain**
1½ pounds bluefish fillets,	**yogurt**
skinned	**1 tablespoon lemon juice**
Salt and pepper	

Soak the mustard seeds in the wine for 20 minutes. Remove any bones
from the fillets and cut the fish into 4 equal portions. Season with salt and
pepper to taste and place in a buttered 13" × 9" baking dish.

Drain the mustard seeds and whisk with the mustard, mayonnaise or
yogurt and lemon juice. Make 4 small mounds of the glaze in the baking
pan. Place a piece of fish on top of each mound and spread the remaining
glaze on top of the fish. (The dish may be prepared up to this point 2 hours
ahead of time.)

Bake in a preheated 450° oven for 10 to 15 minutes, or until the fish
flakes easily with a fork. Place under the broiler for 30 seconds, or until the
glaze puffs and browns.

Serves 4.

Sounds Delicious
Cape Ann Symphony Association, Gloucester, Massachusetts

$\mathcal{S}$WORDFISH CAPER

If the season is not appropriate for grilling outdoors,
you can broil these steaks with excellent results. Either way, be sure
to include the capers—they are an essential ingredient.

2 pounds swordfish steaks, ¾" thick	**2 teaspoons Worcestershire sauce**
⅓ cup lemon juice	**2 teaspoons sugar**
¼ cup oil	**4 bay leaves**
¼ cup chopped onions	**2 cloves garlic, finely chopped**
2 tablespoons capers and juice	**Paprika**
2 tablespoons ketchup	

Cut the steaks into serving-size portions and place in a single layer in a shallow, nonreactive baking dish. In a small bowl, combine the lemon juice, oil, onions, capers and juice, ketchup, Worcestershire sauce, sugar, bay leaves and garlic. Pour over the fish and refrigerate for 30 minutes, turning once.

Remove the fish from the marinade, reserving the marinade for basting. Place the fish in well-greased hinged wire grills. Sprinkle with paprika. Spoon on some of the marinade and grill about 4 inches from moderately hot coals for 8 minutes. Baste with the marinade, turn, sprinkle with paprika, spoon on some of the marinade and grill for 7 to 10 minutes more, or until the fish flakes easily when tested with a fork. Discard any remaining marinade.

Serves 4 to 6.

The Taste of Gloucester
The Fishermen's Wives of Gloucester and The Cape Ann League of Women Voters,
Gloucester, Massachusetts

HALIBUT À LA GRECO

One of the beauties of fish is that it generally doesn't
need to be cooked long. Thus, you can have a fancy main dish
like this on the table in less than 30 minutes.

4 halibut steaks, ¾" thick
(about 1½ pounds total)

2 tablespoons butter or
margarine

1 egg, beaten

⅓ cup milk

1 cup crumbled feta cheese

⅛ teaspoon ground red pepper

1 large tomato, chopped (about
1 cup)

¼ cup pitted ripe olives cut into
halves

¼ cup toasted, slivered pine
nuts or almonds

1 tablespoon lemon juice

1 tablespoon snipped fresh
parsley

⅛ teaspoon ground black
pepper

In a large skillet, cook the fish in the butter or margarine over medium-
high heat for 3 minutes per side. Transfer the steaks to a greased 11" × 7"
baking dish.

In a small bowl, combine the egg and milk. Stir in the cheese and red
pepper and spoon over the halibut. Sprinkle with the tomatoes, olives and
pine nuts or almonds. Bake in a preheated 400° oven for 10 minutes, or
until the fish flakes easily when tested with a fork. Sprinkle with the lemon
juice, parsley and pepper and serve.

Serves 4.

Doorway to Healthy Eating
Trinity Church on the Green: Episcopal Church Women, Branford, Connecticut

GRILLED SALMON STEAKS

For an elegant dinner party or extra-special occasion,
serve these beautiful salmon steaks grilled to golden-brown perfection.
A light pasta (without a heavy sauce) and a lightly dressed,
crisp green salad will round out the meal.

4 **salmon steaks, ³⁄₄" thick
(1¹⁄₂ – 2 pounds total)**
¹⁄₄ **cup plus 2 tablespoons dry
vermouth**
¹⁄₄ **cup plus 2 tablespoons oil**
2 **teaspoons lemon juice**
¹⁄₂ **teaspoon salt**

Pinch of ground black pepper
¹⁄₈ **teaspoon dried thyme**
¹⁄₈ **teaspoon dried marjoram**
Pinch of dried sage
2 **teaspoons finely chopped
fresh parsley**

Place the steaks in a large nonreactive pan. In a small bowl, mix the vermouth, oil, lemon juice, salt, pepper, thyme, marjoram, sage and parsley
and pour over the salmon. Let stand for 3 to 4 hours in the refrigerator,
turning once.

Remove the dish from the refrigerator and place on a greased broiler
rack, reserving the marinade. In a preheated broiler, cook the fish until
browned, turn carefully and brown the other side. Cook for a total of about
15 minutes, or until fork-tender, brushing frequently with the marinade.

Serves 4.

The Civic Women's Guilford Sampler
Guilford Civic Women, Guilford, Connecticut

WHOLE ROAST SALMON WITH PARSLEY-DILL SAUCE

The sauce must be made several hours in advance so that the flavors have time to mingle. It can be lightened slightly by substituting ½ cup nonfat plain yogurt for ½ cup of the mayonnaise. When ready to serve the fish, surround it with fresh peas and boiled new potatoes.

SAUCE

- 1½ cups mayonnaise
- 3 tablespoons chopped fresh parsley
- 3 tablespoons chopped fresh dill
- 1 tablespoon lemon juice
- 2 sweet gherkins, minced
- ½ teaspoon ground white pepper

SALMON

- 1 salmon (6 pounds), cleaned, with head and tail still on
- ¼ cup olive oil
  Handful of fresh herbs such as dill, parsley or fennel, with stems
- 2 onions, thinly sliced
- 2 lemons, thinly sliced
- 2 cups white wine
- 1 tablespoon black peppercorns

To make the sauce: Combine the mayonnaise, parsley, dill, lemon juice, gherkins and white pepper in a nonreactive bowl and mix well. Cover and refrigerate for several hours until ready to use.

To make the salmon: Rinse the salmon inside and out and pat dry. Rub it all over with the oil and place in a well-oiled roasting pan. Stuff the cavity with the herbs, half of the onions and half of the lemon slices. Arrange the remaining onions and lemons on top. Pour the wine over the fish and sprinkle the peppercorns in the pan.

Measure the thickness of the fish at its thickest part and bake in a preheated 400° oven for 8 to 10 minutes per inch, basting occasionally with the pan juices. Transfer to a large oval platter, garnish with more herbs and serve with the sauce on the side

Serves 6.

Mystic Seaport's Seafood Secrets Cookbook
Mystic Seaport Museum Stores, Mystic, Connecticut

BAY SCALLOPS WITH VEGETABLES

Both sea scallops and bay scallops are found off the coast of New England. Of the two, bay scallops are generally smaller and sweeter.

3 tablespoons butter or margarine, divided
1 tablespoon olive oil
2 cups cubed zucchini
2 teaspoons finely minced garlic

1½ cups peeled, seeded and cubed tomatoes
2 tablespoons Pernod
1½ pounds bay scallops
¼ cup finely chopped fresh parsley
Salt and pepper

Heat 1 tablespoon of the butter or margarine and the oil in a large, fairly deep skillet or casserole and add the zucchini. Cook, stirring, for 1 minute, then add the garlic. Stir and add the tomatoes. Continue cooking, stirring often, for 2 minutes. Sprinkle with Pernod and stir. Mix in the scallops, parsley, remaining 2 tablespoons butter or margarine and salt and pepper to taste. Let simmer for 2 to 3 minutes and serve immediately.

Serves 4.

A Taste of New England
Junior League of Worcester, Massachusetts

BROILED SEA SCALLOPS

This dish has a sophisticated taste and appearance.
Serve it with a green salad, linguine (or pasta of choice) and plenty of
French or Italian bread to soak up every drop of the heavenly sauce.

½ **cup dry vermouth**
2 **tablespoons chopped fresh**
 parsley
1 **tablespoon oil**
1 **clove garlic, crushed**
½ **teaspoon salt**

1 **pound sea scallops, cut into**
 bite-size pieces
½ **cup fresh bread crumbs**
1 **tablespoon butter or**
 margarine, melted
 Paprika

In a medium bowl, mix the vermouth, parsley, oil, garlic and salt. Add
the scallops and stir. Marinate for 1 hour in the refrigerator.

Preheat the broiler. Toss the bread crumbs in the butter or margarine.
Spoon the scallops and marinade into a shallow dish or 4 ramekins. Place
2" from the broiler and broil for 3 minutes. Turn over the scallops, sprinkle
on the buttered bread crumbs and paprika and broil for 3 minutes more.

Serves 4.

Divine Cooking
St. Giles' Church: Episcopal Church Women, Jefferson, Maine

SHRIMP & FETA CHEESE CASSEROLE

When the shrimp are added to the casserole,
try to arrange them in an orderly fashion so that they will be
easy to remove and serve as described below with rice.

Juice of 1 lemon
2 pounds shrimp, peeled and deveined
2 bunches scallions, finely chopped
1 clove garlic, minced
1 stalk celery, finely chopped
2 tablespoons chopped fresh parsley
1 can (16 ounces) whole tomatoes

1 tablespoon olive oil
1 cup bottled clam juice
1 tablespoon butter or margarine
1 large tomato, peeled and cored
Salt and pepper
1 teaspoon dried oregano
½ cup white wine
½ pound feta cheese, crumbled

In a large bowl, pour the lemon juice over the shrimp, toss to combine and set aside.

In a skillet, sauté the scallions, garlic, celery, parsley and canned tomatoes in the oil until the scallions and celery are tender. Reduce the heat and simmer for about 30 minutes. Add the clam juice, cook for 5 minutes more and remove from the heat.

In another skillet, sauté the shrimp in the butter or margarine until pink. Pour the tomato mixture into the bottom of a casserole, place the whole tomato in the center, surround it with the shrimp and sprinkle the entire casserole with salt and pepper to taste and the oregano. Pour the white wine around the shrimp and sprinkle the cheese over the shrimp and into the tomato center. Bake in a preheated 400° oven for 15 minutes, or until the cheese melts.

To serve, remove the shrimp carefully with a spatula so that the cheese stays intact. Cut the tomato into sixths or eighths to garnish each serving.

Serves 6 to 8.

The Mark Twain Library Cookbook, Vol. III
Mark Twain Library Association, Redding, Connecticut

SHRIMP SCAMPI

Large shrimp are necessary for this rich dish. When buying shrimp, check to make sure they are still firm to the touch and have no offensive ammonia smell. To peel a shrimp, hold it between your thumb and forefinger and with the other hand pull off the feelers and then the entire shell. Remove the tail end with your fingers. Use a small, sharp knife to make a shallow cut along the back of the shrimp to expose the dark vein. While holding the shrimp under running water, scrape away and discard the vein. Place the shrimp on paper towels and pat dry before using.

2 **scallions, minced**	1 **tablespoon olive oil**
1–2 **cloves garlic, minced**	2 **teaspoons lemon juice**
2 **tablespoons minced fresh parsley**	½ **teaspoon salt**
1 **tablespoon butter or margarine, melted**	1¼ **pounds large shrimp, shelled and deveined**
	Lemon wedges

About 20 minutes before serving, preheat the broiler. In a broiler pan, combine the scallions, garlic, parsley, butter or margarine, oil, lemon juice and salt. Place the shrimp in the pan, turning to coat with the mixture on all sides. Arrange in a single layer. Broil, turning once, for 5 to 8 minutes, or until the shrimp are opaque and curled. Serve with the pan juices and garnish with lemon wedges.

Serves 4.

Smith Neck Friends Meeting Cookbook
Smith Neck Friends Meeting of Dartmouth Monthly Meeting,
South Dartmouth, Massachusetts

How to Cook a Lobster
The Cape Cod Way

꙳

Steaming rather than boiling is the method of choice when cooking lobsters, as steaming appears to enhance the flavor. As one Chatham fisherman said, "You only want to cook 'em, not drown 'em."

Lobsters, 1–1½ pounds each **Melted butter or margarine**
(1 per person) **Lemon wedges**
2 **teaspoons salt**

Boil about 3″ of water in a large kettle. Add the salt, then plunge the lobsters into the water headfirst and cover the kettle. Rapidly bring back to the steaming point and begin timing: 17 minutes for 1 pounders, 18 to 20 minutes for 1¼ to 1½ pounders.

Remove the lobsters from the water and place each on its back. Using a heavy knife, cut from head to tip of tail. Spread open and remove the intestinal vein and small sac just below the head. Crack the large claws. Serve with a small dish of melted butter or margarine and lemon wedges.

Serves as many people as there are lobsters.

Cape Cod Kitchen Secrets
Cape Cod Hospital Auxiliary, Chatham, Massachusetts

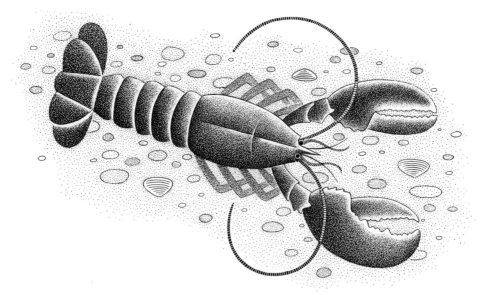

LOBSTER QUICHE

Although many recipes suggest using a partially baked pie shell for quiche, it really isn't necessary. What is important is to let the quiche sit for a while before cutting it into servings. When it has a lobster filling, such a recommendation may be absolutely impossible to follow.

Pastry for single-crust 9" pie
2 tablespoons finely chopped onions
2 teaspoons butter or margarine
1¼ cups diced cooked lobster
1 tablespoon chopped fresh dill

4 eggs, lightly beaten
2 tablespoons dry white wine
½ teaspoon salt
¼ teaspoon ground white pepper
1½ cups light cream, scalded

Line a 9" pie pan with the pastry and flute the edges.

In a small skillet, sauté the onions in the butter or margarine until tender, then spread in the bottom of the pie shell. Distribute the lobster over the onions and sprinkle with the dill.

In a small bowl, combine the eggs, wine, salt and white pepper. Slowly stir in the cream, mixing well. Pour over the lobster in the pie shell and bake in a preheated 375° oven for 25 to 30 minutes, or until a knife inserted in the center comes out clean.

Serves 6 to 8.

Cape Cod Kitchen Secrets
Cape Cod Hospital Auxiliary, Chatham, Massachusetts

KENNEBUNKPORT CRABMEAT SOUFFLÉ

*This is crunchy on top and light and fluffy inside,
and it has just the right amount of crabmeat.*

8 slices white bread, trimmed
and diced, divided
2 cups crabmeat
1 medium onion, finely diced
1 cup finely diced celery
1 medium green bell pepper,
finely diced

1½ cups shredded Cheddar
cheese, divided
2 cups milk
4 eggs, beaten
½ cup mayonnaise

Put half the bread in a greased 13" × 9" casserole. In a bowl, combine the
crabmeat, onions, celery, bell peppers, 1¼ cups of the cheese, milk, eggs
and mayonnaise. Mix well and pour over the bread. Cover with the remaining bread and sprinkle with the remaining ¼ cup cheese. Bake in a preheated
350° oven for 1 hour.

Serves 6 to 8.

Portland Symphony Cookbook
Portland Symphony Orchestra Women's Committee, Portland, Maine

CRAB CAKES WITH BASIL TARTAR SAUCE
❧

Whether they are served as an evening entrée, a summer lunch on the porch or an appetizer for a party, these golden-brown cakes will be a big hit. The sauce is an important part of the dish, and fresh basil is a must.

CRAB CAKES
- 1 egg
- 1 egg yolk
- 4½ teaspoons heavy cream
- 1 teaspoon lemon juice
- ½ teaspoon ground red pepper
- ½ teaspoon dry mustard
- ½ teaspoon Worcestershire sauce
- ¼ teaspoon salt
- ¼ teaspoon ground black pepper
- 1 pound crabmeat
- 2 tablespoons chopped scallions
- 2 tablespoons chopped fresh parsley

- 2 tablespoons cracker crumbs
- ¼ cup dry bread crumbs
- 2 tablespoons butter or margarine, melted

SAUCE
- ½ cup packed fresh basil leaves
- ½ cup mayonnaise
- 1 tablespoon sour cream or plain yogurt
- 1 teaspoon lemon juice
- 1 teaspoon minced garlic
- ⅛ teaspoon salt
- Pinch of ground red pepper
- Dash of hot-pepper sauce

To make the crab cakes: In a medium bowl, whisk the egg, egg yolk, cream, lemon juice, red pepper, mustard, Worcestershire sauce, salt and black pepper until well blended. Add the crabmeat, scallions, parsley and cracker crumbs and mix well. Divide the mixture into 8 equal portions and shape into patties (mixture will be crumbly). Sprinkle the bread crumbs on both sides of each patty and place in a greased ovenproof serving dish. Drizzle the butter or margarine on top, cover and refrigerate for 1 hour.

Adjust the oven rack to its highest position and preheat the oven to 475°. Bake the crab cakes for 10 minutes, or until lightly browned.

To make the sauce: While the crab cakes are baking, rinse the basil under very hot water, then pat dry. Place in a food processor or blender along with the mayonnaise, sour cream or yogurt, lemon juice, garlic, salt, red pepper and hot-pepper sauce. Puree until thoroughly blended. Serve with the crab cakes.

Serves 4.

Saint Gabriel's Horn of Plenty
Saint Gabriel's Episcopal Church, Marion, Massachusetts

OYSTER-NOODLE CASSEROLE
※

Oysters are most flavorful in the fall and winter, so the
old saying that they should be eaten only in those months that
have the letter *r* in their names is a pretty reliable rule of thumb.

1 **pint oysters**	3 **tablespoons flour**
3 **tablespoons butter or**	1¼ **cups milk**
margarine	**Salt and pepper**
3 **tablespoons finely chopped**	1½ **cups cooked noodles**
onions	½ **cup fresh bread crumbs**
2 **tablespoons minced green bell**	1 **tablespoon butter or**
peppers	**margarine, melted**

Drain the oysters and reserve their liquor. Melt the 3 tablespoons butter
or margarine in a saucepan and sauté the onions and bell peppers until the
onions wilt. Whisk in the flour. When blended, add the milk and stir vigorously. When the mixture is smooth and thickened, stir in the oyster liquor
and salt and pepper to taste.

Butter a 1½-quart casserole and add half the noodles. Cover with the
oysters, season with salt and pepper to taste and add the remaining noodles. Pour the sauce over all. Combine the bread crumbs and melted butter
and sprinkle on top. Bake in a preheated 350° oven for 30 minutes, or until
browned and bubbly.

Serves 4.

Cape Cod Kitchen Secrets
Cape Cod Hospital Auxiliary, Chatham, Massachusetts

$\mathcal{S}$CALLOPED OYSTERS

This dish is very delicate in texture—like a soufflé. Let it sit for about 5 minutes after removing it from the oven so it will be easier to serve. Oyster lovers may want to increase the amount to 1½ or 2 pints.

1 **pint oysters**	3 **tablespoons butter or**
1 **cup cracker crumbs**	**margarine, melted**
½ **cup dry bread crumbs**	**Salt and pepper**
	2 **cups milk or cream, divided**

Drain the oysters and reserve their liquor. Mix the cracker crumbs and bread crumbs and stir in the butter or margarine. Spread a thin layer of crumbs in the bottom of a buttered shallow baking dish and cover with half the oysters. Sprinkle with salt and pepper to taste and 2 tablespoons of the reserved oyster liquor. Pour 1 cup of the milk or cream over all. Layer the remaining oysters, oyster liquor, salt and pepper and milk or cream and cover with the remaining crumbs. Bake in a preheated 400° oven for about 25 to 30 minutes.

Serves 4.

Bulfinch's Boston Faire
Doric Dames, Boston, Massachusetts

$\mathcal{S}$QUID WITH LEEKS & RED WINE

When buying fresh squid, select those that are ivory in color and have small dark blue spots on their translucent skin. Avoid any that have a strong chlorine smell. Serve this dish over rice or pasta and accompany it with French or Italian bread to sop up the flavorful broth.

1	pound squid, cleaned	2	teaspoons unbleached flour
2	tablespoons olive oil, divided	½	tablespoon chopped fresh
	Salt and pepper		parsley
1	cup red wine (approximately)	½	teaspoon dried thyme
1	tomato, chopped	1	bay leaf
2	leeks, chopped		Several strips of orange rind
2	cloves garlic, minced		

Slice the squid into 1″ rings. Heat 1 tablespoon of the oil in a skillet and sauté the squid. Season with salt and pepper to taste. Deglaze the skillet with the red wine and remove from the heat.

In a separate pan, heat the remaining 1 tablespoon oil and sauté the tomatoes, leeks and garlic until tender. Add salt and pepper to taste. Combine the squid and wine with the tomato mixture and stir in the flour. Pour in enough additional wine and water to barely cover the ingredients. Stir in the parsley, thyme, bay leaf and orange rind, cover and simmer until the squid is tender, about 30 to 40 minutes.

Serves 4.

350th Guilford, Connecticut, Birthday Cook Book
Leete's Island Garden Club, Guilford, Connecticut

MUSSELS & PASTA IN RED SAUCE

Mussels are nutritious, inexpensive and easy to prepare. Debearding them is simple, too. Rinse them under running water, then pull off the small tuft of hair, called the beard, which is attached to each one.

20–30 **mussels, scrubbed and debearded**

4 or 5 **fresh or canned plum tomatoes, crushed**

½ **cup chopped fresh parsley**

3–4 **cloves garlic, finely chopped**

¼ **cup olive oil**

1 **pound linguine or spaghetti**

1 **teaspoon salt (optional) Chopped fresh parsley for garnish**

In a large, heavy pot, mix the mussels, tomatoes, ½ cup parsley, garlic and oil. Cover and cook over medium heat until the mussels open, then cook for 5 to 10 minutes more. Remove the mussels from the pot to a serving platter and keep warm. Cook the sauce, uncovered, over low heat for 6 minutes.

Meanwhile, in a separate pot, cook the linguine or spaghetti until just tender and drain. Transfer the mussels to the pot with the sauce, add the salt (if using) and combine. Transfer the pasta to a serving platter and pour the sauce and mussels on top. Garnish with parsley.

Serves 4.

History in the Baking
Sunapee 2000 Beautification Committee, Sunapee, New Hampshire

CLAMBURGER SPECIAL
❦

If you are digging your own clams for this recipe, wash them
well with seawater and place them in a pail. Cover them with fresh
seawater and let them stand for 10 to 15 minutes to allow the clams to
cleanse themselves of sand, which will settle to the bottom. Then carefully
remove the clams without disturbing the sand. Serve these burgers on
toasted rolls with sliced tomatoes, lettuce and tartar sauce.

1 **pint clams, finely chopped**	½ **teaspoon salt**
1 **cup cracker crumbs**	¼ **teaspoon ground black**
1 **egg, well beaten**	**pepper**
½ **teaspoon dried parsley**	2 **tablespoons oil**

In a medium bowl, mix the clams, cracker crumbs, egg, parsley, salt and
pepper. Refrigerate for 30 minutes.

Form the mixture into 3″ round cakes. Heat the oil in a large skillet and
fry the cakes for 2 minutes per side, or until crisp. Drain on paper towels.

Serves 4 to 6.

Mystic Seaport's Seafood Secrets Cookbook
Mystic Seaport Museum Stores, Mystic, Connecticut

CAPE COD CLAMBAKE
❦

Here's how to put on a traditional Cape Cod clambake.
When buying lobsters and broiler-fryers, all should be of a uniform
size for uniform baking—no larger than 1 to 1½ pounds.

Lobsters	**Oysters**
Corn (with husks)	**Mussels**
Broiler-fryer chickens	**Melted butter or margarine**
Fish of choice	**Salt**
Clams	

To prepare the baking area: Make a round bed of stones on the ground, using field or beach rock or any type of stones available. The best size stone is about as large as a cabbage. Cover an area about a yard in diameter, and pile the stones about a foot high. Stack firewood on top, set afire and keep feeding the fire steadily, letting it burn for at least 4 hours.

Rake away all the charred wood and embers, leaving just the heated stones, then cover with a heavy layer (6" to 8") of rockweed or seaweed.

To prepare the food to be cooked: Take a large square of cheesecloth, lay 3 or 4 lobsters side by side and tie and knot the 4 corners together. This makes it easy to remove the bundle from the hot seaweed later.

Corn should be stripped to the last two layers of husk. Put 3 or 4 ears to a bundle, using the same method as for the lobsters.

Cut the chicken so that it lies flat and tie it in a bundle in the same way as the lobsters. Tie the fish in a bundle, too. If clams, oysters or mussels are to be baked, wash them well in seawater to remove all the sand or mud but do not tie them in a bundle.

To arrange the food: Leave a space in the center of the seaweed and arrange the food in a circular fashion for an attractive bake. Start the inner circle with alternate bundles of corn and lobsters, side by side. Use the same circle arrangement for the broiler-fryers and fish. Last, on the outer edges (where the heat is less intense), place the clams, oysters or mussels.

Cover everything with a 4" to 6" layer of seaweed. Cover the entire pile with a piece of canvas large enough to extend over the ground and be fastened down tightly by placing rocks around the edges. This is important to prevent any steam from escaping.

Allow a full 45 minutes for baking. Remove the canvas and top layer of seaweed. The bake will be very colorful and picturesque if foods have been artfully placed. The rich red lobster set off by the alternate bundles of light green corn combine with the fringe of white shellfish to charm the eye and elicit the admiration of waiting guests. The luscious fragrance that wafts through the air as the bake is "undone" is certain to linger long in the memory of all seafood gourmets.

Clams can be raked off the edges into small wooden bowls or sturdy paper plates. Keep a can of melted butter or margarine near the hot rocks and small paper cups for individual helpings. Several tin saltshakers also should be provided.

Serves a crowd.

Cape Cod Kitchen Secrets
Cape Cod Hospital Auxiliary, Chatham, Massachusetts

$\mathcal{E}$D'S BAKED STUFFED QUAHOGS

These will be clamored (!) for, whether they are
presented as a main course or an appetizer.

1 tablespoon butter or oil
1 medium onion, chopped
1 pound quahogs, minced
2 medium potatoes, boiled and
  mashed
2 bottles (8 ounces each) clam
  juice (approximately)

1½ cups dry bread crumbs
  (approximately)
  Seasonings such as ground
  black pepper, ground red
  pepper and celery salt
  Paprika
  Bacon strips (optional)

Heat the butter or oil in a skillet and sauté the onions until golden. In
a large bowl, mix the quahogs, onions, potatoes, clam juice and bread
crumbs. Season to taste. The consistency of the mixture should be very
moist but not soupy. If it is too dry, add more clam juice; if too wet, add
more crumbs.

Lightly oil 16 scallop shells, fill with the clam mixture and sprinkle with
paprika. (If shells are not available, cook as a loaf or fill greased muffin
cups.)

Place a small piece of bacon (if using) on top of the stuffing. Bake in a
preheated 450° oven for 30 minutes, or until the center is cooked.

Serves 4.

Our Saviour's Parish 65th Anniversary Cookbook
Our Saviour's Parish School of Christian Living, Woonsocket, Rhode Island

SEAFOOD LASAGNA

Easy yet somewhat time-consuming, this dish is a tradition in households all along the New England coast.

1 can (28 ounces) whole tomatoes	3 eggs
½ cup diced onions	1 pound ricotta cheese
2 cloves garlic, minced	2 tablespoons grated Parmesan cheese
3 tablespoons olive oil, divided	1 pound lasagna, cooked according to package directions and drained, divided
1½ pounds haddock, cusk or pollack fillets	
Salt and pepper	
1 can (6 ounces) tomato paste	1½ cups shredded provolone cheese, divided
1 pound shrimp, peeled and deveined	

Blend the tomatoes in a blender or food processor, then strain to remove the seeds.

In a large saucepan, sauté the onions and garlic in 2 tablespoons of the oil. Add the fish and salt and pepper to taste. Cover the pan and simmer, stirring occasionally, until the fish flakes easily, about 7 to 10 minutes.

Add the tomatoes, bring to a boil, lower the heat, cover and simmer for 5 minutes. Add the tomato paste and simmer, uncovered, for 10 minutes, stirring occasionally.

Meanwhile, in a medium skillet, heat the remaining 1 tablespoon oil. Add the shrimp and cook lightly until they curl. Strain and add to the fish sauce. (If the shrimp are large, cut them into bite-size pieces before adding.)

Beat the eggs in a medium bowl, add the ricotta and Parmesan cheeses and season with pepper to taste. Mix well.

Pour about ¼ of the fish sauce into a 15" × 11" lasagna pan and cover with ⅓ of the lasagna. Dot with about ⅓ of the cheese mixture and sprinkle with ⅓ of the provolone. Continue to layer the fish sauce, lasagna and cheeses until you have 3 layers of each. Top with the remaining sauce, cover with foil and bake in a preheated 350° oven for 30 minutes.

Serves 10 to 12.

The Taste of Gloucester
The Fishermen's Wives of Gloucester and The Cape Ann League of Women Voters, Gloucester, Massachusetts

SEAFOOD PIE

Because this pie is so rich and filling,
it's ideal cut into small portions for a buffet.

2 cups chicken stock
1 dozen oysters
½ pound scallops
1 cod fillet (½-pound)
¼ cup butter or margarine
1 small onion, finely minced
1 tender stalk celery, finely minced

¼ cup unbleached flour
1 cup diced cooked lobster
¼ cup dry sherry
Salt and pepper
Pastry for double-crust 10" pie

In a large pot, bring the stock to a boil. Add the oysters, scallops and cod, lower the heat and cook for 4 to 5 minutes, or until the oysters curl at the edges and the fish flakes easily with a fork. Separate the fish into bite-size pieces as it cooks. Do not overcook. Using a slotted spoon, transfer the fish and shellfish to a bowl, reserving the stock.

Melt the butter or margarine in a saucepan over medium heat. Add the onions and celery and cook until soft, but do not brown. Stir in the flour and cook for about 1 minute. Add the reserved stock and cook, stirring, until thickened. Carefully fold in the lobster, scallops, cod, oysters and sherry. Season with salt and pepper to taste and set aside to cool.

Line a deep-dish 10" pie plate with half the pastry. Pour in the seafood mixture. Cut three small fish shapes from the top crust for vents and reserve the cutouts. Place the top crust on the pie and seal and crimp the edges. Dampen the underside of the fish cutouts with water and place between the vents on the top crust. Bake in the center of a preheated 375° oven for about 30 to 35 minutes, or until golden brown.

Serves 6 to 8.

Flavors of Cape Cod
Thornton W. Burgess Society, East Sandwich, Massachusetts

SEAFOOD VERMICELLI

*The choice of seafood can be varied here
depending on what is available in the market.*

2 tablespoons olive oil	1/2 teaspoon salt
1 large onion, chopped	1/8 teaspoon ground black
1 large green bell pepper, diced	pepper
2 cloves garlic, minced	1/2 pound shrimp, peeled and
1 can (16 ounces) crushed	deveined
tomatoes	1/2 pound sea scallops
1 can (8 ounces) tomato sauce	1/2 pound monkfish or halibut,
1 can (6 ounces) tomato paste	cut into 1 1/2" chunks
3/4 cup white wine	1 dozen littleneck clams,
1/4 cup dry vermouth (optional)	scrubbed
1/2 cup chopped fresh parsley	1 pound vermicelli, cooked and
1 teaspoon dried oregano	drained

Heat the oil in a large saucepan and add the onions, bell peppers and
garlic. Cook over medium heat for 2 to 3 minutes. Add the tomatoes,
tomato sauce, tomato paste, wine, vermouth (if using), parsley, oregano,
salt and pepper. Bring to a boil, lower the heat and simmer, covered, for
30 minutes.

Add the shrimp, scallops, monkfish or halibut and clams and cook for
about 10 minutes, or until the clams open. Serve immediately over the
vermicelli.

Serves 6.

Off the Hook
The Junior League of Stamford-Norwalk, Darien, Connecticut

VEGETARIAN

NO-CRUST CHEESE & SPINACH PIE

Delicious and substantial, this meal-in-a-dish travels well
and is a fine contribution to a potluck supper.

1   package (10 ounces) frozen
    chopped spinach, cooked and
    well drained
1   cup shredded mozzarella or
    Cheddar cheese or 1 cup
    crumbled feta cheese, or a
    combination
3   eggs, lightly beaten
2   tablespoons oil
½   teaspoon onion salt
½   teaspoon garlic salt
½   teaspoon ground black
    pepper

1   cup sliced zucchini, sautéed
    in a small amount of oil
    (optional)
1   cup sliced mushrooms,
    sautéed in a small amount of
    oil (optional)
½   cup diced green bell peppers,
    sautéed in a small amount of
    oil (optional)
1   tablespoon butter or
    margarine

Combine the spinach, cheese, eggs, oil, onion salt, garlic salt and pepper.
Add the zucchini, mushrooms and bell peppers (if using). Pour into a deep,
lightly oiled 9" pie plate and dot with the butter or margarine. Bake in a
preheated 350° oven for 40 minutes, or until a knife inserted in the center
comes out clean.

Serves 6 to 8.

The Fine Arts Cookbook II
Museum of Fine Arts, Boston, Massachusetts

$\mathcal{Y}$UMMY ZUCCHINI-MUSHROOM PIE

When they are overrunning the garden, it's hard to acknowledge the virtues of zucchini—the vegetable we all love to hate. Combined as it is here with mushrooms and onions and baked in a flaky crust, this prolific vegetable will be well received for brunch, lunch or supper.

2 tablespoons butter or margarine	½ teaspoon salt
1 cup chopped onions	¼ teaspoon ground black pepper
1 package (12 ounces) mushrooms, sliced	2 cups shredded Swiss cheese
¾ pound zucchini, thinly sliced	Pastry for double-crust 9" pie
2 tablespoons unbleached flour	1 egg yolk, lightly beaten with 3 tablespoons water
½ teaspoon dried thyme	

In a large pan, melt the butter or margarine and sauté the onions, mushrooms and zucchini for 5 minutes. Drain. Add the flour, thyme, salt and pepper and stir. Set aside to cool a bit.

Line a 9" pie plate with ½ of the pastry. Mix the cheese with the vegetables and pour into the pastry shell. Cover with the top crust and prick with a fork. Brush the egg wash over the top and bake in a preheated 375° oven for 45 minutes.

Serves 4 to 6.

Poker Hill Cookbook
Poker Hill School, Underhill, Vermont

CAULIFLOWER-CHEESE PIE

❧

This recipe has a lot of steps, but it is not at all difficult. The cauliflower is cooked to perfection—tender, not mushy—and the layers of cheese and browned potato crust complement the flavor and texture. This vegetarian entrée also could be served as a side dish with meat, poultry or fish.

CRUST
- 2 cups packed grated potatoes
- ½ teaspoon salt
- 1 egg, beaten
- ¼ cup grated onions

FILLING
- 1 cup chopped onions
- 1 clove garlic, crushed
- 3 tablespoons butter or margarine

- 1 medium cauliflower, broken into small florets
- ½ teaspoon dried basil
- ½ teaspoon salt
- Ground black pepper
- Pinch of dried thyme
- 1 cup packed shredded low-fat Cheddar cheese, divided
- 2 eggs, beaten
- ¼ cup milk
- Paprika

To make the crust: Set the freshly grated potatoes in a colander over a bowl. Add the salt and let sit for 10 minutes, then press out the excess water (which can be reserved to use for soup stock or bread). Mix the potatoes with the egg and onions and pat onto the bottom and up the sides of a well-oiled 9″ pie plate. Bake in a preheated 350° oven for 40 minutes, or until browned. After the first 30 minutes, brush the crust with a little oil to crispen it.

To make the filling: In a skillet, sauté the onions and garlic in the butter or margarine for 3 minutes. Add the cauliflower, basil, salt, pepper to taste and thyme. Cook, covered, over medium-low heat for about 10 minutes, stirring occasionally.

Spread half the cheese in the baked crust, add the sautéed vegetables and top with the rest of the cheese. Beat the eggs and milk together and pour over all. Sprinkle the top with paprika and bake for 30 minutes, or until a knife inserted in the center comes out clean.

Serves 4 to 6.

The Kinderhaus Cookbook
Kinderhaus Children's Center, Williston, Vermont

SPINACH-YOGURT QUICHE

This quiche does not use cream, which reduces not only the fat content but also the cost of the dish. Serve it warm or at room temperature.

Pastry for single-crust 9" pie
1 **tablespoon oil**
1 **medium onion, chopped**
½ **cup sliced fresh mushrooms (optional)**
1 **cup shredded sharp Cheddar cheese**
2 **eggs, beaten**
1 **package (10 ounces) frozen chopped spinach, thawed and pressed to remove excess water**

1 **cup plain yogurt**
1 **teaspoon unbleached flour**
¼ **teaspoon salt**
¼ **teaspoon ground black pepper**
¼ **teaspoon ground nutmeg**
  Paprika

Line a 9" pie plate with the pastry. In a skillet, heat the oil and sauté the onions and mushrooms (if using) until tender. Spread over the bottom of the pie shell, then sprinkle with the cheese. In a medium bowl, combine the eggs, spinach, yogurt, flour, salt, pepper and nutmeg and pour over the onions and cheese. Sprinkle the top with paprika and bake in a preheated 350° oven for 45 to 60 minutes, or until a knife inserted in the center comes out clean.

Serves 6.

The Vermont Symphony Cookbook
Vermont Symphony Orchestra, Burlington, Vermont

WINTER SQUASH QUICHE

Those who favor more onion flavor may want to
increase the amount called for, but the quantity of nutmeg
should not be altered. It's just the right amount.

Pastry for single-crust 9″ pie
1 **tablespoon butter or margarine**
3 **tablespoons chopped onions**
1 **cup shredded Swiss cheese**
3 **eggs, beaten**

1½ **cups milk**
1 **cup mashed cooked squash**
½ **teaspoon salt**
 Ground black pepper
⅛ **teaspoon ground nutmeg**

Line a 9″ pie plate with the pastry. Melt the butter or margarine in a
small skillet and sauté the onions until tender. Scatter the onions and
cheese over the bottom of the pie shell. In a bowl, combine the eggs, milk,
squash, salt, pepper to taste and nutmeg. Pour into the pie shell, covering
the cheese and onions. Bake in a preheated 375° oven for 45 minutes, or
until a knife inserted in the center comes out clean.

Serves 6.

Sullivan Sampler
United Congregational Church, Sullivan, New Hampshire

Hometown Cooking in New England

$\mathcal{S}$TUFFED SQUASH

Although substantial enough to serve as a main dish,
this also is suitable as an accompaniment to meat or chicken.
The initial baking time for the squash depends on the kind used.
Test it with a fork, and when it is almost done, remove it from the
oven and fill it with the stuffing, mounding the stuffing above the
surface of the squash. Then proceed with the final baking.

2 **large acorn or butternut squash**	2 **cups low-fat cottage cheese**
2 **medium apples, peeled, cored and cut into chunks**	¾ **cup shredded Cheddar cheese**
½ **cup chopped onions**	½ **cup toasted chopped walnuts or a handful of raisins**
1 **tablespoon butter or oil**	1 **teaspoon lemon juice**
	½ **teaspoon ground cinnamon**

Split the squash in half lengthwise. Remove the seeds and bake, cut side down, on an oiled baking sheet in a 350° for 30 to 50 minutes.

Meanwhile, in a skillet, sauté the apples and onions in the butter or oil until the onions are tender. In a medium bowl, combine the apples and onions with the cottage cheese, Cheddar cheese, walnuts or raisins, lemon juice and cinnamon. Stuff the squash and bake, covered, for 15 to 20 minutes more, or until the stuffing is heated through and the squash is tender.

Serves 4.

The Morrison House Museum Cookbook
Londonderry Historical Society, Londonderry, New Hampshire

$\mathcal{S}$QUASH LISA

This unusual combination of ingredients is absolutely wonderful. Sage is the perfect herb to use with the squash and cheese. If you can't find butternut, another kind of winter squash, such as acorn or Hubbard, may be used.

1 medium butternut squash	1½ cups dry bread crumbs
3 tablespoons butter or margarine, divided	½ teaspoon salt
¾ cup shredded mozzarella cheese	¼ teaspoon ground black pepper
2 medium onions, diced	½ teaspoon dried sage

Peel the squash, cut into pieces and steam or boil until tender. Mash with 1 tablespoon of the butter or margarine. (Makes about 3 cups squash.) Spread the squash evenly over the bottom of a 9″ × 9″ casserole. Sprinkle the cheese evenly over the squash.

In a large skillet, sauté the onions in the remaining 2 tablespoons butter or margarine. Add the bread crumbs, salt, pepper and sage and stir to combine. Spread the crumb mixture over the cheese and squash and bake in a preheated 325° oven for 35 minutes.

Serves 6.

Portland Symphony Cookbook
Portland Symphony Orchestra Women's Committee, Portland, Maine

APPLES, NOODLES & CHEESE CASSEROLE

After a day of leaf peeping and apple picking,
this dish hits the spot and gives you an immediate use
for the apples and Cheddar cheese you just bought.

6 ounces noodles	**2 cups peeled, cored and diced apples**
½ cup shredded Cheddar cheese	**¼ cup firmly packed dark brown sugar**
2 tablespoons butter or margarine	**¼ teaspoon ground mace**

Cook the noodles in 3 quarts boiling salted water for about 3 minutes. Drain, then pour into a greased 1½- to 2-quart casserole. Add the cheese and butter or margarine and stir until melted. Add the apples, brown sugar and mace and stir to blend. Bake, covered, in a preheated 350° oven for 35 minutes. Remove the cover and bake for 15 minutes more.

Serves 4.

Poker Hill Cookbook
Poker Hill School, Underhill, Vermont

$\mathcal{B}$AKED POTATO & ZUCCHINI CASSEROLE

A tasty combination of vegetables, this casserole is hearty
enough to be the centerpiece for Sunday supper.

3 **medium zucchini**	1 **can (8 ounces) tomato sauce**
3 **medium potatoes**	½ **cup chopped fresh parsley**
4 **tablespoons oil, divided**	½ **teaspoon dried basil**
2 **medium onions, chopped**	½ **teaspoon dried oregano**
2 **cloves garlic, minced**	**Salt and pepper**

Cut the zucchini lengthwise into ¼"-thick strips. Peel the potatoes and
cut into similar strips.

Heat 2 tablespoons of the oil in a skillet and cook the onions and garlic
until soft, stirring frequently. Add the tomato sauce, parsley, basil, oregano
and salt and pepper to taste. Simmer for 5 minutes.

Grease a 4-quart casserole and add the potatoes and zucchini in layers,
beginning and ending with the potatoes. Before adding the last layer of
potatoes, pour the tomato sauce over the last layer of zucchini, then add
the potatoes. Drizzle the remaining 2 tablespoons oil over the top and bake
in a preheated 350° oven for 1¼ to 1½ hours, or until the potatoes on top
are crisp and most of the moisture has been absorbed.

Serves 6.

United Methodist Churches Cookbook
United Methodist Church of Litchfield, Connecticut

$\mathcal{S}$WEET POTATO PANCAKES

These are great served with homemade applesauce,
tomato wedges and raw vegetable sticks as an entrée
or as an accompaniment to German sausages.

1 **cup firmly packed grated sweet potatoes**	1 **small clove garlic, crushed (optional)**
1 **cup firmly packed grated white potatoes**	4 **eggs, beaten**
1 **teaspoon salt, divided**	1/3 **cup unbleached flour**
1 **cup firmly packed grated carrots**	**Ground black pepper**
	Pinch of ground nutmeg
2 **tablespoons grated onions**	**Juice of 1/2 lemon**
1/4 **cup chopped fresh parsley**	**Plain yogurt or sour cream and chives**

Place the sweet potatoes and white potatoes in a colander over a bowl.
Salt lightly with 1/2 teaspoon of the salt and let stand for 15 minutes. Rinse
and squeeze out well to get rid of all the extra water.

In a large bowl, combine the potatoes with the carrots, onions, parsley,
garlic (if using), eggs, flour, remaining 1/2 teaspoon salt, pepper, nutmeg
and lemon juice. Mix well and form into 6 to 8 pancakes.

Cook on a lightly greased griddle or in a heavy skillet and fry the pancakes until golden brown and crisp on both sides. Serve topped with
yogurt or sour cream and chives.

Makes 6 to 8.

Marblehead Cooks
Tower School, Marblehead, Massachusetts

ℰGGPLANT-ZUCCHINI PARMIGIANA

Instead of frying the slices of eggplant, as is done in most
recipes of this kind, you bake them first, which cuts
down on preparation time as well as fat content. Sliced
mushrooms may be substituted for the zucchini if desired.

1 medium eggplant, peeled and
cut crosswise into ¼"-thick
slices

1–2 tablespoons mayonnaise

¼ cup Italian-seasoned dry
bread crumbs

1 cup low-fat or regular cottage
cheese

1 egg, lightly beaten

¼ teaspoon garlic powder

1 can (8 ounces) tomato sauce,
divided

1 cup diced mozzarella cheese,
divided

2 tablespoons grated Parmesan
cheese, divided

1 small zucchini, cut into
⅛"-thick slices

Arrange the eggplant slices in a single layer on a foil-lined baking sheet.
Spread them with the mayonnaise and sprinkle with the bread crumbs.
Bake in a preheated 475° oven for 10 minutes. Remove from the oven and
reduce the temperature to 375°.

In a small bowl, mix the cottage cheese, egg and garlic powder. In a
10" × 6" baking dish coated with a no-stick spray or lightly greased, layer
the eggplant, half the cottage cheese mixture, half the tomato sauce, half the
mozzarella and half the Parmesan. Top with the zucchini, then layer the
remaining cottage cheese mixture, tomato sauce, mozzarella and Parmesan.

Bake for 30 minutes, or until bubbly. Remove from the oven and let
stand for 5 minutes before cutting.

Serves 4 to 6.

Berkshire Seasonings
Junior League of Berkshire County, Pittsfield, Massachusetts

$\mathcal{N}$O-COOK SUMMER TOMATO SAUCE WITH TORTELLINI

Whether it's for a high-summer supper or pasta salad for a picnic, the key to success with this dish is using fresh herbs and juicy, ripe tomatoes.

1 pound frozen cheese- or meat-filled tortellini
1 pound ripe fresh tomatoes
⅓ cup finely chopped fresh basil
¼ cup finely chopped fresh parsley
3 cloves garlic, minced

3 tablespoons olive oil
1 tablespoon balsamic vinegar or red wine vinegar
½ teaspoon salt
½ teaspoon ground black pepper
Fresh basil leaves (optional)

Cook the tortellini according to the package directions. Meanwhile, cut the tomatoes into ¼″ dice and place in a large bowl. Add the basil, parsley and garlic and mix well. Stir in the oil, vinegar, salt and pepper.

Drain the tortellini thoroughly and toss with the tomato mixture, coating well. If desired, garnish each serving with 1 or 2 fresh basil leaves.

Serves 4.

Recipe Sampler
Shoreline Quilters' Guild, Branford, Connecticut

PASTA WITH GREEN TOMATOES

This is another great way to put an abundant crop to good use.
Double or triple the recipe for a quick and easy supper for a crowd.

1 tablespoon oil
1 medium onion, finely chopped
1 teaspoon finely chopped garlic
2 large green tomatoes, thinly sliced (about 4 cups)
¼–½ cup chicken stock
1½ tablespoons coarsely chopped fresh basil

1 tablespoon finely chopped fresh parsley
   Salt and pepper
8 ounces rigatoni or tubular pasta
3 tablespoons grated Parmesan cheese
   Chopped fresh parsley

Heat the oil in a large saucepan or skillet. Add the onions and sauté over medium heat until they begin to turn golden. Add the garlic and cook for about 1 minute, then add the tomatoes and simmer, stirring occasionally, for 5 minutes.

Add ¼ cup of the stock and the basil, parsley and salt and pepper to taste. Cover and simmer for 20 minutes, adding more stock if necessary.

When the sauce is nearly done, cook the pasta until just tender. Drain well and toss with the sauce. Add the cheese, mix and serve immediately. Garnish with chopped parsley.

Serves 4.

The Maine Collection
Portland Museum of Art, Portland, Maine

VEGETABLE LASAGNA

Entertaining can be difficult when some of the guests include individuals who do not eat meat. With this recipe, you will not only meet their dietary needs but also treat the others to a hearty and impressive meal.

1	tablespoon butter or margarine	3	tablespoons grated Parmesan cheese
1¼	cups chopped onions	¼	cup chopped fresh parsley, or 1 tablespoon dried
2	cloves garlic, finely minced	2	eggs, beaten
6	ounces mushrooms, coarsely chopped	¼	teaspoon salt (optional)
2	large stalks broccoli, chopped	¼	teaspoon ground black pepper
½	pound spinach, washed and chopped	3	cups tomato sauce, divided
3	tablespoons sherry	8	ounces lasagna noodles, cooked and drained
½	teaspoon dried fines herbes		Grated Parmesan cheese (optional)
1	container (16 ounces) low-fat cottage cheese		
1	cup shredded part-skim mozzarella cheese		

In a large skillet, melt the butter or margarine and sauté the onions, garlic and mushrooms until soft. Add the broccoli, spinach, sherry and fines herbes. Mix well, reduce the heat, cover and simmer for about 5 minutes, or until the broccoli is crisp-tender.

In a medium bowl, combine the cottage cheese, mozzarella, Parmesan, parsley, eggs, salt (if using) and pepper. Spread ½ cup of the tomato sauce on the bottom of a 13" × 9" baking dish. Arrange three lasagna noodles on the sauce, spread half the cheese mixture over the noodles and spread half the vegetable mixture over the cheese mixture. Top with 1 cup of the sauce. Repeat the layering, starting with the noodles and ending with a layer of noodles topped with the remaining ½ cup tomato sauce.

Sprinkle the top of the lasagna with additional Parmesan cheese (if using), then bake in a preheated 375° oven for 25 to 30 minutes. Let stand for about 10 minutes before cutting and serving.

Serves 6 to 8.

The Andover Cookbook II
Phillips Academy: The Ladies' Benevolent Society, Andover, Massachusetts

VEGETABLES
&
SIDE DISHES

ASPARAGUS PARMESAN

This is a great do-ahead dish for an evening with guests. An alternative to using all mayonnaise or all yogurt is to combine ¼ cup of each. This not only reduces the fat but also smoothes the texture of the sauce.

1 pound asparagus	¼ teaspoon salt
1 tablespoon butter or margarine	⅛ teaspoon ground black pepper
½ cup chopped scallions	⅛ teaspoon dry mustard
½ cup mayonnaise or plain yogurt	½ cup dry bread crumbs
2 tablespoons lemon juice	⅓ cup grated Parmesan cheese

Trim and discard the tough ends of the asparagus, drop the spears into a pan of boiling, salted water and cook for 3 to 4 minutes, or until crisp-tender. Drain and immediately rinse with cold water to retain the color. Redrain and lay the spears in a 2-quart baking dish.

Heat the butter or margarine in a skillet and sauté the scallions for 1 minute. Remove the skillet from the heat and add the mayonnaise or yogurt, lemon juice, salt, pepper and mustard. Pour the mixture over the asparagus spears and sprinkle the bread crumbs over all. Top with the cheese and bake in a preheated 350° oven for 10 to 15 minutes, or until lightly browned.

Serves 4 to 6.

Mystic Seaport's Seafood Secrets Cookbook
Mystic Seaport Museum Stores, Mystic, Connecticut

HARVARD BEETS

The burgundy color of this old-time favorite is especially beautiful when in the company of dark green vegetables like broccoli, spinach or beet greens.

2½ **cups cooked or canned beets**	2 **tablespoons butter or**
⅓ **cup sugar**	**margarine**
4 **tablespoons lemon juice or**	1 **tablespoon cornstarch**
3 tablespoons vinegar	**Pinch of salt**
¼ **cup water (approximately)**	

Cube or slice the beets. In a saucepan, combine the sugar, lemon juice or vinegar, water, butter or margarine, cornstarch and salt and boil for 5 minutes. Add the beets and stir over low heat until thoroughly heated. Serve immediately.

Serves 4.

A Century of Good Cooking
Waldoboro Woman's Club, Waldoboro, Maine

BROCCOLI & WINE SAUCE

Finding new ways to serve broccoli can become a challenge, so having a repertoire of sauce recipes comes in handy. This one is versatile enough to use with other vegetables such as cauliflower, carrots and green beans. It takes about 10 to 15 minutes for the sauce to thicken, so keep that in mind as you prepare the vegetables and other foods on the menu. When the sauce begins to thicken slightly, keep an eye on it and stir more often to prevent it from scorching.

1 **bunch broccoli**	2 **tablespoons olive oil**
2 **cloves garlic, minced**	½ **cup orange juice**
2 **tablespoons butter or**	**Grated rind of 1 orange**
margarine	½ **cup dry white wine**

Cut the broccoli into serving-size portions and steam until crisp-tender. Meanwhile, sauté the garlic in the butter or margarine and oil in a skillet, but do not brown. Add the orange juice, orange rind and wine and cook over medium-high heat until reduced to a syrup, stirring frequently. Pour over the fresh steamed broccoli, toss and serve immediately.

Serves 4.

Derry Community Playground Cookbook
Derry Playground Committee, East Derry, New Hampshire

ℬRUSSELS SPROUTS DELUXE

"You'll never eat plain sprouts again!" wrote the contributor of this recipe. If brussels sprouts are definitely verboten at your family's meals, substitute broccoli, cauliflower, carrots or onions.

2 **pints fresh brussels sprouts**	½ **teaspoon salt**
½ **cup chopped onions**	½ **teaspoon dry mustard**
2 **tablespoons butter or margarine**	½ **cup milk**
1 **tablespoon unbleached flour**	1 **cup sour cream or plain yogurt**
1 **tablespoon firmly packed brown sugar**	**Snipped fresh parsley**

Wash and trim the brussels sprouts. Cook, covered, in salted water for 15 to 20 minutes, or until tender.

Meanwhile, in a saucepan cook the onions in the butter or margarine until tender but not browned. Stir in the flour, brown sugar, salt and mustard, mixing well. Add the milk slowly and cook, stirring, until thick and bubbly. Slowly blend in the sour cream or yogurt, but do not let boil. Add the drained sprouts, stir and heat through. Garnish with the parsley.

Serves 6.

Cohasset Entertains
The Community Garden Club, Cohasett, Massachusetts

RED CABBAGE WITH CRANBERRIES

Delicious and different, this colorful, piquant dish is ideal for
Thanksgiving or Christmas dinner, but it really deserves to be enjoyed
more often. It is outstanding with pork and duckling, too.

2 **cups cranberries**	½ **cup firmly packed brown**
8 **cups finely shredded red**	**sugar**
cabbage	3 **tablespoons butter or**
2 **apples, peeled, cored and**	**margarine, melted**
shredded	½ **teaspoon salt (or to taste)**
1 **cup apple cider or apple juice**	¼ **teaspoon ground black**
	pepper

Pick over the cranberries and rinse them thoroughly. In a large bowl, toss
together the cranberries, cabbage and apples. Stir in the apple cider or
apple juice, brown sugar, butter or margarine, salt and pepper, mixing
thoroughly. Place in a buttered casserole, cover and bake in a preheated
350° oven for 1 hour, or until the cabbage is tender. Serve hot.

Serves 6 to 8.

The Mystic Seaport All Seasons Cookbook
Mystic Seaport Museum Stores, Mystic, Connecticut

NUTTY CARROTS

This is an appetizing way to get your family to eat carrots.
For a slightly sweeter taste, increase the honey to 1 tablespoon.
Brown sugar or maple syrup also may be used.

2½ **cups carrot sticks cut into**	2 **teaspoons honey**
3″ pieces	½ **teaspoon salt**
¼ **cup butter or margarine,**	¼ **teaspoon ground black**
melted	**pepper**
2 **tablespoons lemon juice**	¼ **cup coarsely chopped**
¼ **teaspoon grated lemon rind**	**walnuts**

HOMETOWN COOKING IN NEW ENGLAND

Steam the carrots until crisp-tender. Meanwhile, combine the butter or margarine, lemon juice, lemon rind, honey, salt and pepper in a small saucepan and heat thoroughly. When the carrots are done, place them in a large bowl, toss with the walnuts, pour on the sauce and toss again.

Serves 4.

Bouquet of Recipes
Sherman Garden Club, Sherman, Connecticut

$\mathscr{B}$UTTERED ROASTING EARS
❧

You may want to double this recipe,
for 1 ear per person generally is not enough.

¼ **cup butter or margarine, softened**	¼ **teaspoon salt**
1 **clove garlic, minced**	⅛ **teaspoon ground black pepper**
1½ **teaspoons minced fresh basil**	4 **large ears corn, husked**
½ **teaspoon dried oregano**	½ **cup grated Romano cheese**

In a small bowl, combine the butter or margarine, garlic, basil, oregano, salt and pepper. Spread evenly on the corn and wrap each ear in foil, making a lengthwise fold and sealing the ends securely. Roast on a grill 4″ from the coals for 15 to 20 minutes, turning every 5 minutes. (The corn also may be roasted in a preheated 350° oven for 20 to 25 minutes.) Open the foil, sprinkle with the cheese and serve immediately.

Serves 4.

Watch Hill Cooks
Watch Hill Improvement Society, Watch Hill, Rhode Island

$\mathcal{E}$ASY CORN FRITTERS
※

You don't have to wait until August, when fresh corn is abundant,
to make these fritters. Use frozen corn, briefly processed in a
food processor to resemble the texture of corn cut from the cob.
These fritters are beautiful, with a lot of loft, when they are hot off the
griddle—crisp on the outside and soufflé-like on the inside—
but they fall in a matter of minutes, so serve them immediately.
Place on a warm plate and accompany with maple syrup or butter.

6 **ears fresh corn**	2 **tablespoons unbleached flour**
2 **eggs, separated**	½ **teaspoon salt**
3 **tablespoons milk**	

Cut the corn from the cob. In a bowl, beat the egg yolks until light
yellow and add the corn, milk, flour and salt, blending well. Beat the egg
whites until they hold their shape, then fold into the corn mixture. Drop
by rounded tablespoonfuls into a hot greased skillet or onto a griddle and
cook until golden brown on both sides.

Serves 4.

The Maine Collection
Portland Museum of Art, Portland, Maine

$\mathcal{G}$RANDMA MILLER'S CORN PUDDING
※

Deep golden on top, this custardy,
light pudding is easy to make for any occasion.

12 **ears fresh corn or 6 cups frozen**	1 **teaspoon unbleached flour**
4 **eggs, separated**	2 **cups milk**
1–2 **teaspoons sugar**	1 **teaspoon salt**
1 **tablespoon butter or margarine, melted**	¼ **teaspoon ground black pepper**

If using fresh corn, scrape the kernels from the ears. If using frozen corn, chop it finely using a food processor to approximate the texture of fresh corn scraped from the cob. Set aside.

In a large bowl, beat the egg yolks until golden. Add 1 teaspoon of the sugar if using fresh corn, 2 teaspoons if using frozen. In a small bowl, combine the butter or margarine and flour and add to the beaten yolks along with the milk, salt and pepper. Add the corn and mix well.

Beat the egg whites in a medium bowl until stiff but not dry. Fold into the corn mixture and transfer to a greased 2½-quart casserole. Bake in a preheated 350° oven for 45 to 50 minutes, or until a knife inserted in the center comes out clean.

Serves 8 to 10.

Vernon Bicentennial Cookbook
Vernon Bicentennial Cookbook Committee, Vernon, Vermont

CRANBERRY ICE

This festive, colorful side dish can be scooped out into
small chilled bowls and served as an accompaniment to fruit
salad, chicken salad or even turkey sandwiches.

2 cups cranberries	**½ tablespoon lemon juice**
2 cups water	**(optional)**
1¼ cups sugar	

Pick over the cranberries and rinse them thoroughly. In a saucepan, bring the water to a boil, add the cranberries and cook until soft. Sieve into a bowl and stir in the sugar and lemon juice (if using) while the cranberries are still hot. Cool the mixture and pour into an ice-cube tray with the dividers removed. When partially frozen, beat and then refreeze. Use an ice cream scoop to serve.

Serves 4 to 6.

Portland Symphony Cookbook
Portland Symphony Orchestra Women's Committee, Portland, Maine

CRANBERRY BREAD PUDDING

This unique dish can be served as an accompaniment
to poultry or meat, or it can be topped with whipped cream
or vanilla ice cream and presented as dessert.

PUDDING
- 1 **cup cranberries**
- ¼ **cup butter or margarine, softened**
- 2 **eggs, well beaten**
- ½ **cup sugar**
- ½ **teaspoon salt**
- 2 **cups soft bread cubes**
- ⅓ **cup milk**

SAUCE
- ½ **cup water**
- ¼ **cup dark corn syrup or maple syrup**
- ¼ **cup firmly packed brown sugar**
- 2 **teaspoons unbleached flour**
- 1 **teaspoon butter or margarine**
- ⅛ **teaspoon salt**
- ½ **teaspoon vanilla**

To make the pudding: Pick over the cranberries and rinse them thoroughly.
Set aside.

In a large bowl, cream the butter or margarine. Add the eggs, sugar and
salt and beat until smooth. Add the bread cubes, cranberries and milk,
tossing until well mixed. Pour into a greased 1½-quart casserole, set inside
a larger pan and pour enough hot water into the larger pan so it comes
halfway up the sides of the casserole. Bake in a preheated 350° oven for
1 hour.

To make the sauce: In a heavy-bottomed pot, combine the water, corn
syrup or maple syrup, brown sugar, flour, butter or margarine and salt.
Cook at a rolling boil for 10 minutes, stirring often. Remove from the heat
and stir in the vanilla. Just before serving, pour the warm sauce over the
pudding.

Serves 6.

Marshfield's Overdue Cookbook
Cliff Rodgers Free Library, Marshfield Hills, Massachusetts

MUSHROOM CASSEROLE

For a crunchy top, reserve ½ cup of the croutons and sprinkle them on top of the casserole during the last 10 minutes of baking.

1½ **pounds mushrooms, sliced**	¼ **teaspoon ground black pepper**
2 **tablespoons oil**	2 **cups milk**
2 **tablespoons butter or margarine**	1 **tablespoon dry sherry**
¼ **cup unbleached flour**	2 **cups seasoned croutons, divided**
1 **tablespoon chopped fresh parsley**	**Paprika**
½ **teaspoon salt**	

In a skillet, sauté the mushrooms in the oil until tender. Remove the mushrooms with a slotted spoon and set aside.

Melt the butter or margarine in the same skillet, stir in the flour, parsley, salt and pepper and cook, stirring, for 1 minute. Set aside. In a saucepan, heat the milk until warm, blend into the flour mixture and cook over medium heat, stirring until the mixture thickens. Blend in the sherry.

Place 1 cup of the croutons in a buttered casserole, top with half the mushrooms and pour half the white sauce over the mixture. Repeat the layers, sprinkle with paprika and bake in a preheated 375° oven for 20 minutes.

Serves 6.

Family Recipe Cookbook
Habitat for Humanity, Providence, Rhode Island

GREENS & VINEGAR

This is a traditional New England recipe. For a variation,
sauté 1 or 2 cloves garlic in 1 tablespoon olive oil, stir in the rinsed
greens with water still clinging to the leaves, cover and simmer until
tender. Let diners add their own vinegar at the table. Any kind will do,
but balsamic vinegar and brown rice vinegar are excellent.

½ **cup water**
3–4 **cups rinsed and chopped**
     kale, mustard greens or
     collard greens

1–2 **tablespoons vinegar**

In a large pot, bring the water to a boil. Add the greens, cover and
reduce the heat to medium. Simmer for about 30 minutes, or until tender.
Toss with the vinegar and serve.

Serves 4.

Vernon Bicentennial Cookbook
Vernon Bicentennial Cookbook Committee, Vernon, Vermont

HOLIDAY CREAMED ONIONS

Although frozen small white onions can be substituted,
fresh ones are better—especially for the holidays.

24 **small white onions (about**
    1¼ pounds), blanched and
    peeled
2   **tablespoons unsalted butter**
    or margarine
2   **tablespoons unbleached flour**
1   **cup milk or half-and-half**

¼ **cup minced fresh parsley**
   Freshly grated nutmeg
   Salt and pepper (preferably
   white pepper)
½ **cup dry bread crumbs**
2 **tablespoons butter or**
   margarine, melted

Place the onions in a large saucepan, cover with salted water and bring to a boil. Reduce the heat, cover and simmer for about 40 minutes, or until just tender. Drain and set aside.

In a saucepan, melt the unsalted butter or margarine over low heat, stir in the flour and cook, stirring, for 3 minutes. Add the milk or half-and-half in a steady stream, whisking. Bring to a boil, whisking constantly, then reduce the heat and simmer, stirring occasionally, for 5 minutes. Add the parsley, nutmeg, salt and pepper to taste and onions. In a small bowl, combine the bread crumbs and melted butter or margarine. Pour the creamed onions into a small, shallow casserole, cover with the buttered bread crumbs and bake in a preheated 350° oven for 20 minutes, or until bubbly.

Serves 4 to 6.

Saint Gabriel's Horn of Plenty
Saint Gabriel's Episcopal Church, Marion, Massachusetts

$\mathcal{S}$HAKER SCALLOPED ONIONS

This is an example of good, basic cooking at its best—
true to the Shaker tradition.

6 **medium onions, sliced**	½ **teaspoon salt**
¼ **cup butter or margarine**	⅛ **teaspoon ground black**
½ **cup shredded Cheddar cheese**	**pepper**
⅓ **cup dry bread crumbs**	**Paprika**
2 **tablespoons heavy cream**	

In a large pot, sauté the onions in the butter or margarine until tender. Place them in a buttered baking dish, then sprinkle with the cheese, bread crumbs, cream, salt, pepper and paprika. Bake in a preheated 350° oven for 20 minutes, or until lightly browned.

Serves 4.

South Newbury Union Church and Society Cookbook
South Newbury Union Church, South Newbury, New Hampshire

DILLY ONION RINGS

These keep indefinitely in the refrigerator. Serve them with
beef or fish, on sandwiches, in salads and any number of other ways.
Let your culinary whim be your guide.

½ cup white vinegar	½ teaspoon salt
½ cup sugar	1 large sweet onion, thinly
¼ cup water	sliced and separated into
1 teaspoon dried dill	rings

In a medium bowl, combine the vinegar, sugar, water, dill and salt, stirring to dissolve the sugar and salt. Pour over the onion rings and toss to
coat. Cover and refrigerate overnight, stirring occasionally.

Serves 4 to 6.

Vermont Kitchens Revisited
The Women of the Cathedral Church of St. Paul, Burlington, Vermont

FRIED PARSNIPS IN BATTER

This recipe can easily be tailored to fit your family's preferences. Add a
little cinnamon, nutmeg and sugar to the batter for a slightly sweet and
spicy effect, or add parsley, oregano and thyme for something more savory.

4–6 parsnips, peeled and	¼ cup unbleached flour
quartered lengthwise	Salt and pepper
1 egg, beaten	2–3 tablespoons oil
2 tablespoons milk	

Boil or steam the parsnips until crisp-tender. Drain and set aside.
In a small bowl, beat the egg with the milk. Add the flour and salt and
pepper to taste, stirring until the batter is smooth and thick. Add more
flour to get the proper consistency if necessary.

Heat 2 tablespoons of the oil in a large skillet. Dip the parsnips in the batter to coat, then fry them in the hot oil. (Add the remaining 1 tablespoon oil if necessary.) Drain on paper towels and serve piping hot.

Serves 4 to 6.

Our Daily Bread
St. Patrick's Church: Our Lady's Guild, Bennington, New Hampshire

$\mathcal{P}$OTATO KUGEL

This yummy, easy-to-make side dish is appropriate with any meal—even breakfast. Similar to hash browns, it has a light brown, crispy top and just the right blend of potatoes, onions and seasonings.

2 **cups grated potatoes**	½ **teaspoon salt**
1 **large onion, grated**	**Ground black pepper**
1 **large carrot, grated**	4 **tablespoons butter or**
2 **eggs, beaten**	**margarine, melted and**
¼ **cup unbleached flour**	**divided**
¼ **cup matzo meal**	**Water (if needed)**
1 **teaspoon baking powder**	

In a large bowl, combine the potatoes, onions and carrots. Add the eggs, flour, matzo meal, baking powder, salt, pepper and 2 tablespoons of the butter or margarine. Mix together well. If the mixture seems a little too dry, add a little water. Pour into a greased 9″ × 9″ baking dish and drizzle the remaining 2 tablespoons butter or margarine on top. Bake in a preheated 350° oven for about 1 hour, or until the top is crisp and brown.

Serves 4 to 6.

The Kosher Yankee II
Sisterhood of the Rutland Jewish Center, Rutland, Vermont

$\mathcal{G}$ARLIC ROASTED POTATOES
❧

The aroma from the garlic as these potatoes bake in the oven will whet everyone's appetite. This dish goes well with meat, poultry or fish.

3 pounds medium red potatoes, cut into ½" slices	**1 tablespoon chopped fresh parsley**
¼ cup olive oil	**1 teaspoon lemon rind (yellow part only), cut into thin strips**
6–8 cloves garlic, chopped	
Ground black pepper	**½ teaspoon salt**

In a large, shallow glass baking dish, toss the potatoes with the oil, garlic to taste and pepper. Bake in a preheated 375° oven, turning several times, for 1 hour, or until the potatoes are golden and tender.

Transfer to a serving dish, add the parsley, lemon rind, salt and more pepper (if desired). Toss lightly and serve warm or at room temperature.

Serves 6 to 8.

Hospitality
Salem Hospital Aid Association, Salem, Massachusetts

$\mathcal{G}$REEK OVEN FRIES
❧

These guilt-free fries are simple, savory and satisfying.

2 medium baking potatoes, unpeeled	**¼ teaspoon salt**
1 teaspoon olive oil	**⅛ teaspoon ground black pepper**
1 teaspoon dried oregano	**2 tablespoons malt vinegar**

Scrub the potatoes, then cut each lengthwise into 8 wedges. Place the wedges in a bowl and cover with cold water. Let sit for 30 minutes, then drain. Pat dry with paper towels. Toss the potatoes with the oil and place them skin side down on a baking sheet coated with no-stick spray or oil.

Combine the oregano, salt and pepper and sprinkle evenly over the potatoes. Bake in a preheated 400° oven for 45 to 50 minutes, or until the potatoes are tender and browned. Remove from the oven, sprinkle with the vinegar and serve immediately.

Serves 4.

Recipe Sampler
Shoreline Quilters' Guild, Branford, Connecticut

$\mathcal{Y}$ANKEE BAKED SWEET POTATOES WITH APPLES

Use apples that have body and won't fall apart from the sautéing and baking, like Granny Smith or Cortland.

3 **large apples**	3 **large sweet potatoes, boiled,**
3 **tablespoons butter or**	**peeled and sliced**
margarine, divided	½ **teaspoon salt**
	¼ – ½ **cup maple syrup**

Peel, core and slice the apples. Sauté them in a skillet in 2 tablespoons of the butter or margarine until slightly softened. Arrange the apples and sweet potatoes in alternate layers in a buttered 9″ × 9″ baking dish. Sprinkle with the salt, pour the syrup over the top and dot with the remaining 1 tablespoon butter. Bake in a preheated 350° oven for about 35 minutes.

Serves 4 to 6.

The Civic Women's Guilford Sampler
Guilford Civic Women, Guilford, Connecticut

MAPLE MASHED SWEET POTATOES

Sweet simplicity, this dish will be a hit with kids as well as adults.

- **4 sweet potatoes, cooked, peeled and mashed**
- **1 teaspoon grated orange rind**
- **3 tablespoons maple syrup**
- **2 tablespoons butter or margarine, melted**

In a medium bowl, mix the mashed sweet potatoes and orange rind. Spread the mixture in a greased baking dish. In a small bowl, mix the maple syrup and butter or margarine and pour over the top of the potatoes. Bake in a preheated 350° oven for 25 minutes.

Serves 4.

Favorite Recipes
St. Elizabeth Ann Seton Church of Fryeburg, Maine: Mission of St. Joseph's Church, Bridgton, Maine

BUTTERNUT SQUASH SOUFFLÉ

Butterscotch-colored, light and somewhat puddinglike, this soufflé straddles the line between side dish and dessert. Decrease or increase the amount of sweetener, depending on how you wish to present it. If you can't find butternut squash, any other winter squash will do.

- **2 cups mashed cooked butternut squash**
- **¼ cup maple syrup**
- **3 tablespoons cornstarch**
- **2 tablespoons firmly packed brown sugar**
- **½ teaspoon salt**
- **3 eggs, separated**
- **1¼ cups half-and-half**
- **2 tablespoons butter or margarine, melted**

In a large bowl, combine the squash, maple syrup, cornstarch, brown sugar and salt and beat until fluffy. Add the egg yolks, half-and-half and butter or margarine. Mix well.

In a separate bowl, beat the egg whites until stiff and fold into the squash mixture. Pour into a buttered 2-quart casserole. Bake in a preheated 350° oven for 1 hour, or until a knife inserted in the center comes out clean.

Serves 8 to 10.

Country Classics
Welcome Wagon Club, Londonderry, New Hampshire

*N*EW ENGLAND–STYLE BUTTERNUT SQUASH

This delicious combination of winter squash and spices has the added treat of plump raisins. Either dark or golden raisins will work just fine.

1	**medium butternut squash**	
1½	**cups water**	
¾	**cup raisins**	
1	**teaspoon ground cinnamon**	

¼ **teaspoon ground cloves**
¼ **teaspoon ground nutmeg**
Salt and pepper

Cut the squash in half, scrape out and discard the seeds, peel and cut into bite-size pieces. Combine with the water and raisins in a saucepan. Simmer, loosely covered, for 20 minutes, or until the squash is tender. Drain. Add the cinnamon, cloves, nutmeg and salt and pepper to taste and mash the squash to the desired consistency.

Serves 4.

Rhode Island Cooks
American Cancer Society: Rhode Island Division, Pawtucket, Rhode Island

$\mathscr{B}$AKED SUMMER SQUASH
❦

Quichelike but without the crust,
this dish also can be made with zucchini.

6 **cups sliced small yellow summer squash**	**Salt and pepper**
1½ **cups chopped onions**	½ **cup milk**
4 **tablespoons butter or margarine, divided**	2 **large eggs**
	½ **cup cracker crumbs**

Steam the squash until crisp-tender. Transfer to a shallow 2-quart baking dish and toss with the onions, 2 tablespoons of the butter or margarine and salt and pepper to taste. Beat the milk and eggs together in a small bowl and mix well with the squash. Melt the remaining 2 tablespoons butter or margarine, combine with the cracker crumbs and sprinkle over the top. Bake in a preheated 450° oven for 10 minutes, or until browned.

Serves 6 to 8.

Cohasset Entertains, Encore
The Community Garden Club, Cohasset, Massachusetts

$\mathscr{B}$AKED STUFFED TOMATOES
❦

Using a grapefruit spoon with a serrated edge simplifies the task of hollowing out the tomatoes. This simple but impressive presentation is best made in the summer, when ripe fresh tomatoes are readily available.

4 **firm ripe tomatoes**	1½ **cups dry bread crumbs**
2 **tablespoons olive oil**	1 **tablespoon grated Parmesan cheese**
1 **clove garlic, minced**	1 **tablespoon marsala**
1 **teaspoon minced onions**	**Salt and pepper**
1 **teaspoon minced fresh parsley**	

Hollow out the tomatoes and set aside the pulp in a sieve to drain. Heat the oil in a skillet, add the garlic, onions and parsley and sauté until tender. Do not overcook. Chop the tomato pulp and add to the skillet. Simmer for 5 minutes more.

Remove from the heat, transfer to a large bowl and add the bread crumbs, cheese, marsala and salt and pepper to taste, mixing well. Fill the tomato shells with the mixture, place in an oiled baking dish and bake in a preheated 350° oven until tender, about 30 minutes.

Serves 4.

A Collection of Favorite Italian Recipes
St. Anthony's Church: The Women's Guild, Woonsocket, Rhode Island

$\mathcal{T}$URNIP WITH MAPLE SYRUP

If chunks of turnip turn your kids off, mash them by hand or puree them in a food processor, then combine with the maple syrup.

1 large turnip, peeled	**½ cup water**
1 tablespoon butter or oil	**2 tablespoons maple syrup**

Cut the turnip into chunks. Heat the butter or oil in a saucepan and sauté the turnip for 3 to 5 minutes. Add the water, bring to a boil, reduce the heat and cook until tender. Add the maple syrup, stir to coat and serve.

Serves 4.

The Community Cooks
Pine Hill Waldorf School, Wilton, New Hampshire

CIDER RICE PILAF
※

Especially good with pork or lamb,
this rice perks up just about any meal.

2 tablespoons butter or
margarine
1 cup uncooked white or brown
rice
¾ cup chopped celery
½ cup chopped onions
1 teaspoon grated orange rind

Salt and pepper
4 tablespoons minced fresh
parsley, divided
¾ teaspoon fresh rosemary,
or ¼ teaspoon dried
1¾ cups apple cider

Melt the butter or margarine in a skillet, add the rice and stir until golden. Add the celery, onions, orange rind and salt and pepper to taste. Sauté for 5 minutes more. Stir in 2 tablespoons of the parsley and the rosemary.

In a separate pan, bring the cider to a boil, then stir it into the rice. Cover the skillet and cook over low heat for about 30 minutes for white rice, 50 minutes for brown rice. Serve sprinkled with the remaining 2 tablespoons parsley.

Serves 4.

Vermont Kitchens Revisited
The Women of the Cathedral Church of St. Paul, Burlington, Vermont

RICE WITH HERBS

Herbs and chicken stock turn ordinary rice into
a superior dish. Flavorful and attractive, it is superb
with roast chicken, turkey or Cornish game hens.

1 **medium onion, finely chopped**	¾ **teaspoon dried basil**
1 **cup uncooked rice**	¾ **teaspoon dried marjoram**
1 **tablespoon butter or margarine**	½ **teaspoon dried sage**
3 **cups chicken stock**	¼ **teaspoon dried thyme**
	¼ **teaspoon curry powder**
	½ **teaspoon salt**

In a saucepan, sauté the onions and rice in the butter or margarine for
5 minutes. Add the stock, basil, marjoram, sage, thyme, curry powder and
salt and heat to boiling. Reduce the heat, cover and cook slowly for 30 minutes, or until the rice has absorbed the stock.

Serves 6.

The Fine Arts Cookbook I
Museum of Fine Arts, Boston, Massachusetts

SKILLET RICE WITH TOMATOES

In addition to its excellent flavor and ease of preparation,
which make this dish appealing in its own right, is the added bonus
of its being low in fat and high in complex carbohydrates.

1 tablespoon olive oil	1 cup chicken stock
3 tablespoons minced shallots	¼ cup apple juice
3 tablespoons chopped green bell peppers	1 teaspoon ground ginger
	1 teaspoon dried tarragon
½ cup uncooked rice	4 dashes of hot-pepper sauce
1 cup canned tomatoes, undrained	2 tablespoons minced fresh parsley

Heat the oil in a skillet until hot. Sauté the shallots and bell peppers in
the oil until wilted but not browned, stirring constantly. Add the rice and
stir, sautéing for 1 minute more. Stir in the tomatoes, stock, apple juice,
ginger, tarragon and hot-pepper sauce. Bring to a simmer, cover and cook
for 20 minutes, stirring once after the first 10 minutes. Remove from the
heat and let sit for 5 minutes. Fluff with a fork, sprinkle with the parsley
and serve.

Serves 4.

Vernon Bicentennial Cookbook
Vernon Bicentennial Cookbook Committee, Vernon, Vermont

Hometown Cooking in New England

MAPLE BAKED BEANS

Classic New England fare, especially when accompanied
with steamed brown bread and served on Saturday night. For an
updated version, substitute bacon for the salt pork.

2	pounds yellow eye or pea beans	1	teaspoon salt
1½	teaspoons baking soda	½	teaspoon dry mustard
½	cup maple syrup	1	bay leaf
¼	cup molasses	¼	pound salt pork, rinsed and sliced
¼	cup chopped onions		

Wash the beans and discard any imperfect ones. Place them in a large
bowl, add enough water to cover them by 2 inches and soak overnight.

In the morning, drain and rinse the beans and put in a large pot. Add
water to cover, stir in the baking soda and simmer for 30 minutes. Drain,
rinse and return to the pot.

In a bowl, combine the maple syrup, molasses, onions, salt, mustard
and bay leaf. Pour over the beans, add the salt pork and mix well. Cover
with boiling water, cover the pot and bake in a 300° oven for 6 to 8 hours,
adding water as needed. Remove the cover during the last 30 minutes
of baking.

Serves 12 to 14.

College Street Congregational Church 125th Anniversary Cookbook
College Street Congregational Church, Burlington, Vermont

CURRIED KIDNEY BEANS
❧

It is recommended that canned kidney beans be rinsed
before using, for this removes the thick canning liquid that
often contains a great deal of sodium.

2　tablespoons oil
1　onion, chopped
1　green bell pepper, chopped
1　apple, cored and chopped
2　cans (15 ounces each) kidney
　　beans, rinsed and well
　　drained
1　can (28 ounces) tomatoes,
　　well drained

½　cup firmly packed brown
　　sugar
1　tablespoon white vinegar
1　teaspoon curry powder
¼　teaspoon salt
⅛　teaspoon ground black
　　pepper
　　Grated Parmesan cheese

Heat the oil in a large pot and sauté the onions, bell peppers and apples
until tender. Mix in the beans, tomatoes, brown sugar, vinegar, curry powder,
salt and pepper. Transfer to a greased casserole and bake in a preheated 350°
oven for 30 minutes. Top with the cheese and serve immediately.

Serves 8 to 10.

The Vermont Symphony Cookbook
Vermont Symphony Orchestra, Burlington, Vermont

GARDEN SPECIAL
❧

In addition to serving this as a side dish, you may use it in soups, stews,
casseroles, spaghetti sauces and omelets. To freeze, cool the mixture, then
put it in clean pint- or quart-size freezer containers. Cover and freeze.

1　cup diced celery
1　cup diced onions
1½　red or green bell peppers,
　　diced
1　cup tomato juice

4　cups peeled and coarsely
　　chopped ripe tomatoes
1½　teaspoons salt (or to taste)
1½　teaspoons sugar

Place the celery, onions and bell peppers in a large pot. Add the tomato juice and cook for 20 minutes. Add the tomatoes, bring to a boil and stir in the salt and sugar. Simmer for 40 minutes more.

Makes about 7 cups.

Bulfinch's Boston Faire
Doric Dames, Boston, Massachusetts

$\mathcal{A}$PPLE-PRUNE STUFFING

Another excellent stuffing for winter squash as well as poultry. Doubled in quantity, it will provide enough stuffing for a 10- to 12-pound bird.

¼ **cup butter or margarine**	1 **cup cooked prunes, diced**
1 **small onion, finely chopped**	½ **cup coarsely chopped**
3 **cups day-old bread crumbs**	**walnuts**
1 **cup peeled, cored and**	1 **tablespoon lemon juice**
coarsely chopped tart apples	½ **teaspoon salt**

Melt the butter or margarine in a large skillet and sauté the onions until translucent. Transfer to a large bowl and combine with the bread crumbs, apples, prunes, walnuts, lemon juice and salt, mixing well.

Makes 5 cups.

Christmas Memories Cookbook
Mystic Seaport Museum Stores, Mystic, Connecticut

CHESTNUT-APPLE STUFFING

In addition to poultry and meat, this stuffing can be used
to fill acorn squash. It also can be served as a side dish or even
as a main dish. The recipe can easily be cut in half.

4 slices smoked bacon
2 tablespoons butter or
   margarine
1 medium onion, chopped
1 cup diced celery
6 cups soft bread crumbs
4 large red baking apples, cored
   and chopped
2 cups chopped roasted
   chestnuts

2 eggs, lightly beaten
½ cup apple juice
   (approximately)
½ cup chopped fresh parsley
1½ teaspoons dried sage
1½ teaspoons dried thyme
1 teaspoon ground black
   pepper

Chop the bacon and cook it in a skillet over medium-high heat for
about 10 minutes, or until most of the fat is rendered. Reduce the heat to
medium-low. Add the butter or margarine, onions and celery and sauté the
vegetables until crisp-tender, about 10 minutes. Transfer to a large bowl.
Add the bread crumbs, apples, chestnuts, eggs, apple juice, parsley, sage,
thyme and pepper and mix until well blended and the crumbs are lightly
moistened. Add a bit more apple juice for a moister stuffing.

Makes about 14 cups, or enough to stuff an 18- to 20-pound turkey.

Watch Hill Cooks
Watch Hill Improvement Society, Watch Hill, Rhode Island

GRANDPA K'S OYSTER STUFFING FOR TURKEY

If you don't have a food processor or meat grinder, finely chop the giblets, bacon, celery and onions by hand.

Turkey giblets (heart, liver, wing tips and neck)
3 strips bacon
½ pound pork sausage
½ teaspoon salt
½ teaspoon ground black pepper

½ teaspoon poultry seasoning
¼ teaspoon dried thyme
2–3 stalks celery
1 medium onion
½ pint oysters, coarsely chopped
Large loaf of French bread

In a saucepan, cook the giblets in water to cover for 45 minutes. Drain. (This can be done a day ahead.)

In a food processor or meat grinder, grind the giblets with the bacon until coarse. Put the sausage in a large pot and add the ground giblets and bacon, salt, pepper, poultry seasoning and thyme. Sauté for 15 minutes.

Coarsely process or grind the celery and onion and add to the sausage-giblets mixture. Cook for 8 minutes, or until the vegetables are tender. Add the oysters and cook for 2 to 3 minutes more. Transfer the mixture to a large bowl.

Soak the bread in water for 5 minutes, then squeeze out the water. Break up the bread and combine well with the other ingredients in the bowl, then stuff the bird.

Makes about 8 cups, or enough to stuff a 12-pound turkey.

Mystic Seaport's Seafood Secrets Cookbook
Mystic Seaport Museum Stores, Mystic, Connecticut

DESSERTS

 Pies, Puddings & Cobblers

First-Prize Apple Pie

Definitely a winner by anyone's standards, this sweet and cinnamon-flavored pie with its lightly browned, flaky crust not only tastes splendid but also looks as if it was made by a professional pastry chef.

CRUST
- 1 cup shortening
- 2½ cups unbleached flour
- 1 egg
- 1 teaspoon white vinegar
- 6 tablespoons ice water (approximately), divided

FILLING
- 8–9 medium McIntosh apples
- ¾ cup sugar
- ¼ cup unbleached flour
- 2 teaspoons ground cinnamon
- 2 tablespoons butter or margarine
- Milk

To make the crust: In a large bowl, cut the shortening into the flour until crumbly. Beat in the egg, add the vinegar and slowly add the water, 1 tablespoon at a time, stirring until all the ingredients are moistened. Form the dough into 2 balls and refrigerate.

To make the filling: Peel, core and slice the apples. Toss in a large bowl with the sugar, flour and cinnamon.

Roll out 1 ball of dough and place in a 9″ pie plate. Arrange the apples in the bottom crust. Cut the butter or margarine into small bits and arrange on top. Roll out the remaining ball of dough and cover the apples. Flute and seal the edges and cut vents in the top. Brush milk over the top and bake in a preheated 425° oven until the filling begins to bubble through the vents, about 50 to 60 minutes. Let cool before serving.

Serves 6 to 8.

The Civic Women's Guilford Sampler
Guilford Civic Women, Guilford, Connecticut

SPECIAL APPLE PIE

Rich and creamy with a crumbly, crunchy topping, this pie is unlike many similar recipes, for the crust and topping carry the spices.

CRUST
- 1¾ cups unbleached flour
- 3 tablespoons sugar
- 1 teaspoon ground cinnamon
- ¼ teaspoon salt
- ½ cup plus 2 tablespoons butter or margarine
- ¼ cup apple cider or apple juice (approximately)

FILLING
- 1⅔ cups sour cream (low-fat may be used)
- ¾ cup sugar
- ⅓ cup unbleached flour
- 1 egg
- 2 teaspoons vanilla
- ¼ teaspoon salt
- 8 McIntosh apples, peeled, cored and sliced

TOPPING
- 1 cup chopped walnuts
- ½ cup unbleached flour
- ¼ cup granulated sugar
- ¼ cup firmly packed brown sugar
- 1 tablespoon ground cinnamon
- Pinch of salt
- ¼ cup butter or margarine, softened

To make the crust: Combine the flour, sugar, cinnamon and salt in a large bowl. Add the butter or margarine and cut it in using 2 forks or a pastry blender. Add the apple cider or apple juice and toss until moistened. (An additional 1 to 2 teaspoons may be needed to make the dough easy to work.) Roll out to make a single crust and place in a 10″ pie plate. Build up the sides and flute the edges. Cover with plastic wrap while preparing the filling.

To make the filling: Beat the sour cream, sugar, flour, egg, vanilla and salt. Stir in the apples and pour into the prepared crust. Bake in a preheated 450° oven for 10 minutes, reduce the temperature to 350° and continue baking until the filling is slightly puffed and golden brown, about 45 minutes.

To make the topping: Combine the walnuts, flour, granulated sugar, brown sugar, cinnamon and salt in a small bowl. Cut in the butter or margarine until the mixture is crumbly. Sprinkle over the pie. Bake for 15 minutes more.

Serves 8 to 12.

Sounds Delicious
Cape Ann Symphony Association, Gloucester, Massachusetts

$\mathcal{S}$EAPORT MOM'S TREASURED BLUEBERRY PIE

This is a treasure indeed! The Chambord and raspberry preserves add a sweet surprise, and the combination of cooked and uncooked fresh blueberries is an exquisite match.

3 cups blueberries, divided
1½ cups sugar
¾ cup water
¾ cup Chambord or raspberry liqueur

3 tablespoons cornstarch, combined with 2 tablespoons water
⅓ cup raspberry preserves
9" baked piecrust
Whipped cream

Put 1½ cups of the blueberries, the sugar and the water in a saucepan and bring to a boil. Add the Chambord and the combined cornstarch and water. Cook over medium heat, stirring gently, for 2 to 3 minutes, or until thick and clear.

Remove the pan from the heat and cool for 15 minutes. Fold in the remaining 1½ cups blueberries.

Spread the preserves evenly over the piecrust and pour in the blueberry mixture. Chill for several hours before serving. Top with a dollop of the whipped cream.

Serves 6 to 8.

Mystic Seaport's Seafood Secrets Cookbook
Mystic Seaport Museum Stores, Mystic, Connecticut

MOCK CHERRY PIE

This cranberry and raisin combination in a flaky pastry crust is out of this world. To make it even easier, leave the fruit whole rather than chopping it. Let the pie cool for at least 20 minutes before cutting and serving, and accompany it with vanilla ice cream or frozen yogurt.

CRUST
- ⅔ **cup shortening**
- 2 **cups unbleached flour**
- ½ **teaspoon salt**
- 4–5 **tablespoons cold water**

FILLING
- 1 **cup sugar**
- 3 **tablespoons unbleached flour**
- 2 **cups cranberries, chopped**
  (see Note below)
- 1 **cup raisins, chopped**
- 2 **tablespoons butter or margarine**

To make the crust: In a medium bowl, cut the shortening into the flour and salt until crumbly. Add the water, 1 tablespoon at a time, stirring until the mixture forms a ball. Chill in the refrigerator.

Roll out half the dough on a floured surface to fit a 9″ pie plate. Line the plate with the bottom crust.

To make the filling: Mix the sugar and flour in a medium bowl. Stir in the cranberries and raisins, coating well. Pour into the piecrust and dot with the butter or margarine.

Roll out the remaining dough on a floured surface, fit over the pie, seal the edges and cut vents in the top. Bake in a preheated 425° oven for 15 minutes. Reduce the oven temperature to 350° and bake for 35 to 45 minutes more, or until golden.

Note: Before chopping the cranberries, pick them over carefully, discarding any that are bad. Rinse them under running water and pat dry.

Serves 8.

Boston Cooks
Women's Educational & Industrial Union, Boston, Massachusetts

GINGERED PEAR PIE

This juicy pie with a slight bite from candied ginger needs
to sit for 30 to 45 minutes before it is cut. This allows the
filling to firm up a bit and makes for easier serving.

Pastry for double-crust 9" pie
6 **medium pears, peeled, cored
and sliced**
¾ **cup sugar**
¼ **cup unbleached flour**

¼ **cup minced candied ginger**
2 **teaspoons grated lemon rind**
3 **tablespoons lemon juice**
2 **tablespoons butter or
margarine**

Place the bottom crust in a pie plate. Arrange the pears in the crust.
In a small bowl, combine the sugar, flour, ginger and lemon rind and
sprinkle over the pears. Drizzle on the lemon juice and dot with the butter
or margarine. Cover with the top crust, seal or crimp the edges and cut
vent holes in the top. Bake in a preheated 450° oven for 15 minutes.
Reduce the oven temperature to 375° and bake for 40 minutes more.

Serves 8.

Flavors of a Vermont Village
West Newbury Women's Fellowship, West Newbury, Vermont

OATMEAL PIE

This tastes like a pecan pie without the pecans. It is quick and easy to make and relatively inexpensive. Serve it with a dollop of whipped cream.

1 **cup rolled oats**	¹/₂ **teaspoon ground cinnamon**
1 **cup maple syrup**	¹/₂ **teaspoon ground cloves**
¹/₂ **cup sugar**	¹/₄ **teaspoon salt**
¹/₄ **cup butter or margarine,**	3 **eggs, divided**
softened	**9" unbaked piecrust**

In a large bowl, beat together the oats, maple syrup, sugar, butter or margarine, cinnamon, cloves and salt. Add the eggs, 1 at a time, beating well after each addition. Pour into the piecrust and bake in a preheated 350° oven for 1 hour. Cool completely before serving.

Serves 8.

Still Alarm Recipes
Brattleboro Benefit Association, Brattleboro, Vermont

PUMPKIN ICE CREAM PIE WITH GINGERSNAP CRUST

Keep the tradition of serving pumpkin pie at Thanksgiving, but to win the approval of diners of all ages, serve this one. It makes an excellent, easy dessert year-round, too.

22 **gingersnaps**	¹/₂ **teaspoon ground cinnamon**
1³/₄ **cups or 1 can (15 ounces)**	¹/₄ **teaspoon ground nutmeg**
mashed cooked pumpkin	¹/₂ **cup chopped nuts**
¹/₂ **cup sugar**	1 **quart vanilla ice cream or**
¹/₂ **teaspoon salt**	**frozen yogurt, softened slightly**

Arrange 19 or 20 whole gingersnaps on the bottom and sides of a 9" pie plate. Crush the remaining gingersnaps and set aside.

In a medium bowl, combine the pumpkin, sugar, salt, cinnamon and nutmeg and mix well. Stir in the nuts and chill.

Fold the chilled mixture into the softened ice cream or frozen yogurt and spoon into the piecrust. Sprinkle the reserved gingersnap crumbs over the top and freeze. Remove the pie from the freezer 15 to 20 minutes before serving.

Serves 8 to 10.

Patchwork Pantry
Monadnock Community Hospital, Peterborough, New Hampshire

$\mathcal{L}$EMON-CAKE PIE

This unusual dessert has a light, delicate cake layer
on top of a luscious, lemony pie filling.

1 **cup sugar**	2 **eggs, separated**
¼ **cup unbleached flour**	**Juice and grated rind of**
¼ **cup butter or margarine,**	**1 lemon**
melted and cooled	1 **cup milk**
⅛ **teaspoon salt**	**9″ unbaked piecrust**

In a large bowl, combine the sugar, flour, butter or margarine, salt, egg yolks, lemon juice and lemon rind. Beat until smooth. Add the milk and mix thoroughly.

Bake the piecrust in a preheated 350° oven for 5 minutes. Meanwhile, beat the egg whites until stiff but not dry, then fold into the sugar-butter mixture. Pour into the partially baked crust and bake for 40 minutes more, or until the filling is firm.

Serves 6 to 8.

Crossroads Cookbook
Somers Congregational Church, Somers, Connecticut

VERMONT MAPLE-WALNUT PIE

This rivals any pecan pie, which it resembles in appearance,
but the flavor is not so intensely sweet. Mellowed by the
maple syrup and cream, it is a fine way to finish off any meal.

¾ cup granulated sugar
½ cup firmly packed light
  brown sugar
⅓ cup butter or margarine,
  softened
3 eggs
½ cup light cream

¼ cup maple syrup
¼ teaspoon salt
1 cup walnuts, broken into
  pieces
1 teaspoon vanilla
  9" unbaked piecrust

In a saucepan, cream the granulated sugar, brown sugar and butter or
margarine. Add the eggs and beat well. Add the cream, maple syrup and
salt and cook over low heat for 5 minutes, stirring constantly. Remove from
the heat and stir in the walnuts and vanilla. Pour into the piecrust and bake
in a preheated 350° oven for 1 hour. Serve warm.

Serves 6 to 8.

RRMC Family Favorites
Rutland Regional Medical Center Auxiliary, Rutland, Vermont

TOLL HOUSE PIE

Either walnuts or pecans can be used in this sumptuously
chocolaty pie, but to enhance their flavor and preserve their
texture, you might want to toast them first.

2 eggs
½ cup unbleached flour
½ cup granulated sugar
½ cup firmly packed brown
  sugar

1 cup butter or margarine,
  melted and cooled
1 cup chopped nuts
1 package (6 ounces) semisweet
  chocolate chips
  9" unbaked piecrust

In a medium bowl, beat the eggs until foamy. Beat in the flour, granulated sugar and brown sugar until well blended. Stir in the butter or margarine, nuts and chocolate chips. Pour the mixture into the piecrust and bake in a preheated 325° oven for 1 hour.

Serves 6.

Our Daily Bread
St. Patrick's Church: Our Lady's Guild, Bennington, New Hampshire

*E*ASY OIL PIECRUST

Easy enough for a novice, this recipe yields a fine crust that is perfect for dessert pies or savory quiches. To facilitate rolling out the dough between waxed paper, put a few drops of water on the work surface and cover with the bottom sheet of waxed paper; the water will hold the paper in place.

2 cups unbleached flour	**¹⁄₂ cup oil**
1 teaspoon salt	**¹⁄₄ cup plus 2 tablespoons milk**

Combine the flour and salt in a medium bowl. Add the oil and milk and stir until the dough forms a ball. Roll out between 2 sheets of waxed paper.

Makes enough pastry for 1 single-crust 9″ pie.

College Street Congregational Church 125th Anniversary Cookbook
College Street Congregational Church, Burlington, Vermont

PERFECT PIECRUST

Here are step-by-step directions for an unfailingly tender,
flaky piecrust. No matter how much you handle this dough (you
can beat it with your rolling pin if you like), it will always be flaky,
tender and delicious. Scraps can be rerolled if necessary, and the
crust will never be tough. The dough can be left in the refrigerator
for up to 3 days; it will remain soft and can be taken out and rolled at once.
Or it can be frozen until you're ready to use it. Just thaw until it's soft
enough to roll. Give the recipe your undivided attention.

4 cups unbleached flour (not
   instant or self-rising), lightly
   spooned into measuring cup
   and leveled
1 tablespoon sugar
2 teaspoons salt

1¾ cups shortening (not chilled;
   do not use oil, lard,
   margarine or butter)
½ cup water
1 tablespoon white or cider
   vinegar
1 egg

Put the flour, sugar and salt in a large bowl and mix well with a fork.
Add the shortening and cut in with the fork until the ingredients are
crumbly.

In a small bowl, beat the water, vinegar and egg with a fork. Add to the
flour mixture, stirring until all the ingredients are moistened.

Divide the dough into 5 portions. Using your hands, shape each portion
into a flat, round patty ready for rolling. Wrap each patty in plastic wrap or
waxed paper and chill for at least 30 minutes.

When you're ready to roll out the piecrust, lightly flour both sides of a
patty and place on a lightly floured surface or pastry cloth. Cover the
rolling pin with a stockinette and rub in a little flour. Keeping the pastry
round and starting from the center, roll out to a ⅛" thickness and 2" larger
than the inverted pie plate.

Fold in half, transfer to the pie plate, unfold and fit loosely in the plate.
Press with your fingers to remove any air pockets.

**Makes enough pastry for 2 double-crust 9" pies
and 1 single-crust 9" pie or 20 tart shells.**

Patchwork Pantry
Monadnock Community Hospital, Peterborough, New Hampshire

SANDY'S CHOCOLATE TRUFFLE CAKE

❦

Intensely chocolaty but not densely textured, this is a rich
and decadent dessert. Although it's called a cake, it is baked and sliced
like a pie. Serve it with whipped cream or ice cream.
(Yes, the small amount of flour is correct.)

2 cups semisweet chocolate chips	**1½ teaspoons sugar**
½ cup butter or margarine	**1 teaspoon hot water**
1½ teaspoons unbleached flour	**4 eggs, separated**

In a double boiler or heavy-bottomed saucepan, melt the chocolate chips
and butter or margarine. Remove from the heat and stir in the flour, sugar
and hot water. Let cool slightly.

In a small bowl, beat the egg whites until stiff. Beat the egg yolks, 1 at a
time, into the cooled chocolate mixture, then fold in the egg whites. Pour
into a 9" pie plate and bake in a preheated 425° oven for 15 minutes. Chill
before slicing into small portions but serve at room temperature.

Serves 6 to 8.

The Kinderhaus Cookbook
Kinderhaus Children's Center, Williston, Vermont

BAKED INDIAN PUDDING

A traditional New England dish, this pudding is absolutely wonderful—luscious, smooth and rich. To ensure the smooth consistency, use a whisk to mix the ingredients and stir the pudding frequently. Serve warm with a scoop of vanilla ice cream, whipped cream or plain cream.

4 cups milk, divided	1/2 teaspoon ground cinnamon
1/2 cup molasses	1/2 teaspoon ground ginger
1/2 cup cornmeal	1 tablespoon butter or
1/4 cup firmly packed brown	margarine
sugar	1 egg, beaten
1/2 teaspoon salt	

Mix 2 cups of the milk and the molasses in a double boiler. Combine the cornmeal, brown sugar, salt, cinnamon and ginger in a small bowl and add to the milk-molasses mixture. Add the butter or margarine and cook for 20 minutes, stirring frequently.

Mix the egg with 1 cup of the remaining milk and stir into the cornmeal mixture. Pour into a greased 2-quart baking dish and bake in a preheated 325° oven for 1 hour. Pour the remaining 1 cup milk over the top of the pudding, but do not stir. Bake for 1 hour more.

Serves 6.

The Fine Arts Cookbook I
Museum of Fine Arts, Boston, Massachusetts

BAKED CUSTARD WITH MAPLE SYRUP

This familiar all-time favorite also can be served for breakfast or brunch, or even as a light supper when you're in need of some comfort food.

5 eggs	5 cups milk, scalded
1 cup sugar	1 cup plus 2 tablespoons maple
2 teaspoons vanilla	syrup
Pinch of salt	Ground nutmeg

In a medium bowl, beat the eggs, sugar, vanilla and salt. Slowly add the milk, stirring constantly until well mixed.

Put 1½ tablespoons maple syrup in the bottom of each of 12 (½-cup) custard cups. Pour the custard mixture over the syrup, filling the cups ⅔ full. Sprinkle with nutmeg. Place the cups in a shallow pan of water and bake in a preheated 350° oven for about 20 to 30 minutes, or until a knife inserted in the center comes out clean.

Serves 12.

Vermont II: Kitchen Memories
Montpelier, Vermont

ℬANANAS WITH RUM
❧

Simple yet elegant, this dessert can follow just about any meal.
Serve it hot, warm or at room temperature; with ice cream,
sour cream, whipped cream or plain.

¼ **cup unsalted butter or margarine**
4 **medium bananas, peeled and halved lengthwise**

¼ **cup firmly packed brown sugar**
¼ **cup dark rum**

Use a portion of the butter or margarine to grease a glass baking dish large enough to hold all the bananas in 1 layer. Place the bananas in the dish cut side down. Sprinkle with the brown sugar and rum and dot with the remaining butter or margarine. Bake in a preheated 400° oven until the bananas are tender but not mushy, about 10 to 15 minutes.

Serves 4.

Recipe Sampler
Shoreline Quilters' Guild, Branford, Connecticut

PPLE CRISP

Most New Englanders have a tried-and-true favorite
recipe for this traditional treat. Devoted though one may be to a
particular combination of ingredients, this crisp is likely to be rated
as a close second—if not move into first place. Serve with
ice cream, frozen yogurt or sweetened whipped cream.

1 **cup graham cracker crumbs**	½ **teaspoon ground cinnamon**
1 **tablespoon unbleached flour**	½ **teaspoon ground nutmeg**
1 **cup chopped walnuts or**	**Pinch of salt**
pecans	½ **cup butter or margarine,**
1 **cup firmly packed brown**	**melted**
sugar	4 **large tart apples (early**
¼ **cup granulated sugar**	**McIntosh are best)**
1 **tablespoon grated orange**	
rind	

In a medium bowl, combine the graham cracker crumbs, flour, walnuts
or pecans, brown sugar and granulated sugar. Stir in the orange rind, cinnamon, nutmeg and salt, then blend in the butter or margarine.

Lightly butter a 13″ × 9″ baking dish. Peel, core and thinly slice the
apples. Place the slices on the bottom of the dish and scatter the crumb
mixture over the top. Bake in a preheated 350° oven for 45 minutes.

Serves 6 to 8.

The Maine Collection
Portland Museum of Art, Portland, Maine

HOMETOWN COOKING IN NEW ENGLAND

GALLIMAUFRY'S APPLE BROWN BETTY

A tasty variation of this ever-popular dessert. The maple syrup and lemon provide a distinctive sweet-tart flavor. Serve with cream or hard sauce.

1 **cup fairly coarse dry bread crumbs**

2 **tablespoons butter or margarine, melted**

2 **cups peeled, cored and chopped tart apples, divided**

½ **cup maple syrup, divided**

Juice and grated rind of 1 lemon, divided

¼ **teaspoon ground cinnamon, divided**

⅛ **teaspoon ground nutmeg, divided**

½ **cup apple cider**

In a medium bowl, combine the bread crumbs and butter or margarine. Sprinkle a few crumbs on the bottom of a 10" pie plate or baking dish. Cover with half the apples, half the buttered bread crumbs and half the maple syrup. Sprinkle with half the lemon juice, lemon rind, cinnamon and nutmeg. Repeat the layers. Pour the cider over all and bake in a preheated 350° oven for 30 minutes, or until the apples are tender.

Serves 4 to 6.

Seasoned with Love
Eastman House, Cranston, Rhode Island

ℒEMON-ROSEMARY APPLE COBBLER

ᔥ

Rosemary gives an appealing new twist to this old-time favorite,
although traditionalists may be reluctant to try it. When making this
for the first time, use only ⅛ teaspoon dried rosemary in the
filling and ⅛ teaspoon in the crust. For those who want more
rosemary flavor, increase the amount to ¼ teaspoon, and for a
totally new experience, use the original amount called for—½ teaspoon.
This is excellent warm with vanilla ice cream, but it's equally
delectable at room temperature for breakfast or brunch.

FILLING
- ⅛–½ **teaspoon dried rosemary**
- ⅓ **cup sugar**
- 2 **tablespoons lemon juice**
- **Grated rind of ½ lemon**
- 5 **cups peeled, cored and thinly sliced apples**

CRUST
- ⅛–½ **teaspoon dried rosemary**
- 1 **cup unbleached flour**
- 1 **tablespoon sugar**
- 1 **teaspoon baking powder**
- ⅛ **teaspoon salt**
- 3 **tablespoons cold unsalted butter or margarine, cut up**
- ⅓ **cup light cream or milk**

To make the filling: Crush the rosemary as fine as possible and put in a
large bowl. Add the sugar, lemon juice and lemon rind and stir to mix. Add
the apples, stirring to coat, and arrange in a 9″ pie plate or similar size
baking dish.

To make the crust: Finely crush the rosemary and mix with the flour,
sugar, baking powder and salt in a medium bowl. Add the butter or margarine and cut in with a pastry blender or knives until the mixture is the
consistency of coarse cornmeal. Add the cream or milk and stir until a soft
dough forms. Knead on a lightly floured surface 10 to 12 times. Roll out
the dough to fit the baking dish. Place it over the apples, seal the edges and
cut slits in the top. Bake in a preheated 400° oven for 25 to 30 minutes, or
until golden.

Serves 6.

Vermont Kitchens Revisited
The Women of the Cathedral Church of St. Paul, Burlington, Vermont

$\mathcal{R}$HUBARB-STRAWBERRY COBBLER

To boost the nutritive value of this luscious dessert, substitute 2 table-spoons wheat germ for part of the flour in the biscuit topping and add 3 tablespoons instant nonfat dry milk to the dry ingredients before mixing in the oil and milk. Serve warm with ice cream or nonfat frozen yogurt.

BASE

- 3 cups rhubarb cut into 1" pieces
- 2 cups strawberries cut into halves
- 1 egg, beaten
- 1 tablespoon lemon juice
- 1¼ cups sugar
- 3 tablespoons unbleached flour

CRUST

- 1 cup unbleached flour
- 2 tablespoons sugar
- 1 teaspoon baking powder
- ½ teaspoon salt
- ¼ cup milk
- 3 tablespoons oil

To make the base: Combine the rhubarb and strawberries and pour into a shallow 9" × 9" baking dish. In a small bowl, beat the egg and lemon juice, stir in the sugar and blend in the flour. Pour over the rhubarb-strawberry mixture.

To make the crust: In a small bowl, combine the flour, sugar, baking powder and salt. In another bowl, combine the milk and oil and add to the dry ingredients, mixing well. Roll out to a 9" × 9" square and place over the rhubarb-strawberry mixture. Bake in a preheated 425° oven for 15 to 20 minutes.

Serves 4.

South Newbury Union Church and Society Cookbook
South Newbury Union Church, South Newbury, New Hampshire

$\mathscr{B}$LUEBERRY SLUMP & GRUNT

ᴥ

Maine folklore credits the name of this recipe to the known
fact that menfolk on the farm, when served this dessert at noon,
were inclined to "slump" into a porch chair and "grunt"
instead of returning to complete their chores!

4	cups fresh or frozen blueberries	2	teaspoons baking powder
1	cup sugar, divided	½	teaspoon salt
½	cup water	½	cup milk
2	tablespoons butter or margarine		Fresh cream, sour cream or ice cream
1	cup unbleached flour		Ground cinnamon or ground nutmeg (optional)

To make the slump: Combine the blueberries, ¾ cup of the sugar, the
water and the butter or margarine in a saucepan. Bring to a boil, reduce the
heat and simmer.

In a small bowl, mix the flour, baking powder, salt, remaining ¼ cup
sugar and milk to make a stiff batter. Spoon over the hot mixture as for
dumplings. Cover tightly and simmer for 12 minutes. Do not uncover
during the cooking time. Serve hot with fresh cream or sour cream.

To make the grunt: Combine the blueberries, ¾ cup of the sugar and the
water in a large bowl. Pour into a greased 2-quart casserole. Bake in a preheated 400° oven until the mixture simmers.

Meanwhile, blend the flour, baking powder, salt and remaining ¼ cup
sugar in a large bowl. Cut in the butter or margarine until the mixture
is crumbly, then add the milk, stirring to combine. Spoon over the hot
berries. Bake in a preheated 350° oven for 20 minutes. Serve hot with fresh
cream or ice cream. Sprinkle with cinnamon or nutmeg (if using).

Serves 6 to 8.

Merrymeeting Merry Eating
Mid Coast Hospital/Brunswick Auxiliary, Brunswick, Maine

CAKES, COOKIES & CANDIES

SHAKER PINEAPPLE CAKE

This moist cake is great with or without the creamy sauce.
The nuts are recommended, as they enhance the texture.

CAKE
- 2 cups unbleached flour
- 2 cups sugar
- 2 teaspoons baking powder
- 2 eggs
- 1 can (20 ounces) crushed unsweetened pineapple, with juice
- ½–1 cup chopped walnuts (optional)

SAUCE
- 2 cups sifted confectioners' sugar
- 3 tablespoons butter or margarine, softened
- 3 tablespoons milk
- ½ package (3-ounce size) cream cheese, softened
- ¼ teaspoon salt

To make the cake: Combine the flour, sugar and baking powder in a medium bowl. Beat the eggs in a large bowl, then add the pineapple and juice. Blend in the flour mixture. Add the walnuts (if using) and pour the mixture into an ungreased 13" × 9" baking pan. Bake in a preheated 350° oven for 30 to 40 minutes, or until a toothpick inserted in the center comes out clean.

To make the sauce: In a large bowl, beat the confectioners' sugar, butter or margarine, milk, cream cheese and salt until creamy. Serve on the side with the cake.

Serves 12 to 14.

History in the Baking
Sunapee 2000 Beautification Committee, Sunapee, New Hampshire

BLUEBERRY-LEMON POUND CAKE

Light and luscious, rich and moist, this cake satisfies any
craving for something sweet. Serve it for dessert, at brunch or tea or
as a snack. It's a surefire moneymaker for a bake sale, too.

1 cup butter or margarine,
   softened
2 cups sugar, divided
6 eggs, separated
   Grated rind of 3 lemons
2 tablespoons lemon juice
3 cups unbleached flour
½ teaspoon baking soda

1 cup plain yogurt
   Pinch of cream of tartar
   Pinch of salt
1½ cups blueberries, tossed with
   1½ tablespoons unbleached
   flour
   Confectioners' sugar

In a large bowl, cream the butter or margarine and add 1½ cups of the
sugar, beating until the mixture is light and fluffy. Beat in the egg yolks, 1 at
a time, and add the lemon rind and lemon juice. Sift the flour and baking
soda into a medium bowl and add alternately with the yogurt to the butter-
sugar mixture.

Beat the egg whites with the cream of tartar and salt until they hold soft
peaks. Gradually beat in the remaining ½ cup sugar until the mixture holds
stiff peaks. Stir ¼ of the egg white mixture into the yogurt batter; fold in
the rest. Fold the blueberries into the batter and spoon into a buttered and
floured 10" tube pan or two 9" × 5" loaf pans. Bake in a preheated 375°
oven for 60 to 70 minutes, or until a toothpick inserted in the center comes
out clean. Let cool, then sift confectioners' sugar over the cake.

Serves 12 to 16.

The Charlotte Central Cooks' Book
Charlotte Central PTO, Charlotte, Vermont

$\mathcal{S}$TONE FENCE APPLESAUCE CAKE
❧

A cross between apple cake and carrot cake, this is moist,
wholesome and chunky. The quantity of walnuts can easily
be reduced by half, since nuts are high in fat.

½ **cup butter or margarine, softened**	1½ **teaspoons ground cinnamon**
1 **cup granulated sugar**	½ **teaspoon ground nutmeg**
1 **cup firmly packed brown sugar**	½ **teaspoon ground allspice**
2 **eggs**	2¼ **cups applesauce**
3 **cups unbleached flour**	¾ **cup shredded carrots**
1½ **cups whole-wheat flour**	1½ **cups coarsely broken walnuts**
1 **tablespoon baking soda**	1½ **cups raisins**
	Confectioners' sugar

In a large bowl, cream the butter or margarine until light and fluffy.
Gradually beat in the granulated sugar and brown sugar. Beat in the eggs.

In another bowl, combine the unbleached flour and whole-wheat flour.
Add the baking soda, cinnamon, nutmeg and allspice and mix well.

Add the dry ingredients alternately with the applesauce and carrots to
the creamed mixture. Fold in the walnuts and raisins. Transfer to a greased
and floured 10″ Bundt pan. Bake in a preheated 350° oven for 1¼ to
1½ hours, or until the top springs back when lightly pressed with a finger.

Cool in the pan for 10 minutes, tap to loosen and unmold. Cool thoroughly before cutting into thin slices. Serve sprinkled with confectioners'
sugar.

Serves 10 to 12.

Cohasset Entertains, Encore
The Community Garden Club, Cohasset, Massachusetts

DOWNEAST RASPBERRY CAKE

Serve this cake soon after frosting, while the berries are still colorful.
Light and delicate, it requires careful handling when it is being cut into
portions. Frozen raspberries work perfectly fine, making this an ideal
choice when the winter blahs beg for a boost to one's spirits.

CAKE

- 1/3 **cup butter or margarine,
  softened**
- 1 **cup sugar**
- 1 **egg**
- 1 **cup milk**
- 1 **teaspoon vanilla**
- 2 **cups unbleached flour**
- 3 **teaspoons baking powder**
- 1/2 **teaspoon salt**
- 1 **pint fresh or frozen
  raspberries**

GLAZE

- 1 1/2 **cups sifted confectioners'
  sugar**
- 3 **tablespoons heavy cream**
- 1 **teaspoon butter or margarine,
  melted**

To make the cake: Cream the butter or margarine and sugar in a large
bowl. Add the egg and beat. Combine the milk and vanilla in a small bowl.
Sift the flour, baking powder and salt and add alternately with the combined
milk and vanilla to the creamed mixture. Mix until smooth. Pour the batter
into a greased and floured 13" × 9" baking pan. Sprinkle the raspberries
evenly over the batter and bake in a preheated 375° oven for 30 minutes.

To make the glaze: Mix the confectioners' sugar, cream and butter or
margarine until smooth. Frost the cake while it is still warm.

Serves 10 to 12.

Merrymeeting Merry Eating
Mid Coast Hospital/Brunswick Auxiliary, Brunswick, Maine

$\int$TRAWBERRY-ALMOND SHORTCAKE

Who doesn't love strawberry shortcake? And if there is such a soul,
this almond-amended version will certainly do the trick.
Instead of canned almond paste, you can use a 7-ounce roll of
the soft type, but add an additional 3 tablespoons flour.

2 cups unbleached flour	1/2 cup milk
2 teaspoons baking powder	1 egg
1 cup unsalted butter or	1/2 teaspoon almond extract
margarine, softened	1 quart ripe strawberries,
1 can (8 ounces) almond paste,	rinsed, drained and hulled
cut into small pieces	1 cup whipping cream
1/4 cup plus 3 tablespoons sugar,	1/2 teaspoon vanilla
divided	1/4 cup toasted sliced almonds

In a small bowl, combine the flour and baking powder. In a large bowl,
beat the butter or margarine, almond paste and 1/4 cup of the sugar until
light and fluffy. Beat in the milk, egg and almond extract. Stir in the flour
mixture until blended.

Spoon equal amounts of batter into 2 ungreased 9" round cake pans.
Spread evenly and smooth the tops. Bake in a preheated 375° oven for
20 minutes, or until the cakes pull away from the sides of the pans and the
tops are light golden brown. Cool in the pans on wire racks for 10 minutes,
then remove to the racks to cool completely.

Meanwhile, cut enough strawberries in half to equal 2 cups, leaving the
remainder whole. In a small bowl, sprinkle 2 tablespoons of the remaining
sugar over the halved berries. Let stand at room temperature, stirring occasionally, for 30 minutes to extract the juices.

In a small bowl, beat the cream, remaining 1 tablespoon sugar and
vanilla until soft peaks form.

To assemble, put 1 shortcake on a serving plate, top side up. Top with
the halved berries and their juices, then half the whipped cream. Cover
with the second shortcake and spread with the remaining whipped cream.
Arrange the whole berries on top with the stem ends down. Sprinkle the
almonds in the spaces between the berries. Serve immediately.

Serves 12.

Recipe Sampler
Shoreline Quilters' Guild, Branford, Connecticut

ORANGE KISS-ME CAKE

When you need an appealing dessert to follow a heavy meal, serve this cake. It is neither too sweet nor too rich, and garnished with thin orange slices, it makes a fine presentation.

1 large orange	1 cup milk, divided
1 cup raisins	½ cup shortening
⅓ cup walnuts	2 eggs
2 cups unbleached flour	⅓ cup firmly packed brown
1 cup granulated sugar	sugar
1 teaspoon baking soda	¼ cup chopped walnuts
½ teaspoon salt	1 teaspoon ground cinnamon

Juice the orange and set aside ⅓ cup of the juice. Grind together the orange rind and pulp, raisins and ⅓ cup walnuts. Set aside.

In a large bowl, sift together the flour, granulated sugar, baking soda and salt. Add ¾ cup of the milk and the shortening and beat for 2 minutes. Add the eggs and remaining ¼ cup milk and beat for 2 minutes more. Fold the orange-raisin mixture into the batter. Pour into a well-greased, lightly floured 12" × 8" baking pan and bake in a preheated 350° oven for 40 to 50 minutes.

Drizzle the reserved orange juice over the warm cake. In a small bowl, combine the brown sugar, chopped walnuts and cinnamon and sprinkle over the top of the cake.

Serves 12 to 16.

Stowe Community Church Cookbook
Stowe Community Church: United Ladies Aid, Stowe, Vermont

THANKSGIVING RUM-DATE CAKE

Moist, chunky and delicious, this is a good keeper and would make an excellent substitute for the more traditional type of fruitcake that calls for citron and candied cherries. It can be drizzled with a rum-sugar or butter-cream icing and garnished with cranberries, or served with ice cream or whipped cream. A small portion is appropriate.

¾ cup butter or margarine, softened
1½ cups firmly packed brown sugar
1 pound dates, pitted and chopped
1 pound pecans, chopped

1 cup boiling water
1 teaspoon baking soda
3 eggs, beaten
2¼ cups unbleached flour
¼ teaspoon salt
½ cup rum

In a large bowl, cream the butter or margarine and brown sugar until well blended. Fold in the dates and pecans.

In a small bowl, combine the water and baking soda and pour over the sugar mixture, stirring to blend. Add the eggs, flour and salt and beat until smooth. Add the rum and blend well. Pour into a well-greased 10″ Bundt pan and bake in a preheated 300° oven for 1½ hours. Cool in the pan on a wire rack for 10 minutes, then invert onto a serving plate.

Serves 18 to 20.

A Taste of New England
Junior League of Worcester, Massachusetts

CAN'T-BE-BEET CAKE

Unusual and appealing, this is a fun cake to take to a party, where you can ask samplers to guess the secret ingredient.

1½ cups unbleached flour
2 tablespoons unsweetened cocoa powder
1½ teaspoons baking soda
1 teaspoon ground ginger
1 teaspoon ground cinnamon
¼ teaspoon ground cloves
¼ teaspoon ground nutmeg
¼ teaspoon salt
1 jar (16 ounces) sliced pickled beets, well drained
3 eggs
1½ cups firmly packed brown sugar
½ cup oil
Confectioners' sugar or whipped cream

In a medium bowl, combine the flour, cocoa, baking soda, ginger, cinnamon, cloves, nutmeg and salt. Puree the beets in a blender or food processor.

Whisk the eggs, brown sugar and oil together in a large bowl. Add the beets and stir. Blend in the flour mixture. Pour into a greased 9" × 9" baking pan and bake in a preheated 350° oven for 30 to 35 minutes, or until a toothpick inserted in the center comes out clean.

Cool in the pan on a wire rack for 10 minutes. Turn out on the rack, invert onto a plate and sprinkle with confectioners' sugar or serve with whipped cream.

Serves 8 to 10.

Vernon Bicentennial Cookbook
Vernon Bicentennial Cookbook Committee, Vernon, Vermont

CARAMEL CAKE

Topped with a glossy caramel frosting, this is not the kind of
cake that can be made quickly, but it is a beauty.

CAKE

- 7 **egg whites**
- 2 **cups sugar, divided**
- 1 **cup butter or margarine,
  softened**
- 1 **teaspoon vanilla**
- 1½ **cups unbleached flour**
- 1 **cup cornstarch**
- 1 **tablespoon baking powder**
- ½ **teaspoon salt**
- 1 **cup minus 1 tablespoon milk**

FROSTING

- 1 **cup plus 2 tablespoons brown
  sugar**
- 4 **squares (1 ounce each)
  unsweetened chocolate**
- ½ **cup evaporated milk**
- 2 **tablespoons butter or
  margarine**
- 2 **teaspoons vanilla**

To make the cake: In a large bowl, beat the egg whites until soft peaks
form. Gradually add ⅔ cup of the sugar and continue beating until stiff
peaks form. Set aside.

In another bowl, cream the butter or margarine and the remaining
1⅓ cups sugar. Stir in the vanilla.

Sift the flour, cornstarch, baking powder and salt in a bowl and add to
the creamed mixture alternately with the milk. Fold in the egg whites. Pour
into a greased and waxed paper–lined 13" × 9" baking pan and bake in a
preheated 325° oven for 50 to 60 minutes, or until a toothpick inserted in
the center comes out clean.

Cool for about 15 minutes, remove from the pan and finish cooling on a
wire rack. When completely cooled, invert onto a plate.

To make the frosting: Combine the brown sugar, chocolate, milk, butter or
margarine and vanilla in a saucepan and cook, stirring, until the chocolate
melts and the mixture begins to thicken, about 5 minutes after it starts to
boil. Remove from the heat and beat with a wooden spoon until cool and
thick enough to spread. Frost the cooled cake.

Serves 16.

A Taste of Glocester
Glocester Heritage Society, Chepachet, Rhode Island

WELLESLEY FUDGE CAKE

This cake is well worth the time and the investment in a candy thermometer, which is very useful when making the fudge frosting.

CAKE

- **4** squares (1 ounce each) unsweetened chocolate
- **½** cup hot water
- **1¾** cups sugar, divided
- **2** cups unbleached flour
- **1** teaspoon baking soda
- **½** teaspoon salt
- **½** cup butter or margarine, softened
- **3** eggs
- **1** teaspoon vanilla
- **⅔** cup milk

FROSTING

- **1½** cups milk
- **4** cups sugar
- **4** teaspoons light corn syrup
- **4** squares (1 ounce each) unsweetened chocolate
- Pinch of salt
- **¼** cup butter or margarine
- **2** teaspoons vanilla

To make the cake: Combine the chocolate and water in a double boiler. Cook over hot water until the chocolate is melted. Stir in ½ cup of the sugar and cook for 2 minutes more. Remove from the heat and set aside.

In a medium bowl, sift the flour, baking soda and salt three times. In a large bowl, cream the butter or margarine. Add the remaining 1¼ cups sugar, beating until light and fluffy. Add the eggs, 1 at a time, beating thoroughly after each addition. Stir in the vanilla. Add the flour mixture alternately with the milk, beating well after each addition. Add the melted chocolate and blend well.

Pour the batter into 2 well-greased 9″ round cake pans. Bake in a preheated 350° oven for 25 to 30 minutes, or until a toothpick inserted in the center comes out clean.

To make the frosting: In a saucepan, heat the milk just to boiling. Remove from the heat and add the sugar, corn syrup, chocolate and salt, stirring until the sugar dissolves.

Place the saucepan over medium-low heat and bring back to a boil. Boil for 2 to 3 minutes, stirring constantly. Reduce the heat to low and cook, stirring occasionally, to the soft-ball stage (238°). This may take as long as 30 minutes depending on your stove. When the temperature nears 238°, the mixture should have a fine bubbling overall. Remove from the heat carefully. Cool the mixture to 110°. This can be quickened by placing the hot pan in a larger pan of cold water, cooling the bottom of the pan. When cooled, beat in the butter or margarine and vanilla. Spread the frosting between the layers of the cooled cake and then on the top and sides.

Serves 8 to 12.

The Longyear Cookbook
Longyear Museum and Historical Society, Brookline, Massachusetts

ZUCCHINI CHOCOLATE CHIP CAKE

A good keeper, this is a scrumptious holiday dessert or snack cake. Pop a slice into the microwave to warm slightly and top with vanilla ice cream or frozen yogurt. Yum!

2½ cups unbleached flour	3 eggs
½ cup unsweetened cocoa powder	2 cups coarsely chopped zucchini
2½ teaspoons baking powder	1 package (12 ounces) semisweet chocolate chips
1½ teaspoons baking soda	1 cup chopped walnuts (optional)
1 teaspoon ground cinnamon	
½ teaspoon salt	½ cup milk
¾ cup butter or margarine, softened	2 teaspoons vanilla
2 cups sugar	2 teaspoons grated orange rind

In a medium bowl, sift the flour, cocoa, baking powder, baking soda, cinnamon and salt. In a large bowl, cream the butter or margarine and sugar, then beat in the eggs, 1 at a time. Stir in the zucchini, chocolate chips, walnuts (if using), milk, vanilla and orange rind. Add the dry ingredients and blend well. Pour into a well-greased 10" Bundt or angel food cake pan and bake in a preheated 350° oven for 1 hour, or until a toothpick inserted in the center comes out clean.

Serves 20 to 24.

Cracker Barrel Cookbook
First Congregational Church: Newbury Women's Fellowship, Newbury, Vermont

BOSTON CREAM PIE

This pie is really a 2-layer cake with a custard filling and glossy chocolate frosting. It involves a lot of steps but is the "real thing." You may find that there's more than enough frosting for the cake, so use what's left over for something else, like cupcakes.

CAKE
- 2 eggs, separated
- 1 cup superfine sugar
- 1 cup unbleached flour
- 1 teaspoon baking powder
  Pinch of salt
- 1 tablespoon butter or margarine
- ½ cup milk, heated
- ½ teaspoon vanilla
- ½ teaspoon lemon extract (optional)

FILLING
- ½ cup sugar
- 3 tablespoons unbleached flour
  Pinch of salt
- 1 cup milk or cream, scalded
- 1 egg, lightly beaten
- ½ teaspoon vanilla or orange extract

FROSTING
- 1 cup sugar
- 3 tablespoons cornstarch
- 2 squares (1 ounce each) unsweetened chocolate, shaved
- ¼ teaspoon salt
- 1 cup boiling water
- 1 tablespoon butter or margarine
- 1 teaspoon vanilla

To make the cake: In a large bowl, beat the egg whites until stiff. In a small bowl, beat the egg yolks until light, add to the whites and beat together. Slowly add the sugar, beating for 5 minutes.

In a separate bowl, sift the flour, baking powder and salt. Melt the butter or margarine in the hot milk. Add the dry ingredients and milk mixture to the egg mixture as quickly as possible. Stir in the vanilla and lemon extract (if using). Turn into a well-greased and floured 8" round cake pan and bake in a preheated 350° oven for 25 to 30 minutes. Cool on a wire rack. When completely cool, cut into 2 layers.

To make the filling: Combine the sugar, flour and salt with the milk in a double boiler. Cook for 15 minutes, stirring constantly. Stir a spoonful of the mixture into the egg and pour back into the double boiler. Cook for 3 to 5 minutes more, or until thickened. Cool and add the vanilla or orange extract. Spread on 1 cake layer, then place the other layer on top.

To make the frosting: Combine the sugar, cornstarch, chocolate and salt in a saucepan. Add the water, stir and boil until the mixture thickens enough to be spreadable. Watch carefully, for chocolate burns easily. Remove from the heat and stir in the butter or margarine and vanilla. Spread while hot on top of the cake. The frosting will be glossy.

Serves 10 to 12.

The Fine Arts Cookbook I
Museum of Fine Arts, Boston, Massachusetts

ROWN SUGARS

An excellent recipe for children to make, these cookies are easy and taste great. For dessert, serve them crumbled over vanilla ice cream.

½ **cup butter or margarine, softened**	1 **teaspoon vanilla**
	2 **cups sifted unbleached flour**
½ **cup firmly packed dark brown sugar**	½ **teaspoon salt**
	½ **teaspoon baking soda**
½ **cup granulated sugar**	½ **cup ground walnuts**
1 **egg**	**Granulated sugar for rolling**

In a large bowl, cream the butter or margarine, brown sugar and granulated sugar. Beat in the egg and vanilla.

In a separate bowl, mix the flour, salt and baking soda and add to the creamed mixture. Blend in the walnuts. Form the mixture into walnut-size balls, then roll in granulated sugar. Place the balls on ungreased cookie sheets and flatten with the bottom of a glass. Bake in a preheated 350° oven for 10 to 12 minutes.

Makes 24 to 36.

The Mark Twain Library Cookbook, Vol. III
Mark Twain Library Association, Redding, Connecticut

$\mathcal{S}$NICKER DOODLES

An old-fashioned cookie that remains a New England favorite.
These are similar to sugar cookies but have a cinnamon flavor,
crisp edges and a tender, moist center. They are easy to make,
inexpensive and a nice change from oatmeal or chocolate chip cookies.
They store well in an airtight container with a piece of bread inside.

1 **cup shortening**	2 **teaspoons cream of tartar**
1½ **cups plus 2 tablespoons**	1 **teaspoon baking soda**
sugar, divided	½ **teaspoon salt**
2 **eggs**	2 **tablespoons ground**
2¾ **cups unbleached flour**	**cinnamon**

In a large bowl, cream the shortening and 1½ cups of the sugar. Add the
eggs and beat until light.

In a separate bowl, sift the flour, cream of tartar, baking soda and salt.
Stir into the creamed mixture until thoroughly blended. Chill for 2 hours.

Pinch off pieces of the dough and roll into walnut-size balls. Combine
the remaining 2 tablespoons sugar and cinnamon. Roll the balls in the cinnamon sugar and place 2″ apart on ungreased cookie sheets. Bake in a preheated 400° oven for 8 to 10 minutes, or until lightly browned but still soft.

Makes about 60.

Favorite Recipes
St. Elizabeth Ann Seton Church of Fryeburg, Maine: Mission of St. Joseph's Church,
Bridgton, Maine

$\mathcal{G}$LAZED AUTUMN APPLE COOKIES

Orange juice or milk can be substituted for the apple cider in
this recipe, but if orange juice is used, omit the vanilla. These cookies
spread out quite a bit while baking, so don't place them too close
together. Given their tender texture and attractive glaze, they are somewhat
delicate and may not be suitable for stacking in a cookie jar. Serve
them at teatime or following an autumn outing of leaf peeping.

COOKIES

- 2¼ **cups unbleached flour**
- 1 **teaspoon baking soda**
- 1 **teaspoon ground cinnamon**
- ½ **teaspoon ground cloves**
- ½ **teaspoon ground nutmeg**
- ½ **teaspoon salt**
- 1⅓ **cups firmly packed brown sugar**
- ½ **cup butter or margarine, softened**
- 1 **cup cored and shredded apples (McIntosh or Jonathan)**
- ½ **cup apple cider**
- 1 **egg, beaten**
- ¾ **cup chopped nuts**
- ½ **cup raisins**

GLAZE

- 1 **tablespoon butter or margarine, softened**
- 1½ **cups confectioners' sugar**
- ⅛ **teaspoon salt**
- 3½ **teaspoons apple cider**
- ½ **teaspoon vanilla**

To make the cookies: In a medium bowl, sift the flour, baking soda, cinnamon, cloves, nutmeg and salt. In a large bowl, cream the brown sugar and butter or margarine. Add the apples, cider and egg and mix well. Stir in the dry ingredients, nuts and raisins, mixing thoroughly. Drop the dough by tablespoonfuls onto greased cookie sheets and bake in a preheated 375° oven for 10 minutes.

To make the glaze: In a small bowl, cream the butter or margarine, confectioners' sugar and salt. Stir in the cider and vanilla, mixing well. Glaze the cookies as soon as you remove them from the oven and cool on a wire rack.

Makes 24.

Mystic Seaport's Moveable Feasts Cookbook
Mystic Seaport Museum Stores, Mystic, Connecticut

$\mathcal{F}$RESH GINGER COOKIES

These golden brown, crunchy cookies have a slight bite from the fresh ginger that tingles your tongue and pleases your palate.

½ cup blanched almonds
1½ cups unbleached flour, divided
½ teaspoon baking soda
¼ teaspoon salt
½ teaspoon ground cinnamon
¼ teaspoon ground ginger
⅛ teaspoon ground cloves
⅛ teaspoon ground nutmeg

½ cup unsalted butter or margarine, softened
½ cup firmly packed dark brown sugar
2 tablespoons minced fresh ginger (*see Note below*)
1 egg
2 tablespoons molasses

Using a food processor, process the almonds and ½ cup of the flour. Add the remaining flour, baking soda, salt, cinnamon, ginger, cloves and nutmeg and process until mixed. Transfer to waxed paper.

In the empty processor, place the butter or margarine, brown sugar and ginger, mixing until smooth. Mix in the egg and molasses. Add the flour mixture and process until well incorporated.

Turn out onto waxed paper and shape into a 14″ × 1″ roll. Wrap in waxed paper and chill overnight. Slice thinly, place on greased cookie sheets and bake in a preheated 350° oven for 8 to 10 minutes.

Note: To mince ginger, drop cut-up pieces of fresh ginger in the food processor while the motor is running, then measure out 2 tablespoons of minced ginger.

Makes 60.

Boston Tea Parties
Museum of Fine Arts, Boston, Massachusetts

CHOCOLATE CHIP–APPLE DATERS

This high-energy treat will earn you high marks from cookie connoisseurs. The balanced combination of ingredients yields soft, chewy cookies about 3" in diameter.

1 cup chopped dates	1 teaspoon vanilla
½ cup boiling water	1¾ cups unbleached flour
1 teaspoon baking soda	½ teaspoon salt
¾ cup shortening	1 cup peeled, cored and chopped apples
¾ cup sugar	
2 eggs	1 cup semisweet chocolate chips

In a small bowl, combine the dates, boiling water and baking soda and set aside to cool.

In a large bowl, cream the shortening and sugar until light. Beat in the eggs and vanilla. Add the flour and salt, beating until thoroughly blended. Stir in the apples, chocolate chips and cooled date mixture.

Drop by tablespoonfuls onto greased cookie sheets and bake in a pre-heated 350° oven for 15 to 18 minutes.

Makes about 36.

Cooking with Love
Morris Congregational Church: Women's Fellowship, Morris, Connecticut

CRANBERRY–CHOCOLATE CHIP COOKIES

The tartness of cranberries blended into New England's traditional Toll House cookie dough produces an unexpectedly spectacular treat.

1 cup cranberries	3/4 cup firmly packed brown sugar
2 1/4 cups unbleached flour	1 teaspoon vanilla
1 teaspoon baking soda	2 eggs
1/2 teaspoon salt	1 package (12 ounces) semisweet chocolate chips
1 cup butter or margarine, softened	
3/4 cup granulated sugar	

Pick over the cranberries and rinse them thoroughly. Set aside. In a medium bowl, combine the flour, baking soda and salt. In a large bowl, combine the butter, granulated sugar, brown sugar and vanilla and beat until creamy. Beat in the eggs. Gradually add the flour mixture to the creamed mixture, blending thoroughly. Stir in the chocolate chips and cranberries. Drop by rounded tablespoonfuls onto ungreased cookie sheets and bake in a preheated 375° oven for 10 to 12 minutes.

Makes 36.

Saint Michael's Cooks By Design
Saint Michael's Episcopal Church, Litchfield, Connecticut

CRANBERRY DROPS

These tangy, crunchy cookies are even better the day after they are baked.

1/2 cup butter or margarine	3 cups unbleached flour
1 cup granulated sugar	1 teaspoon baking powder
3/4 cup firmly packed brown sugar	1/4 teaspoon baking soda
1/4 cup milk	1/2 teaspoon salt
2 tablespoons orange juice	2 1/2 cups coarsely chopped cranberries (*see Note next page*)
1 egg	1 cup chopped nuts

In a large bowl, cream the butter or margarine, granulated sugar and brown sugar. Beat in the milk, orange juice and egg.

In a separate bowl, sift the flour, baking powder, baking soda and salt. Add to the creamed mixture and blend well. Stir in the cranberries and nuts. Drop by tablespoonfuls onto greased cookie sheets and bake in a pre-heated 375° oven for 10 to 15 minutes.

Note: Before chopping the cranberries, pick them over carefully, discarding any that are bad. Rinse them under running water and pat dry.

Makes 60.

Cooking with Babes in School Land
Babes in School Land, Lyndeborough, New Hampshire

$\mathcal{B}$EACON HILL COOKIES

Classy, crunchy, chewy and chocolaty, these bite-size treats are somewhat fragile. To preserve their shape, remove them immediately from the cookie sheet—but be sure to use a spatula with a thin metal blade or a knife. A plastic spatula is too thick and will tear the cookies.

1 **package (6 ounces) semisweet chocolate chips**	½ **cup sugar**
2 **egg whites**	½ **teaspoon vinegar**
Pinch of salt	½ **teaspoon vanilla**
	¾ **cup chopped nuts**

Melt the chocolate chips over hot water and set aside. In a medium bowl, beat the egg whites with the salt until foamy. Gradually beat in the sugar until stiff peaks form, then beat in the vinegar and vanilla. Fold in the chocolate and nuts. Drop by teaspoonfuls onto greased cookie sheets and bake in a preheated 350° oven for 10 minutes. Remove immediately.

Makes 36.

Boston Tea Parties
Museum of Fine Arts, Boston, Massachusetts

MAPLE SYRUP–OATMEAL COOKIES

Subtly sweet, these superb cookies are light yet substantial. Accompanied with a glass of milk, they are a satisfying treat at mid morning, after lunch or supper or late at night when the munchies lead you to the kitchen.

1 **cup unbleached flour**	½ **cup shortening**
1 **teaspoon baking powder**	2 **eggs**
¼ **teaspoon salt**	¾ **cup maple syrup**
1 **cup rolled oats**	½ **teaspoon vanilla**
½ **cup chopped walnuts**	

Sift the flour, baking powder and salt into a large bowl. Add the oats and walnuts, mix well and set aside.

Cream the shortening in a medium bowl, add the eggs and beat until light and fluffy. Stir in the maple syrup and vanilla. Pour into the dry ingredients and mix well. Drop by tablespoonfuls onto greased cookie sheets and bake in a preheated 400° oven for 12 minutes.

Makes about 48.

A Collection of Maple Recipes
New Hampshire Maple Producers Association, Londonderry, New Hampshire

SUGARED RYE COOKIES

If you try these once, you'll return to this recipe time and again.
Their flavor is hard to describe—other than delicious!

1 **cup butter or margarine,**	1 **cup rye flour**
softened	1 **teaspoon baking soda**
1 **cup sugar**	½ **teaspoon salt**
2 **teaspoons vanilla**	**Grated rind of 1 orange**
1 **cup unbleached flour**	

In a large bowl, cream the butter or margarine, sugar and vanilla. In another bowl, combine the unbleached flour, rye flour, baking soda, salt and orange rind. Add to the creamed mixture, stirring well. Form into 1" balls and place 2" apart on ungreased cookie sheets. Flatten slightly with the bottom of a glass that has been greased and then dipped in sugar. Bake in a preheated 350° oven for 10 to 14 minutes, or until golden brown.

Makes 36 to 48.

The Joy of Sharing Cookbook
Ascutney Union Church, Ascutney, Vermont

*M*ORNING COOKIES

These are about as hearty and wholesome as you can make a cookie. The name must come from the fact that the nutritious ingredients make them appropriate for a morning snack. They also are a high-energy food that travels well on hiking trips.

¼ **cup butter or margarine, softened**
¼ **cup firmly packed brown sugar**
1 **egg (optional)**
¾ **cup whole-wheat flour**
¾ **cup applesauce**
½ **cup rolled oats**
⅓ **cup wheat bran**

¼ **cup instant nonfat dry milk**
½ **teaspoon baking soda**
¼ **teaspoon baking powder**
½ **teaspoon ground cinnamon**
¼ **teaspoon ground cloves**
¼ **teaspoon salt**
⅓ **cup raisins**
¼ **cup chopped nuts**

In a large bowl, cream the butter or margarine and brown sugar until smooth. Add the egg (if using) and beat until light. Stir in the flour, applesauce, oats, bran, milk, baking soda, baking powder, cinnamon, cloves and salt. Beat until just combined. Stir in the raisins and nuts. Drop by tablespoonfuls about 2" to 3" apart on greased cookie sheets. Bake in a preheated 375° oven for about 10 minutes. Cool on a wire rack.

Makes 24 to 36.

A Taste of Harrisville
Wells Memorial School PTA, Harrisville, New Hampshire

RAISIN ROUGHS

Chewy, chunky and full of treats, these cookies are
rough textured as their name implies. A great after-school snack,
backpacking booster or teatime treat.

1 **cup unbleached flour**	2 **cups sugar**
2 **teaspoons ground cinnamon**	3 **eggs**
¾ **teaspoon baking soda**	¼ **cup milk**
¼ **teaspoon salt**	2 **teaspoons vanilla**
1 **cup shortening**	3½ **cups rolled oats**
½ **cup smooth or chunky peanut butter**	2 **cups raisins**

In a medium bowl, combine the flour, cinnamon, baking soda and salt.
In a large bowl, cream the shortening and peanut butter. Add the sugar and
beat until light. Add the eggs, milk and vanilla and beat well. Stir in the
flour mixture, oats and raisins, blending thoroughly. Drop by tablespoonfuls
onto greased cookie sheets and bake in a preheated 375° oven for 10 to
15 minutes.

Makes about 36.

From the Galleys of Nantucket
First Congregational Church: Ladies' Union Circle, Nantucket, Massachusetts

$\mathcal{J}$OE FROGGERS

These cookies are not really Joe Froggers unless they are
cut with a 4″ round cookie cutter. The recipe for these big
molasses cookies is more than 100 years old. It was the pride of one man,
"Uncle Joe," as he was known to the people of Marblehead,
Massachusetts. Since he lived on the edge of a frog pond, the cookies
soon became known as "Joe Froggers." As the recipe was passed down,
they became available for a penny apiece in the local bake shop.

4⅓ **cups unbleached flour**	¼ **teaspoon ground allspice**
1 **teaspoon baking soda**	¾ **cup shortening**
½ **teaspoon salt**	¾ **cup sugar**
1½ **teaspoons ground ginger**	1 **cup light molasses**
¾ **teaspoon ground cloves**	1 **tablespoon rum extract**
¾ **teaspoon ground nutmeg**	⅓ **cup water**

Sift the flour, baking soda, salt, ginger, cloves, nutmeg and allspice into
a medium bowl and mix. In a large bowl, cream the shortening and sugar.
Add the molasses and rum extract, beating well. Add the flour mixture and
water alternately, beating well after each addition. Wrap the dough in foil
and chill overnight.

Roll the dough to a ¼″ thickness. Cut with a floured 4″ round cookie
cutter and bake on lightly greased cookie sheets in a preheated 375° oven
for 8 to 9 minutes.

Makes 24.

A Taste of New England
Junior League of Worcester, Massachusetts

DATE-FILLED MOLASSES COOKIES

For a simple variation, use raspberry preserves
in place of the date filling.

FILLING
- 1 pound pitted dates
- 1 cup water
- 1 cup firmly packed brown sugar
- 2 tablespoons unbleached flour
- 1 tablespoon butter or margarine
- 1 teaspoon vanilla

COOKIE DOUGH
- 2 eggs
- 1 cup firmly packed brown sugar
- 1 cup shortening
- ¾ cup molasses
- 1 teaspoon vanilla
- 4 cups unbleached flour
- 2 teaspoons baking soda
- ½ teaspoon salt

To make the filling: Combine the dates, water, brown sugar, flour, butter or margarine and vanilla in a saucepan. Cook until the dates soften and the mixture thickens. Set aside to cool.

To make the cookie dough: Combine the eggs, brown sugar, shortening, molasses and vanilla in a large bowl. Sift in the flour, baking soda and salt and mix well.

Place about 2 cups of the dough at a time on a floured surface, roll out thin and cut into 2½" circles. Place a spoonful of filling on half of the circles, top with the remaining circles and press around the edges to seal. Place on ungreased cookie sheets and bake in a preheated 350° oven for 10 to 12 minutes.

Makes about 36.

Maine-ly Good Eatin'
American Cancer Society: Maine Division, Brunswick, Maine

$\mathcal{S}$AND DIMES

These tender cookies have a slightly sticky dough that is a little tricky to roll out. Try different kinds of biscuit and cookie cutters for a variety of shapes and sizes.

FILLING

- 1 **cup raisins**
- ½ **cup sugar**
- ½ **cup orange juice**
- 1 **teaspoon unbleached flour**

COOKIE DOUGH

- ½ **cup butter or margarine, softened**
- 1 **cup sugar**
- 1 **egg**
- ½ **cup milk**
- 3 **cups unbleached flour**
- 2 **teaspoons cream of tartar**
- 1 **teaspoon baking soda**
- 1 **teaspoon vanilla**

To make the filling: Combine the raisins, sugar, orange juice and flour in a small saucepan and cook until thickened. Remove from the heat and set aside to cool.

To make the cookie dough: In a large bowl, cream the butter or margarine and sugar. Beat in the egg, milk, flour, cream of tartar, baking soda and vanilla and mix well. Chill the dough, then roll out thin and cut out 3″ rounds.

Place 1 to 1½ tablespoons of the filling on half the rounds, cover with the remaining rounds and seal the edges. Bake on greased cookie sheets in a preheated 350° oven for 8 to 10 minutes. Cool on a wire rack.

Makes about 24.

Cohasset Entertains
The Community Garden Club, Cohasset, Massachusetts

CHARLOTTE CENTRAL'S CARROT-RAISIN BROWNIES

꒱꒰

Scrumptious and nutritious treats for brown-bag lunches,
after-school snacks or late-night munching.

1½ cups firmly packed light brown sugar	½ teaspoon baking soda
½ cup butter or margarine, softened	½ teaspoon baking powder
	¼ teaspoon salt
2 eggs	1½ cups grated carrots
1 teaspoon vanilla	½ cup raisins, chopped
1½ cups unbleached flour	½ cup chopped walnuts

In a large bowl, cream the brown sugar and butter or margarine. Add
the eggs and vanilla and beat well. Stir in the flour, baking soda, baking
powder and salt, blending thoroughly. Add the carrots and raisins and stir.

Spread the mixture into a greased 13" × 9" baking pan and sprinkle with
the walnuts. Bake in a preheated 350° oven for about 40 minutes, or until
a toothpick inserted in the center comes out clean. Cool, then cut into
squares.

Makes about 24.

The Charlotte Central Cooks' Book
Charlotte Central PTO, Charlotte, Vermont

MAPLE-OATMEAL SQUARES

Maple syrup sweetened, chewy and chunky, these
squares are irresistible. You may want to double the recipe
so that they don't disappear too quickly.

½ **cup shortening**	⅔ **cup unbleached flour**
½ **cup sugar**	⅔ **teaspoon baking powder**
½ **cup maple syrup**	½ **teaspoon salt**
1 **teaspoon vanilla**	½ **cup chopped walnuts**
1 **egg, lightly beaten**	1 **cup rolled oats**

In a large bowl, cream the shortening and sugar. Beat in the maple syrup,
vanilla and egg, then set aside.

Sift the flour, baking powder and salt into a bowl. Stir in the walnuts,
then add to the creamed mixture, blending well. Stir in the oats, mixing
thoroughly. Spread in a greased 9" × 9" or 11" × 7" baking pan and bake in
a preheated 350° oven for 30 to 35 minutes. Cut into squares while still
warm.

Makes 12 to 16.

Vernon Bicentennial Cookbook
Vernon Bicentennial Cookbook Committee, Vernon, Vermont

OATMEAL-RASPBERRY BARS

*Unique, fruity and crisp, these cookies are easy to
make and not overly sweet. Kids love them!*

½ **cup butter or margarine,
softened**
1 **cup rolled oats**
1 **cup unbleached flour**

½ **cup firmly packed light
brown sugar**
¼ **teaspoon baking soda**
⅛ **teaspoon salt**
¾ **cup raspberry preserves**

In a medium bowl, combine the butter or margarine, oats, flour, brown
sugar, baking soda and salt until crumbly. Press 2 cups of the mixture into a
greased 8″ × 8″ baking pan. Spread with the preserves, leaving a ¼″ border
around the edge. Sprinkle with the remaining crumb mixture and lightly
press into the preserves. Bake in a preheated 350° oven for 35 to 40 minutes. Cool before cutting.

Makes 16.

Just Desserts
Londonderry Women's Club, Londonderry, New Hampshire

RASPBERRY-ALMOND SQUARES

Rich and buttery, these cookies are fantastic.
The bottom layer is similar to shortbread and holds together well.

⅔ cup blanched whole almonds	1 egg, separated
1 cup unsalted butter or margarine, softened	1 teaspoon vanilla
	2 cups unbleached flour
1 cup granulated sugar	¾ teaspoon ground cinnamon
¼ cup lightly packed light brown sugar	¼ teaspoon salt
	¾ cup raspberry preserves

Using a food processor with a steel blade, process the almonds until finely chopped but not powdered. Or finely chop them in a blender or with a knife by hand. Set aside.

In a large bowl, cream the butter or margarine, granulated sugar and brown sugar. Beat in the egg yolk and vanilla.

In a medium bowl, mix the flour, cinnamon and salt. Stir into the creamed mixture, blending well.

Press the dough into a lightly buttered 14″ × 11″ jelly roll pan. Spread the raspberry preserves evenly over the top. Beat the egg white until frothy and brush over the preserves. Sprinkle with the almonds and gently press into the preserves. Place on a rack in the center of a preheated 350° oven and bake for 30 to 35 minutes, or until the edges are browned and the center is almost browned. Remove from the oven and immediately loosen the sides with a spatula. Let cool in the pan for 40 minutes, then cut into squares.

Makes 54.

Our Town Cookbook
Peterborough Historical Society, Peterborough, New Hampshire

WALNUT-RASPBERRY BROWNIES

✤

"Bring these to a depressed person, and they'll never need therapy!"
wrote our recipe tester. An outstanding combination of chewy brownie,
crunchy nuts and smooth fudge icing. The raspberry preserves
are a perfect foil for the intense chocolate.

BROWNIES

3	squares (1 ounce each) unsweetened chocolate
½	cup shortening
3	eggs
1½	cups sugar
1½	teaspoons vanilla
¼	teaspoon salt
1	cup unbleached flour
1½	cups chopped walnuts
⅓	cup raspberry preserves

GLAZE

1	square (1 ounce) unsweetened chocolate
2	tablespoons butter or margarine
2	tablespoons light corn syrup
1	cup confectioners' sugar
1	tablespoon milk
1	teaspoon vanilla

To make the brownies: Melt the chocolate and shortening in a double
boiler over warm water, then cool slightly. In a large bowl, beat the eggs,
sugar, vanilla and salt. Stir in the chocolate mixture, then the flour. Fold in
the walnuts. Turn out into a well-greased 8″ × 8″ baking pan and bake in a
preheated 325° oven for about 40 minutes. Spoon the preserves over the
hot brownies, spreading carefully. Let cool while preparing the glaze.

To make the glaze: Melt the chocolate in a double boiler over warm water
and remove from the heat. Blend in the butter or margarine and corn
syrup. Sift in the confectioners' sugar and mix thoroughly. Add the milk
and vanilla and blend well. Spread over the cooled brownies.

Makes 12 to 16.

Anniversary Celebration Cookbook
Trinity Lutheran Church, Chelmsford, Massachusetts

 $\mathcal{F}$ROSTED MOLASSES BARS

Packed in lunches, taken on picnics or enjoyed as a late-night snack, these spicy treats will please young and old alike.

BARS

1½ **cups unbleached flour**
1½ **teaspoons baking powder**
¼ **teaspoon baking soda**
½ **teaspoon salt**
1 **teaspoon ground cinnamon**
½ **teaspoon ground cloves**
½ **cup butter or margarine, softened**
½ **cup sugar**
1 **egg**
½ **cup molasses**
⅓ **cup water**

FROSTING

2 **tablespoons butter or margarine**
1 **cup confectioners' sugar**
1 **tablespoon molasses**
1 **tablespoon water**

To make the bars: In a medium bowl, combine the flour, baking powder, baking soda, salt, cinnamon and cloves. In a large bowl, cream the butter or margarine and sugar. Beat in the egg, molasses and water and stir in the dry ingredients, blending well. Turn into a greased 11″ × 7″ baking pan and bake in a preheated 350° oven for 20 to 25 minutes. Let cool while preparing the frosting.

To make the frosting: Combine the butter or margarine, confectioners' sugar, molasses and water, beating until smooth enough to spread. Spread over the bars while they are still warm, but let the frosting firm up before cutting the bars.

Makes 24.

The Maine Ingredient
Planned Parenthood of Northern New England, Portland, Maine

MRS. OLSON'S HERMITS

Nice and spicy—creating a buzz in your mouth.
Hot from the oven, these bars are soft and similar to gingerbread.
Cooled, they are crunchy and great for dunking. Decrease the baking time
if you prefer a softer texture. To store, let the bars cool completely, then
layer in a cookie jar or tin with plastic wrap between the layers.

³/₄ **cup shortening**	1 **teaspoon ground cinnamon**
1 **cup sugar**	³/₄ **teaspoon ground ginger**
1 **egg**	³/₄ **teaspoon ground cloves**
¹/₄ **cup molasses**	¹/₄ **teaspoon salt**
2¹/₄ **cups unbleached flour**	1 **cup raisins**
2 **teaspoons baking soda**	**Sugar for sprinkling**

Cream the shortening and sugar in a large bowl. Add the egg and molasses and beat well. Mix in the flour, baking soda, cinnamon, ginger, cloves and salt (the batter will be thick). Stir in the raisins. Press evenly into a 17" × 11" greased jelly roll pan. Sprinkle with sugar and bake in a preheated 375° oven for 10 minutes (the dough will appear undercooked).

Makes about 36.

Derry Community Playground Cookbook
Derry Playground Committee, East Derry, New Hampshire

MARBLEHEAD FUDGE ECSTASIES

彡℘

Crinkly on top, moist and fudgy inside, these very chocolaty cookies will be in demand all year long. When removing them from the cookie sheet, use a spatula with a thin metal blade so as not to break them apart.

1 **package (12 ounces) semisweet chocolate chips, divided**	¼ **cup unbleached flour**
	¼ **teaspoon baking powder**
	Pinch of salt
2 **squares (1 ounce each) unsweetened chocolate**	2 **eggs**
	⅔ **cup sugar**
2 **tablespoons butter or margarine**	1 **teaspoon vanilla**
	1 **cup chopped nuts**

In a medium saucepan, heat 1 cup of the chocolate chips, the unsweetened chocolate and the butter or margarine until melted, stirring constantly. Pour into a large bowl and set aside to cool slightly.

In a separate bowl, mix the flour, baking powder and salt. Add the eggs, sugar and vanilla to the cooled chocolate mixture and beat well. Add the flour mixture and beat thoroughly. Stir in the remaining chocolate bits and the nuts.

Drop the batter by teaspoonfuls onto lightly greased cookie sheets. Bake in a preheated 350° oven for 8 to 10 minutes, or until the edges are firm and the surface is dull and cracked. Cool for 1 minute before removing from the sheets. Place on wire racks to cool thoroughly.

Makes 36.

Hospitality
Salem Hospital Aid Association, Salem, Massachusetts

APLETS & COTLETS

Unusual and intriguing, this old-fashioned candy has just
enough tang to keep it from being too sweet. Let it dry out for a
while before rolling it in the confectioners' sugar; otherwise, the sugar
will get absorbed rather than staying on the surface.

3 tablespoons unflavored
gelatin
3 cups apple juice or unsweetened apricot juice, divided
1⅓ cups granulated sugar
2 tablespoons lemon juice
(approximately)

2 tablespoons lime juice
(approximately)
⅔ cup cornstarch, divided
2 cups chopped walnuts
1 cup confectioners' sugar

Soften the gelatin in a small bowl with ½ cup of the apple juice or
apricot juice.

In a saucepan, boil the remaining juice with the granulated sugar for
15 minutes to concentrate it.

Meanwhile, combine the lemon juice and lime juice in a small bowl and
add all but ¼ cup of the cornstarch, stirring until it is dissolved. Add the
gelatin mixture and cornstarch mixture to the boiled juice in the saucepan
and boil rapidly, stirring constantly, for 10 minutes, or until very thick.
Taste for sweet and sour and add more lemon juice or lime juice if desired.

Mix in the walnuts and pour the mixture into a 9″ × 9″ baking pan that
has been dipped in cold water. Let the paste harden for 12 hours, then cut
it into squares with a sharp knife.

Mix the reserved ¼ cup cornstarch and the confectioners' sugar in a
small bowl. Remove the squares with a spatula and roll each in the confectioners' sugar mixture (the cornstarch helps keep the sugar dry).

Makes 64.

From Our House to Yours
The Hikers, Melvin Village, New Hampshire

HOMETOWN COOKING IN NEW ENGLAND

OLD-FASHIONED POTATO CANDY

This candy requires no cooking but does need time in the
refrigerator to achieve the proper consistency.

1 medium potato, peeled,
boiled and mashed
1 box (1 pound) confectioners'
sugar
1 package (7 ounces) flaked
coconut

3 heaping tablespoons smooth
or chunky peanut butter
3 squares (1 ounce each)
unsweetened chocolate,
melted

In a bowl, combine the potato with the confectioners' sugar, coconut and
peanut butter, blending thoroughly. Press into a buttered 10" × 6" baking
pan, cover with the chocolate and refrigerate until firm. Cut into squares
and serve.

Makes about 18.

Our Saviour's Parish 65th Anniversary Cookbook
Our Saviour's Parish School of Christian Living, Woonsocket, Rhode Island

BEVERAGES

$\mathcal{M}$APLE SPICED MILK

Milk never tasted so good! Serve warm on cereal. Try it in hot tea, too.

1 cup milk	**1 teaspoon ground cinnamon**
3 tablespoons maple syrup	**½ teaspoon ground ginger**

Heat the milk, maple syrup, cinnamon and ginger in a saucepan.

Serves 1.

A Collection of Maple Recipes
New Hampshire Maple Producers Association, Londonderry, New Hampshire

$\mathcal{M}$APLE-CREAM SODA

This sweet and satisfying drink is suitable for kids of all ages.

3 tablespoons maple syrup	**Ginger ale, chilled**
3 tablespoons cream	

In a glass, whip the maple syrup and cream. Fill with ginger ale and serve.

Serves 1.

Portland Symphony Cookbook
Portland Symphony Orchestra Women's Committee, Portland, Maine

SPARKLING PEACHES & CREAM

If the canned peaches you use are packed in a sugar syrup,
you can eliminate the sugar in this recipe. For a slight variation,
substitute plain yogurt for cream or milk. Serve in chilled punch cups.

1 **can (16 ounces) peach slices, chilled**
½ **cup unsweetened pineapple juice, chilled**
4 **ice cubes (½ cup)**
1 **tablespoon sugar (optional)**

1 **tablespoon lemon juice**
1 **teaspoon vanilla**
⅓ **cup light cream or milk**
1½ **cups sparkling mineral water or carbonated water, chilled**

In a blender, combine the undrained peaches, pineapple juice, ice cubes,
sugar (if using), lemon juice and vanilla. Blend until smooth. Transfer to a
pitcher and stir in the light cream or milk. Slowly pour the mineral water
or carbonated water down the side of the pitcher and stir gently with an up
and down motion to mix.

Serves 4 to 6.

The Civic Women's Guilford Sampler
Guilford Civic Women, Guilford, Connecticut

FOUR-FRUIT COOLER

A great party punch for kids or adults. It also may be
prepared as a slush. Freeze the mixture for 8 hours or until firm.
Remove from the freezer 45 minutes before serving.

3 **cups water**
1½ **cups sugar**
3 **cups unsweetened pineapple juice**
1 **can (6 ounces) frozen orange juice concentrate, thawed**

2 **tablespoons lemon juice**
3 **ripe bananas, mashed**
2 **quarts plus 1 cup lemon-lime carbonated beverage, chilled**

Combine the water and sugar in a large pot. Bring to a boil, boil for 3 minutes and remove from the heat. Add the pineapple juice, orange juice concentrate, lemon juice and bananas, mixing well. Chill. To serve, combine with the lemon-lime beverage, stirring well.

Makes 1 gallon.

Seasoned with Love at St. James Lutheran Church
St. James Lutheran Church, Barrington, Rhode Island

CAPE COD TOMATO JUICE COCKTAIL

This requires more work than opening a can, but the full,
fresh flavor from the ripe homegrown vegetables can't be beat.

4 cups chopped tomatoes	½ teaspoon ground black
¼ cup chopped celery tops	pepper
½ green bell pepper, chopped	4 whole cloves
1 onion, sliced	1 cup water
1 tablespoon sugar	2 teaspoons lemon juice
1 teaspoon salt	

Combine the tomatoes, celery, bell peppers, onions, sugar, salt, pepper,
cloves and water in a saucepan. Cook slowly for 45 minutes. Press through
a sieve, add the lemon juice and chill.

Serves 8.

The Longyear Cookbook
Longyear Museum and Historical Society, Brookline, Massachusetts

RAZZLE-DAZZLE LEMONADE

Serve this lovely dessert drink with a summer brunch
or lunch out on the porch.

¾ cup sugar	1 cup raspberries or blueberries
1¼ cups water	1 pint lemon sherbet
2 teaspoons grated lemon rind	3 cups carbonated water,
1½ cups lemon juice (about	chilled
6–8 lemons)	

Combine the sugar and water in a small saucepan. Cook over medium
heat, stirring occasionally, for 1 to 2 minutes, or until the sugar dissolves.
Remove from the heat, add the lemon rind and let cool.

In a 1-quart pitcher, combine the sugar syrup, lemon juice and raspberries or blueberries. Cover and chill. For each serving, place 1 scoop of sherbet in a tall glass. Pour ½ cup of the syrup mixture and ½ cup of the carbonated water over the sherbet. Serve immediately.

Serves 6.

The Kinderhaus Cookbook
Kinderhaus Children's Center, Williston, Vermont

 PPLE TEA

If the apple has good flavor, this is a most pleasant drink. It may even be given to someone with a fever or to someone who is very thirsty.

1 tart apple (Granny Smith, Cortland or McIntosh)	**1 cup water** **1 teaspoon sugar (or to taste)**

Wash and wipe the apple. Cut into small pieces. Combine with the water in a saucepan and boil until soft. Strain the water into a bowl and add the sugar, stirring to dissolve. Serve hot or cold.

Serves 1.

The Morrison House Museum Cookbook
Londonderry Historical Society, Londonderry, New Hampshire

CRANBERRY TEA

To use this mixture, dilute 1 cup of the concentrate with
4 cups water and ½ cup sugar. Heat and serve.

3 **cups cranberries**
4 **cups water**
2 **cinnamon sticks**
4 **whole cloves**

1 **can (6 ounces) frozen lemon**
   juice concentrate, thawed
1 **can (6 ounces) frozen orange**
   juice concentrate, thawed

Pick over the cranberries and rinse them thoroughly. In a saucepan, combine the cranberries, water, cinnamon sticks and cloves and bring to a boil. Cook for 10 minutes, or until all the berries have popped. Strain through dampened cheesecloth. Add the lemon juice concentrate and orange juice concentrate and stir until thoroughly blended.

Makes about 6 cups.

The Longyear Cookbook
Longyear Museum and Historical Society, Brookline, Massachusetts

$\mathscr{R}$HUBARB TEA

For a festive—and tasty—touch, add a fresh mint sprig
and a sliced fresh strawberry to each serving.

4 cups diced rhubarb	**Grated rind of 1 lemon or**
4 cups water	**orange**
	¾–1 cup sugar

Simmer the rhubarb in the water until very tender, about 20 to 25 minutes. Strain. Add the grated lemon or orange rind and sugar to taste. Stir
until the sugar is dissolved. Chill and serve over ice.

Serves 4.

The Morrison House Museum Cookbook
Londonderry Historical Society, Londonderry, New Hampshire

$\mathscr{A}$PPLE-MINT PUNCH

During the fall, try this with apple cider instead of juice.

5 cups apple juice	**Lemon slices**
2 cups lemonade	**Mint leaves**
1 cup mint tea (made from	
1 tea bag)	

In a large pitcher, mix the apple juice, lemonade and tea. Refrigerate
until thoroughly chilled. Serve cold over ice with lemon slices and mint
leaves.

Serves 6 to 8.

The Haystack Cookbook
Haystack Mountain School of Crafts, Deer Isle, Maine

Hot Cranberry Punch

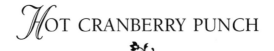

This delicious punch has been enjoyed during the Victorian Christmas celebration at the Thornton W. Burgess Museum for years.

2 cups sugar
1 cup water
1 cup lemon juice
1 quart cranberry juice
1 quart unsweetened pineapple juice

½ teaspoon ground cinnamon
½ teaspoon ground ginger
Lemon slices studded with whole cloves

Boil the sugar and water over medium heat for 10 minutes. Add the lemon juice, cranberry juice, pineapple juice, cinnamon and ginger. Heat slowly until just boiling. Cool slightly and pour into a warmed punch bowl. Garnish with the clove-studded lemon slices.

Serves 20.

Flavors of Cape Cod
Thornton W. Burgess Society, East Sandwich, Massachusetts

Party Punch

This tart and tingly beverage fits any occasion. During strawberry season, put a fresh berry inside each cup before filling with punch.

3 bottles (2 quarts each) pale dry ginger ale
1 package (8 ounces) frozen sliced strawberries
1 can (6 ounces) frozen orange juice concentrate, thawed
1 can (6 ounces) frozen grapefruit juice concentrate, thawed

1 can (6 ounces) frozen lemonade concentrate, thawed
1 can (6 ounces) frozen pineapple juice concentrate, thawed
3 oranges, thinly sliced
3 lemons, thinly sliced

Mix the ginger ale, strawberries, orange juice concentrate, grapefruit juice concentrate, lemonade concentrate and pineapple juice concentrate in a large punch bowl (or large pot and transfer to the punch bowl as needed). Add only as much sliced fruit as will make the bowl attractive.

Makes about 6¹/₂ quarts.

A Collection of Favorite Italian Recipes
St. Anthony's Church: The Women's Guild, Woonsocket, Rhode Island

$\mathcal{C}$ HAMPAGNE PUNCH
$\mathfrak{F}$

This punch is attributed to Abigail Adams. Tea was her unusual addition to a refreshing punch popular for women's gatherings in the 1700s.

1¹/₂ **cups sugar**	1 **cup rum**
1 **cup strong black tea**	1 **bottle (750 milliliters)**
1¹/₂ **cups orange juice**	**champagne, chilled**
¹/₂ **cup lemon juice**	**Orange slices**
Rind of 2 lemons, thinly	**Mint sprigs**
sliced	

In a large pitcher, dissolve the sugar in the tea. Stir in the orange juice, lemon juice, lemon rind and rum. Chill. Just before serving, pour the rum mixture and champagne over ice in a punch bowl. Garnish with the orange slices and mint sprigs.

Makes 2 quarts.

Bulfinch's Boston Faire
Doric Dames, Boston, Massachusetts

$\mathcal{L}$EETE'S ISLAND GARDEN CLUB PUNCH

This spicy, tangy punch can be served at any time of year,
and the ingredients can be added to or subtracted from depending
on the occasion or your preference.

2 cups strong tea
4 cups water, divided
1½ cups sugar
1 cinnamon stick
12 whole cloves
2 cups cranberry juice
1 can (6-ounce size) frozen
orange juice concentrate
1 can (6-ounce size) frozen
grapefruit juice concentrate

1 can (6-ounce size) frozen lime
juice concentrate
1 can (6-ounce size) frozen
lemonade concentrate
½ can (6-ounce size) frozen
pineapple juice concentrate
(or to taste)
1 quart ginger ale (optional)
Mint leaves (optional)
Vodka or rum (optional)

Pour the freshly brewed tea into a large bowl or stainless steel pot. In a saucepan, combine 1 cup of the water with the sugar, cinnamon stick and cloves and simmer, covered, for at least 20 minutes. Strain, cool and add to the tea. Pour in the cranberry juice, orange juice concentrate, grapefruit juice concentrate, lime juice concentrate, lemonade concentrate, pineapple juice concentrate and remaining 3 cups water, stirring until the frozen juices have melted.

When you're ready to serve the punch, pour it over ice in a large punch bowl and add the ginger ale (if using). Float some mint leaves on top (if using), or make a frozen ice mold. Add vodka or rum to taste (if using).

Makes about 1 gallon.

350th Guilford, Connecticut, Birthday Cook Book
Leete's Island Garden Club, Guilford, Connecticut

POINSETTIA PUNCH

To give this a festive touch, make an ice ring out of
cranberry juice and float it on top.

1 gallon cranberry juice	**1 bottle (750 milliliters)**
½ bottle (750 milliliters) triple	**champagne**
sec (or to taste)	

Pour the cranberry juice and triple sec into a punch bowl. Slowly add
the champagne and serve immediately.

Makes about 1¼ gallons.

Country Classics
Welcome Wagon Club, Londonderry, New Hampshire

WASSAIL

An excellent drink for cold-weather entertaining, this also is
enjoyable after a day of snowshoeing or cross-country skiing.

1   quart plus 2 cups apple cider
2   cups cranberry juice
¼   teaspoon aromatic bitters
½   cup sugar
1   tablespoon whole allspice
     berries

4–5 cinnamon sticks
2   oranges studded with whole
     cloves
1–2 cups rum (optional)

In a large pot, simmer the cider, cranberry juice, bitters, sugar, allspice,
cinnamon sticks and oranges until the sugar dissolves and the mixture is
hot. Strain out the spices and chill in the refrigerator. When you're ready to
serve the wassail, reheat it and add the rum (if using).

Makes about 1 gallon.

Northeast Kingdom Cookbook
Caledonia Home Health Care, St. Johnsbury, Vermont

HOT MULLED CIDER

At the end of the day, when the wood has been stacked,
the walkways have been shoveled or the cross-country outing
has been completed, reward yourself with a hot, steaming mug
of this heartwarming, spirit-boosting beverage.

1   quart apple cider
⅓   cup firmly packed brown
     sugar
1   cinnamon stick
8   whole cloves

¼   teaspoon ground nutmeg
¼   teaspoon ground ginger
1   large lemon, thinly sliced
     Whole cloves for garnish

In a saucepan, combine the cider, brown sugar, cinnamon stick, 8 whole cloves, nutmeg and ginger. Add all but 6 of the lemon slices, heat and stir until the sugar dissolves. Bring to a boil, reduce the heat and simmer, covered, for 10 minutes. Meanwhile, stud the remaining lemon slices with whole cloves. Strain the cider and garnish with the clove-studded lemon slices.

Makes about 1 quart.

Favorite Recipes
St. Elizabeth Ann Seton Church of Fryeburg, Maine: Mission of St. Joseph's Church, Bridgton, Maine

MULLED WINE

For a special effect, warm stemmed glasses and serve
this hot wine in them, garnished with a fruit slice and a
couple of whole cloves and allspice berries.

1	cup water	12	whole cloves
½	cup sugar	4	cinnamon sticks
1	lemon, sliced	1	bottle (750 milliliters) dry
1	orange, sliced		red wine such as burgundy or
12	whole allspice berries		claret

In a large saucepan, combine the water, sugar, lemon slices, orange slices, allspice, cloves and cinnamon sticks. Bring to a boil. Reduce the heat and simmer for 5 minutes. Add the wine and bring just to the boiling point, but do not boil. Reduce the heat and simmer for 10 minutes more. Pour the hot wine into warmed mugs and serve immediately.

Serves 4.

Berkshire Seasonings
Junior League of Berkshire County, Pittsfield, Massachusetts

$\mathcal{H}$OT BUTTERED RUM

A little bit of this goes a long way. Serve it on a snowy
evening when you don't have to go out and can kick back
and enjoy all the comforts of hearth and home.

1 pound brown sugar	**½ teaspoon ground cloves**
½ cup butter or margarine, softened	**Rum**
	Boiling water
½ teaspoon ground cinnamon	**Cinnamon sticks**
½ teaspoon ground nutmeg	

In a large bowl, cream the brown sugar and butter or margarine, adding
the cinnamon, nutmeg and cloves as you cream. Store in a covered container in the refrigerator. For each serving, spoon about 2 tablespoons of
this mixture into a mug, add 1 jigger of rum and fill the mug with boiling
water, stirring well. Serve with a cinnamon stick for a stirrer.

Makes about 2 cups.

Marblehead Cooks
Tower School, Marblehead, Massachusetts

$\mathcal{R}$ASPBERRY LIQUEUR

Make 2 or 3 batches of this while fresh raspberries
are available. Divide among fancy glass bottles with corks and
give them away during the holiday season.

1 pint raspberries	**¼ teaspoon whole allspice berries**
2½ cups vodka	
1 vanilla bean	**1 cup sugar**
	½ cup water

Rinse the berries and crush them slightly in a large bowl. Add the vodka,
vanilla bean and allspice. Stir to combine. Pour into a wide-mouth 1-quart
jar, cover and store in a cool, dark place for 3 weeks.

Strain through dampened cheesecloth, squeezing out as much juice as possible. Return to the jar. Boil the sugar and water in a saucepan for about 5 minutes, or until the sugar dissolves. Cool completely. Add to the mixture in the jar, cover and age for 3 to 5 weeks.

Makes about 1 pint.

Recipe Sampler
Shoreline Quilters' Guild, Branford, Connecticut

$\mathscr{C}$RANBERRY CORDIAL
❧

Both the cordial and the cranberries can be given as gifts. The cranberries, which should be kept refrigerated, are fantastic served over ice cream.

4 cups cranberries	**2 cups gin**
3 cups sugar	

Pick over the cranberries, rinse thoroughly and coarsely chop. Place in a large screw-top jar, add the sugar and gin and stir. Cover tightly, invert the jar and let stand for 1 day. Turn the jar upright and let stand for another day. Repeat the daily turning for 3 weeks.

Strain through dampened cheesecloth into a decanter and cover. Spoon the drained berries into a jar, cover and refrigerate.

Makes 3¼ cups cordial and 3 cups berries.

Cohasset Entertains
The Community Garden Club, Cohasset, Massachusetts

DIRECTORY

The following list gives the titles of the cookbooks (arranged alphabetically under each New England state) from which we selected recipes. In addition, we've included the name and address of the organization to contact if you wish to inquire about purchasing a copy of the book. Some of these are no longer for sale, and we have noted this beside the title. Others may have gone out of print while our cookbook was being produced. When you inquire about a book's availability and price, please include a self-addressed, stamped envelope with your letter so the organization doesn't have to pay for the mailing; many of these groups are small and on a tight budget.

CONNECTICUT

350th Guilford, Connecticut,
  Birthday Cook Book
(no longer available)
Leete's Island Garden Club
173 Highwoods Drive
Guilford, CT 06437

Bouquet of Recipes
Sherman Garden Club
P.O. Box 535
Sherman, CT 06784

Christmas Memories Cookbook
Mystic Seaport Museum Stores
47 Greenmanville Avenue
Mystic, CT 06355

The Civic Women's Guilford Sampler
(no longer available)
Guilford Civic Women, Inc.
P.O. Box 296
Guilford, CT 06437

Cooking with Love
Morris Congregational Church:
  Women's Fellowship
Route 109
Morris, CT 06763

Cox Community Cookbook
A.W. Cox PTO: Playground Committee
143 Three Mile Course Road
Guilford, CT 06437

Crossroads Cookbook
Somers Congregational Church
599 Main Street, P.O. Box 295
Somers, CT 06071

Doorway to Healthy Eating
Trinity Church on the Green
Trinity Women's Fellowship
1109 Main Street
Branford, CT 06405

The Mark Twain Library Cookbook, Vol. III
Mark Twain Library Association
P.O. Box 1009
Redding, CT 06875-1009

The Mystic Seaport All Seasons Cookbook
Mystic Seaport Museum Stores
47 Greenmanville Avenue
Mystic, CT 06355

Mystic Seaport's Moveable Feasts Cookbook
Mystic Seaport Museum Stores
47 Greenmanville Avenue
Mystic, CT 06355

Mystic Seaport's Seafood Secrets Cookbook
Mystic Seaport Museum Stores
47 Greenmanville Avenue
Mystic, CT 06355

Off the Hook
The Junior League of Stamford-Norwalk
748 Post Road
Darien, CT 06820

Recipe Sampler
Shoreline Quilters' Guild
P.O. Box 946
Branford, CT 06405

Rumsey Rare Bites
Rumsey Circle: Rumsey Hall
201 Romford Road
Washington, CT 06794

Saint Michael's Cooks By Design
Saint Michael's Episcopal Church
P.O. Box 248
Litchfield, CT 06759

United Methodist Churches Cookbook
United Methodist Church of Litchfield
69 West Street, P.O. Box 65
Litchfield, CT 06759

꙰ ꙰ ꙰ ꙰ ꙰ **MAINE** ꙰ ꙰ ꙰ ꙰ ꙰

A Century of Good Cooking
Waldoboro Women's Club
691 Bremen Road
Waldoboro, ME 04572-6104

Cooking with a Maine Accent
Gorham Woman's Club
c/o Nancy Taber
14 Main Street
Gorham, ME 04038

Divine Cooking
St. Giles' Episcopal Church Women
P.O. Box 259
Jefferson, ME 04348-0259

Favorite Recipes
St. Elizabeth Ann Seton Church of
  Fryeburg, Maine
Mission of St. Joseph's Church
Bridgton, ME 04009

The Haystack Cookbook
Haystack Mountain School of Crafts
P.O. Box 518
Deer Isle, ME 04627

The Maine Collection
Portland Museum of Art
7 Congress Square
Portland, ME 04101

The Maine Ingredient
Planned Parenthood of Northern
  New England
P.O. Box 1519
Portland, ME 04104-1519

Maine-ly Good Eatin'
(no longer available)
American Cancer Society:
  Maine Division
52 Federal Street
Brunswick, ME 04011

Merrymeeting Merry Eating
Mid Coast Hospital/Brunswick Auxiliary
58 Baribeau Drive
Brunswick, ME 04011

Portland Symphony Cookbook
Friends of the Portland Symphony
  Orchestra
P.O. Box 332
Downtown Station
Portland, ME 04112

RSVP
Junior League of Portland
107 Elm Street, #100R
Portland, ME 04101

1717 Meetinghouse Cookbook II
West Parish of Barnstable:
  Women's Guild
P.O. Box 219
West Barnstable, MA 02668

The Andover Cookbook II
Phillips Academy
  The Ladies' Benevolent Society
Andover, MA 01810

Anniversary Celebration Cookbook
Trinity Lutheran Church
170 Old Westford Road
Chelmsford, MA 01824

Berkshire Seasonings
Junior League of Berkshire County, Inc.
379 North Street
Pittsfield, MA 01201

Boston Cooks
Women's Educational & Industrial Union
356 Boylston Street
Boston, MA 02116

Boston Tea Parties
Museum of Fine Arts, Enterprise
295 Huntington Avenue
Boston, MA 02115

Bulfinch's Boston Faire
Doric Dames, Inc.
Massachusetts State House
P.O. Box 45
Boston, MA 02133

Cape Cod Kitchen Secrets
Cape Cod Hospital Auxiliary
P.O. Box 34
Catham, MA 02650

Cohasset Entertains and
  Cohasset Entertains, Encore
The Community Garden Club
  of Cohasset
P.O. Box 502
Cohasset, MA 02025

The Fine Arts Cookbook I and *II*
Museum of Fine Arts, Enterprise
295 Huntington Avenue
Boston, MA 02115

Flavors of Cape Cod
Thornton W. Burgess Society
6 Discovery Hill Road
East Sandwich, MA 02537

From the Galleys of Nantucket
First Congregational Church:
  Ladies' Union Circle
P.O. Box 866
Nantucket, MA 02554

The Harbard Cookbook
Harvard Unitarian Church
P.O. Box 217
Harvard, MA 01451

Hospitality
Salem Hospital Aid Association
81 Highland Avenue
Salem, MA 01970

The Longyear Cookbook
Longyear Museum and Historical Society
120 Seaver Street
Brookline, MA 02146-5797

Marblehead Cooks
Tower School
61 West Shore Drive
Marblehead, MA 01945

Marshfield's Overdue Cookbook
(no longer available)
Clift Rodgers Library
540 Pleasant Street, P.O. Box 168
Marshfield Hills, MA 02051

Saint Gabriel's Horn of Plenty
Saint Gabriel's Episcopal Church
Marion, MA 02738

Smith Neck Friends Meeting Cookbook
Smith Neck Friends Meeting of
  Dartmouth Monthly Meeting
601 Smith Neck Road
South Dartmouth, MA 02748

Sounds Delicious
Cape Ann Symphony Association
Box 1343
Gloucester, MA 01930

The Taste of Gloucester
The Fishermen's Wives of Gloucester and
   The Cape Ann League of Women Voters
P.O. Box 1832
Gloucester, MA 01930

A Taste of New England
Junior League of Worcester
71 Pleasant Street
Worcester, MA 01609

❧ ❧ ❧ ❧ NEW HAMPSHIRE ❧ ❧ ❧ ❧

A Collection of Maple Recipes
New Hampshire Maple Producers
   Association
28 Peabody Row
Londonderry, NH 03053

The Community Cooks
Pine Hill Waldorf School, Wilton, NH
c/o Amazon Publications
35 Adams Road
Townsend, MA 01469

The Community Kitchen Cookbook
The Community Kitchen, Inc.
P.O. Box 1315
Keene, NH 03431

Community Rescue Squad Cookbook
Rescue Squads of Deering, Hillsboro and
   Washington
c/o Route 1, Box 386, Airport Road
Antrim, NH 03440

Cooking Favorites of the St. James Nursery
   School
St. James Nursery School
876 North Main Street
Laconia, NH 03246

Cooking to Beat the Band
(no longer available)
Contoocook Valley Regional
   High School Band
Peterborough, NH 03458

Cooking with Babes in School Land
(no longer available)
Babes in School Land
P.O. Box 67
Lyndeborough, NH 03082

Country Classics
Welcome Wagon Club of Londonderry
35 White Plains Avenue
Londonderry, NH 03053

Derry Community Playground Cookbook
Derry Playground Committee
4 Brookview Drive
Derry, NH 03038

From Our House to Yours
The Hikers
P.O. Box 102
Melvin Village, NH 03850

A Hancock Community Collection
First Congregational Church: The Guild
c/o Guild President
Hancock, NH 03449

History in the Baking
Sunapee 2000 Beautification Committee
P.O. Box 379
Sunapee, NH 03782

Just Desserts
Londonderry Women's Club
P.O. Box 817
Londonderry, NH 03053

Liberal Portions
Unitarian Universalist Church
58 Lowell Street
Nashua, NH 03060

The Morrison House Museum Cookbook
(no longer available)
Londonderry Historical Society
P.O. Box 136
Londonderry, NH 03053

Our Daily Bread (no longer available)
St. Patrick's Church: Our Lady's Guild
Bennington, NH 03442

Our Favorite Recipes (no longer available)
Holy Redeemer Parish
P.O. Box 5484
West Lebanon, NH 03784

Our Town Cookbook
Peterborough Historical Society
P.O. Box 58
Peterborough, NH 03458

Patchwork Pantry
Monadnock Community Hospital
452 Old Street Road
Peterborough, NH 03458

The Sharing & Caring Cookbook
Big Brothers/Big Sisters of the Monadnock
  Region, Inc.
438 Washington Street
Keene, NH 03431

South Newbury Union Church and Society
  Cookbook
South Newbury Union Church
P.O. Box 37
Newbury, NH 03255

Sullivan Sampler
(no longer available)
United Congregational Church
Sullivan, NH 03445

A Taste of Harrissville
Well's Memorial School PTA
38 Chesham Road
Marlborough, NH 03455

❧ ❧ ❧ ❧ RHODE ISLAND ❧ ❧ ❧ ❧

Celebrities Serve
International Tennis Hall of Fame
194 Bellevue Avenue
Newport, RI 02840

A Collection of Favorite Italian Recipes
St. Anthony's Church: The Women's Guild
c/o Charles Lesieur
26 Garden Street
Woonsocket, RI 02895

Family Recipe Cookbook
Habitat for Humanity of RI–Greater
  Providence
83 Stewart Street
Providence, RI 02903

The Hammersmith Farm Cookbook
Hammersmith Farm
Ocean Drive
Newport, RI 02840

Our Saviour's Parish 65th Anniversary
  Cookbook
Our Saviour's Parish School of
  Christian Living
500 Smithfield Road
Woonsocket, RI 02895

People Food
Animal Rescue League of Southern
  Rhode Island
506B Curtis Corner Road
Peacedale, RI 02883

Rhode Island Cooks
American Cancer Society:
  Rhode Island Division
400 Main Street
Pawtucket, RI 02860

Seasoned with Love
Eastman House, Inc.
1545 Pontiac Avenue
Cranston, RI 02920

Seasoned with Love at St. James
  Lutheran Church
St. James Lutheran Church
49 Middle Highway
Barrington, RI 02806

St. John's Episcopal Church Cookbook
St. John's Episcopal Church
c/o Mrs. Robert E. Sprague
3 Donald Ross Road
Barrington, RI 02806

A Taste of Glocester
Glocester Heritage Society
P.O. Box 475
Chepachet, RI 02814

Watch Hill Cooks
Watch Hill Improvement Society
c/o Susanne Knisley
235 Watch Hill Road
Watch Hill, RI 02891

The Charlotte Central Cooks' Book
Charlotte Central PTO
Hinesburg Road
Charlotte, VT 05445

*College Street Congregational Church
  125th Anniversary Cookbook*
(no longer available)
College Street Congregational Church
265 College Street
Burlington, VT 05401

Cracker Barrel Cookbook
First Congregational Church:
  Newbury Women's Fellowship
c/o Virginia Swenson
P.O. Box 65
Newbury, VT 05051

Flavors of a Vermont Village
(no longer available)
West Newbury Women's Fellowship
West Newbury, VT 05085

The Joy of Sharing Cookbook
Ascutney Union Church
P.O. Box 345
Ascutney, VT 05030

The Kinderhaus Cookbook
Kinderhaus Children's Center
RR1, Box 303, Silver Street
Hinesburg, VT 05461

The Kosher Yankee II
Sisterhood of the Rutland Jewish Center
96 Grove Street
Rutland, VT 05701

Northeast Kingdom Cookbook
(no longer available)
Caledonia Home Health Care
St. Johnsbury, VT 05819

Out of Vermont Kitchens
The Women of St. Paul's Cathedral
2 Cherry Street
Burlington, VT 05401

Poker Hill Cookbook
Poker Hill School, Inc.
209 Poker Hill Road
Underhill, VT 05489

RRMC Family Favorites
Rutland Regional Medical Center Auxiliary
160 Allen Street
Rutland, VT 05701

Sharing Recipes
Benson First Response Rescue Squad
Box 199
Benson, VT 05731

Still Alarm Recipes
Brattleboro Firefighters Association
103 Elliot Street
Brattleboro, VT 05301

Stowe Community Church Cookbook
(no longer available)
Stowe Community Church:
  United Ladies Aid
P.O. Box 991
Stowe, VT 05672

Vermont II: Kitchen Memories
(no longer available)
Montpelier, VT 05602

Vermont Kitchens Revisited
The Women of the Cathedral Church of
  St. Paul
2 Cherry Street
Burlington, VT 05401

The Vermont Symphony Cookbook
(no longer available)
Vermont Symphony Orchestra
2 Church Street
Burlington, VT 05401

Vernon Bicentennial Cookbook
Town Beautification Committee
P.O. Box 116
Vernon, VT 05354

$\mathcal{I}$NDEX